D1179030

ZOLA
AND THE VICTORIANS

Also by Eileen Horne
The Pitch (2006)

ZOLA
AND THE VICTORIANS

Censorship in the Age of Hypocrisy

Eileen Horne

with an Introduction by
David Bellos

MACLEHOSE PRESS
QUERCUS · LONDON

First published in Great Britain in 2015 by

MacLehose Press
an imprint of Quercus Publishing Ltd
Carmelite House
50 Victoria Embankment
London EC4Y 0DZ

An Hachette UK Company

A CIP catalogue record for this book is available
from the British Library.

ISBN (HB) 978 0 85705 518 7
ISBN (TPB) 978 0 85705 520 0
ISBN (Ebook) 978 0 85705 517 0

10 9 8 7 6 5 4 3 2 1

Designed and typeset in Miller by Libanus Press
Printed and bound in Great Britain by Clays Ltd, St Ives plc

"Let all be set forth so that all may be healed"

ÉMILE ZOLA

Contents

Illustrations

For Lee Sandlin, *belle-lettrist extraordinaire*, with love

Cross-Channel Traffic

From the reign of Louis XV to the eve of the Great War – from the time of Queen Anne to the Edwardian era, if you prefer – the literatures of England and France were closely, almost inextricably entwined. Richardson's *Pamela* (1740) had as many French as English readers weeping into their handkerchiefs; Scott's Waverley novels (1814–1830) were so popular in France that they prompted Balzac to try to rival them; Hugo's *Notre-Dame de Paris* (1831) was as big a bestseller in London as it was in Paris; *Oliver Twist* (1837) was translated within a couple of years of its appearance and has never been out of print in French since then; Sue's *Mysteries of Paris* (1842–43) prompted *The Mysteries of London* by G. M. W. Reynolds, and Hugo's *Les Misérables* was adapted for the English stage ten times over within a few years of its first appearance in 1862. However, the traffic in novels between Dover and Calais was not symmetrical, and at times it was unfair. The story dramatised by Eileen Horne in this book describes one of the lowest points of justice and equity in the age-old cross-fertilisation of the literatures of England and France.

From the seventeenth to the twentieth century, the French language occupied the same place in Europe as English does in the world nowadays. French was the international language of culture and diplomacy and all middle-class Europeans learned to read and write it as a basic part of their education at school. (Dickens, who missed out on schooling because of his father's constant money troubles, was an exception in that respect.) As a result, French books were sold and read far and wide outside of France and reprinted in French in Leipzig, Amsterdam and even London from time to time. The reverse was not true: English was not a widely known language on the Continent, and access to English fiction in the eighteenth and nineteenth centuries came from translations – which were commonly not at all what would be considered translations nowadays, especially in France.

For centuries, French translators had had no qualms about adapting their sources to conform to French tastes. A long tradition of embellishment, known as the *belles infidèles*, produced cleaned-up versions of Latin and Greek classics from which all mention of bodily functions or amorous improprieties among the gods were removed. As for more modern works, translators in France had no compunction about leaving out words, sentences, paragraphs and whole chapters that seemed to them to fall short of French ideas of literary taste, and gaily added sections or chapters of their own. So the English popular novels that were read in France were also, to a considerable degree, French novels too. That's why the German philosopher Schleiermacher, in his famous essay of 1813 on "the two methods of translating", seriously doubted whether anything had ever been *translated* into French.

The situation was different in the other direction, because it had to be assumed that English-language readers of translations from French were able to check the version against the original, at least to some degree. That's why many French novels came into English under different titles and were attributed to invented names; conversely, the prestige of "Frenchness" was such that many original compositions were published in English as "translations from the French". What counted as a "translation" on both sides of the Channel in the eighteenth and nineteenth centuries was far more flexible and murky than what we expect a translation to be nowadays, and that's the main reason why Émile Zola wasn't over-concerned about the alterations that his English publisher made to his novels about prostitutes', peasants' and miners' lives.

At the start of the nineteenth century, perhaps a quarter of the French population and maybe a third of the English were sufficiently literate to read a novel for pleasure; but with each passing decade, that proportion increased, and by the end of the century more than 90 per cent of the population in both countries was fully literate. This epochal transformation of the social role of reading and writing was not the exclusive result of the expansion of school systems in both countries – though that obviously played a major part – nor was it fostered only by increasing urbanisation and industrial growth. It's a change that seems to have had its own dynamic, and though we may see it as a welcome and thoroughly desirable development, since it brought about the world that we know today, it scared a lot of people on both sides of the Channel. What good would come of it if housemaids, beggars, coachmen and peasants wasted their time on entertainments designed for the leisured classes? What would happen if the labouring masses started to pick up new ideas from books? Universal literacy wasn't a neutral prospect. It was the harbinger of all sorts of dire threats, from demands for extended suffrage to labour unrest. The more the people could read, the more vital it became to make sure they read the right things. The hounding of Zola's English publisher wasn't just about moral proprieties, even if it was couched in those terms. It was an expression of vaguer but more powerful fears of a political and social kind.

Émile Zola's twenty-novel Rougon-Macquart series was by no means an innocent victim of the misplaced anxieties of the propertied class. Conceived in the months before the French Second Empire collapsed in a foolish military confrontation with Prussia, and launched just after the fall of the Paris Commune, the Rougon-Macquart novels are designed overall to show the ineluctable fall of a political and social system grounded in corruption and crime. From a purely French perspective, they are historical fictions, since they are all located in the regime that was swept away in 1870 by the defeat of the French Army at Sedan, and they were all published under the significantly different republican regime that replaced it after 1871. The outcome – defeat, the siege of Paris and the *année terrible* of the Commune and its suppression – was already fixed, so Zola's French readers could take comfort in the novel's exposé of evils that belonged to a past that was now closed. That's the excuse, if you like. But these dramatic, passionate and purportedly scientific investigations of the lives of the different classes under the Second Empire go far beyond their superficial remit of explaining why Louis-Napoléon's regime collapsed. Moreover, once they are removed from their immediate political context – as they are when translated, or read outside of France, or read today – they speak of much deeper and broader kinds of human and social ills. They are contemplations of the wickedness and corruption of individuals, families, social and economic systems, and of life itself. They do not make you feel particularly cheerful about the future of the human race.

The exceptions to the "rule of decline" are almost as scary. *Germinal*, for example, describes the miserable lives of coal miners through the story of a strike for better pay and working conditions. The cruel injustices of joint stock companies, the selfish blindness of the managerial class (who charitably offer *brioche* to peasants in need of bread, seemingly oblivious of the precedent set by Marie-Antoinette), the rampant diseases and sexual indulgence of the mine workers, the presence in the village of a mysterious agitator with a Russian name pursuing a cataclysmic solution to the whole rotten system, a dramatic narration of a mine accident that leaves the hero entombed (to be rescued by a relief shaft that bears an uncanny resemblance to a nightmare of forceps delivery) – all these gripping scenes and situations are connected by the single theme announced in the novel's title, which is the name of the decimal month in the revolutionary calendar corresponding to April and May: that under the ground as under the whole edifice of industrial society, there is something germinating. Like the dragon's teeth of Greek myth, a whole army of angry men will arise from the ground one day soon and sweep the middle-class world away. In the grand finale, the hero Étienne Lantier strides off to fight new battles as a now hardened and convinced labour activist. Zola's manifest sympathy with the miners of his tale doesn't hide the fact that he's as scared of what's pending as any other owner of dividend-bearing stock.

Similarly, Zola's novel of high-class prostitution, *Nana*, shows how a pretty girl from the bottom of the pile can sleep her way into the highest levels of Parisian society. By infecting it, like some "golden fly" from the dung-heap, she brings men, their families, their companies and almost the whole of polite society to ruin. It's an exposé and a searching social critique, but it's also a scare story if you think of it outside the specific frame of explaining why the Second Empire collapsed as it did.

What makes these narratives of social and individual decline so much more than documentary fiction is something Zola himself rarely mentioned. Alongside the main mine in which the action of *Germinal* is set are abandoned shafts that have caught fire and smoulder underground. Of course, it's a mythological netherworld, resuscitating ancient beliefs in hell as a hot place down below. In *The Human Beast*, the locomotive that crashes off the rails and lies panting on its side is also a hydra, a mythological beast, half metal and half flesh, and as it snorts out its last puff of smoke it dies like a wounded horse. Over the whole double family of the Rougons and the Macquarts hangs a "hereditary flaw", a legacy of the past no less terrible and no less abstract than the curse that hangs over the house of Atreus. More like Hugo than Balzac, Zola is a natural creator of modern myths that rival and also feed on more ancient and familiar ones. His English critics were right in at least one respect: Zola's novels have what it takes to appeal to a mass readership, and they arouse strong emotional reactions to the world described, which is at the same time an accurate depiction of social realities, and a fantastical assemblage of universal nightmares and fears.

A second reason why the Rougon-Macquart series aroused alarm lies in the way Zola tells his tales. He doesn't use a lot of dialogue in the manner of Dumas' *Count of Monte-Cristo* or Dickens' *Great Expectations*, in which the spoken words of the fictional characters provide the most memorable and moving passages. Instead, using a device often associated with Flaubert, he blends third-person narrative with the spoken and unspoken thoughts of his characters, creating often quite long passages that hover between narrative and inner speech. This "free indirect style" is part of what makes Zola so easy to read nowadays, since the device has become a convention of modern narrative fiction in French and English; but it also makes it easy to mistake the views of fictional characters for the viewpoint of the novel itself. You could say that the Rougon-Macquart saga presupposes and calls for a slightly more sophisticated kind of reader than the rollicking adventures of three (or four) musketeers, where you know who says what to whom, and when the narrator is speaking on his own behalf. On the other hand, you could also fear that such novels in the hands of unsophisticated readers can spread politically dangerous views with the apparent authority of a great novelist. And in a way, they do: it has taken a long time for even French critics to work out whether or not *Germinal* is a "socialist novel", or a "bourgeois novel" about the birth of socialism and whether *The Dram Shop* (*L'Assommoir*) is a motivated plea for abstinence, or a sympathetic portrait of a sozzled old bag.

Yet none of this explains or excuses the bizarre and savage campaign against Zola's English publisher. Nothing like the story that Eileen Horne tells had happened before in English or French publishing, and although the battle for freedom of expression would have many more episodes before it was won, nobody ever since has suffered the penalties inflicted on Henry Vizetelly for bringing Zola to an English readership. It is a moment of shame in the annals of British justice, and a moment of sheer lunacy in the history of lobbying.

The novel which served as the spark or pretext for the campaign to banish English translations of Zola is without any doubt pretty strong stuff, and it is not hard to see why it ran foul of English sensitivities. *La Terre* (*The Soil* in the first translation, now more commonly called *The Earth*) presents peasant life as a bestial pit of misery at the antipodes of suburban fantasies of the good country life. French laws of inheritance introduced by Napoleon I in the early years of the nineteenth century required landholdings to be divided equally between children. The intention of the law was to break up the great estates of the aristocracy, but its effect, after two or three generations, was to have a large number of farms too small to be managed economically and a large class of almost penniless owners of agricultural land. Generally overpopulated and undercapitalised, the French countryside was not productive enough to generate livelihoods comparable to the growing cities and industrial centres. From the point of view of a city-dweller, as Zola was for the most part, rural France was a different and utterly depressing place, and its inhabitants an almost alien race. Of course, the decline of the peasantry is one part of Zola's overall story of the decline of France under the Second Empire, and *La Terre* is also part of the working-out of the ancestral curse of the "hereditary flaw". Removed from that context, however, it shows how life among animals reduces men and women to beasts, and how desperate poverty can dissolve even the strictest of taboos (on incest, or on the use of human waste, for example). Life on the land is sheer hell – which is absolutely not what the mostly urban readers of England wanted to know. The National Vigilance Association, which began the campaign to put Zola's English publisher behind bars, may have sincerely believed it objected to obscenity (and even today not every reader finds the farting contest funny), but behind its façade of concern for propriety lay a deeper and probably more widely shared reluctance to entertain Zola's dystopian view of country life.

One of the more incomprehensible ironies in the fate that met Henry Vizetelly, Zola's English publisher, is that the French originals of the Rougon-Macquart series remained freely available in Britain. At no point was it even suggested that they too deserved the treatment given to their (highly altered and watered-down) translations. The imbalance underlines the class anxieties of the National Vigilance Association, and makes it obvious that these prudish campaigners were not really interested in protecting young or vulnerable members of the upper classes – because they were able to read the originals anyway. The patently obvious aim of Vizetelly's pursuers was to stop these powerful, disturbing and disruptive portrayals of a society set on a doom-laden path from reaching the growing numbers of readers among the working class.

The strangest things can become political hot potatoes, at least for short periods. I have seen sedate ladies hitting policemen with their parasols to protest at the export of English horses to slaughterhouses in countries where horsemeat is an alternative to beef. Fifty years ago nobody imagined that homosexual marriage would become a divisive issue in French and American political life today. It's therefore worth asking whether the furore over Zola's translation into English was just a bizarre and evanescent wrinkle in the history of literature and censorship, or whether it was a clumsy but genuine response to something of larger social significance.

One issue that Zola's work brings to the fore is whether all classes have the right to see themselves presented in fictional form. Are novels about the poor, the bad, and the despicable to be read only by the middle classes, for their entertainment and instruction, or should they to be accessible to the very classes they depict? Clearly, as England and France moved closer to universal literacy, there were quite powerful groups that did not want new readers to follow the model of their social superiors. The National Vigilance Association may have made a complete fool of itself in running a campaign that put an aged publisher in gaol, but its reactionary view of the proper kind of reading for common folk has been renewed many times by different lobby groups – amongst them, the French Communist Party, which campaigned in the 1950s to ban paperback books on the grounds that they would cheapen the classics and put the wrong kinds of books in workers' hands. Anxiety over the accessibility of reading matter remained a recurrent issue in debates about literature throughout the twentieth century.

Another issue lurking behind the sad story of the Vizetelly publishing house is whether what people read makes any difference to what they do, seek or desire. The universal popularity of cloak-and-dagger adventure stories doesn't seem to have led to any increase in duelling, and the millions of readers of Maigret detective stories haven't spawned an equivalent surge of intuitive sleuths or thwarted criminals either. On the other hand, some novels have changed people's lives and have had lasting impact on social norms. Campaigning writers like the Dickens of *Hard Times* and the Hugo of *Les Misérables* alongside political satires like Zamyatin's *We* and Orwell's *Animal Farm* most certainly changed people's attitudes and led to major changes in practice. On which side of this admittedly very wiggly line should we put Zola's Rougon-Macquart novels?

It's a tricky question. As a historical saga explaining the downfall of the Second Empire, Zola's novel cycle packs the past into a box that is closed, and so his works can't be accused of stoking up resistance to an imperial regime that no longer existed. As a panorama of human vice and folly in a wide range of different social and professional milieux, it is just as unlikely to inspire readers to emulate homicidal train drivers, drunken roofers, dodgy bankers, corrupt market traders, deranged artists or mud-spattered farm workers (especially not them!). But these powerful novels also work on a different, and less blandly representational level. Zola's long gallery of flawed heroes and heroines is in the end not a denunciation, but an appeal for sympathy with even the least appealing representatives of humanity. The entire series, and especially its two most impressive achievements, *Germinal* and *L'Assommoir*, express outrage at injustice. They protest at the cruelty not just of fate, but of the structures that turn random events into disasters for the most vulnerable among us. In their own elaborate but accessible way, blending ancient archetypes with modern documentary research and traditional story telling with a sophisticated narrative technique, the Rougon-Macquart series at its best really does create those strong feelings long associated with stage tragedy. Readers of these great novels are pierced by the twin prongs of pity and fear. Henry Vizetelly was quite right to think that Zola was a classic already.

This story of how a small group of crusading bigots set out to destroy a publishing house to no good purpose takes us into the heart of a legal machine as muddled and murky as the world of *Bleak House*. Henry Vizetelly had the misfortune to be the object of poorly drafted laws manipulated by clever and ambitious men, and to be served by unimpressive counsel that was of little help to him. Could it happen again? Not in quite the same way, to be sure. But you can never be too vigilant when you come across a lobby group that calls itself a National Vigilance Association; and no amount of enlightened legislation is much use without competent and attentive lawyers ready to press for what is right.

DAVID BELLOS

Princeton, 25 July, 2015

PART I:
THE CHALLENGE

1. *April 1888, Médan*

Zola's ever-expanding country villa: two towers overwhelm the original structure gripped between them: the "Nana Tower" in the foreground housing his study, and the "Germinal Tower" beyond.

He is suffocating. Trapped in an underground tunnel, he moves along low, narrow-ceilinged galleries; roots he cannot see are tugging at his legs; he is clambering painfully over sharp stone-falls, then up to his waist in gelatinous sludge, the earth pressing on him, dirt in his eyes and blocking his ears, the mealy, ashy taste of it on his tongue; now it is filling his mouth and making him gag,

27

but there is no pausing, he must burrow forward in the darkness and find his way . . .

Zola wakes with a start. He sits up, propped on his pillows, and breathes deeply for a moment, in, out, and again, slowly, in. His doctor suggests this will ease his panic and slow his racing pulse; he must take care, for he is susceptible to attacks of angina. He pushes back the coverlet and rises to rinse his mouth and start his working day.

There is an oil lamp burning in the corner of the bedroom he shares with his wife Alexandrine, who lies asleep on her back as usual, one arm curved above her head as if to frame her still-handsome face. They have slept with the lamp lit at night since the loss of both his beloved *Maman* and dear friend Flaubert in close succession, eight years earlier. They share a childlike fear of the dark, of its sudden oblivion. Is that the source of his dream too? Unlikely. The dream is not about death, but creation. It has been with him since he was eighteen, when he suffered a brain fever that almost killed him. It is, he thinks, a reminder that there is work to be done; perhaps he was spared thirty years ago in order to keep digging with his pen.

Émile Zola scratching in the dirt – there's an image that would please his enemies in the illustrated press, who love to depict him as a mud-wallowing pig for what they perceive as his "sordid realism" and direct approach to sexual subjects in his work. He is shown not only as a pig, but being mounted by a pig, as an artist sketching pigs in the act of copulation, and even imagined as half-pig and half-man, painting the map of France with the filthy contents of a chamber pot. He is among the most caricatured people in France.

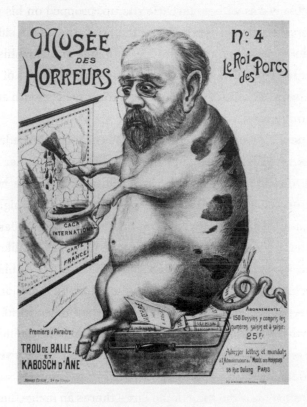

As his bare feet touch the rug, Zola banishes thoughts of his enemies and the sensations of the underground tunnel with the firm resolve that defines him in all things. He can extinguish the lamp now that dawn has come. He dresses himself to walk the dogs, pulling on his brown corduroy suit and heavy boots. Later he will change into his writing clothes: a loose flannel shirt, a padded worker's jacket and wide trousers. He cannot bear restrictive clothing and rough fabrics touching his skin; he devised this peasant's uniform to ensure he works without distraction. This may have become more necessary in recent years – he has steadily gained weight since his thirties and is now nearly sixteen stone, and feels every bit of it as he fastens his coat over a solid, protuberant belly. He adds a white kerchief at his neck; there is always damp in the air here, and he still heeds his late mother's advice to keep the neck covered in all seasons. He clears his throat – is that a tickle he feels, the herald of a spring cold?

One friend calls him "both burly and frail". He is five feet and six inches tall, with a sallow complexion and a thick, round, close-cut beard. Despite the extra weight he carries, his build is robust, his arms and legs muscular. His myopic, small eyes are dark, and still sparkle with boyish mischief now and then, though his hair is greying now and his high forehead is lined like that of a man ten years older. Facing the cheval-glass with comb in hand, he glimpses his father, an Italian engineer who died when he was a boy of seven, and is halted by the memory of a strong arm raised just so, arranging grey-black hair to mask the same bald spot.

He slips from the room and moves down the carved staircase in the half-light, treading quietly at this hour, not so much in deference to others but because he does not wish to engage in banal conversation with servants, or even his wife, most mornings. It is his time to think. Despite the elaborate furnishings and décor, there is an emptiness and gloom about this second home, his country retreat outside of Paris, where they spend at least half of each year. The draperies are heavy at the windows; the tapestries and oil paintings on the walls are mostly dark in hue. It may be that a certain melancholy air pervades the place because its size begs a family to fill it, and the Zolas are childless. If this is a source of secret longing, the writer does not record it in letters or overtly in his fiction, although it escapes nobody, including his wife, that his life's project, the majestic saga of the Rougon-Macquart family, is a history and investigation of procreation and its consequences. "The Rougon-Macquart is his baby," Alexandrine rationalises to friends, and to herself.

She has had a child, in fact, but this is never referred to, even within the privacy of their bedroom. Years ago when they first met in Paris, he a struggling poet, she an artist's model a year his senior, she confided in him that she had been forced to give up an illegitimate child, a baby girl, after an affair a few years earlier with a medical student. "Let us go and find her," Zola had said, filled with the sweet desire to care for this charming, intelligent woman with her dark brows and intense passions. "We shall adopt her ourselves."

Their quest was futile. The child had been left at a foundling hospital and had, they learned, died there as an infant from illness or neglect. With that news, the book was closed, and they never started their own family. Alexandrine was unable to conceive again and Zola may have been too driven by work to crave fatherhood. Now however, in settled middle age, it would have been a pleasure to have children laughing outside under the plane trees that line the long drive, but it is too late.

He steps outside and greets the day, clapping his hands for the dogs. Today some workmen are completing a few refurbishments to the Nana Tower attached to the main house. This and the Germinal Tower on the other side (named for two of the most successful books in his oeuvre) have been grand additions to the original structure during the course of the last decade; he has created what he calls "his rascally big house" on the grounds of a modest villa, designed to his requirements, his taste for comfort, and his professional needs. He had fallen in love with the place when he first saw it, not for its undistinguished architecture (he dubbed it "the rabbit hutch" on sight) but for its picturesque situation. It is a haven from the city, only an hour northwest of Paris on the train line that runs through the valley below. The house is hidden in a nest of pretty foliage, set apart from the rest of the little hamlet of Médan at the end of the long alley of trees.

He lifts a hand towards the workmen in greeting as he strikes off down the lane. It is the same routine every day. He takes one hour's stroll, following the path near the water, with his dogs at his heels. He calls to them by name in a pleasant voice that is surprisingly light for a man of his bulk. His wife's pet is Fan-fan, a wirehaired griffon whom she coddles and kisses so much that her cousin Amelie, a frequent visitor, refers to the dog as "your son". Zola's favourite is a little terrier called Ratón who has a dislike of strangers, especially the parade of interviewers who frequent Médan now that his fame has grown great. He has become so well known that he had to express surprise recently when a correspondent in Holland complained that his letters had not been delivered. "Why, you have only to write *Émile Zola, France* on the envelope and it will get to me," he replied.

The dogs jump and bark in the fresh air as he carelessly throws them a stick. For one who is known for his extraordinary observational powers, he sees little – not white buds or river reeds or rusting hooks on the side of a fishing dinghy on the bank – his photographic mind is entirely selective. His latest novel is about knights and angels; he has no need for details of buds or boats. This is Zola's way; if he is writing about a banker, politicians hold no interest. It saves waste to focus only on his topic, lest his mind become too crowded. He is impatient with people who assume writers are necessarily interested in everything at all times.

Anyone might breathe deeply on such a morning stroll, tipping their face to the spring sky to marvel at God's gifts – and though he is an ardent atheist, Zola is truly grateful for the rewards that life has brought him; yet his ingrained habit, as each day begins, is to enumerate his worries. Even if he has slept well he can find something to fret about. Soon he will be made a Knight of the Legion of Honour, for example – but is that as prestigious as being invited to join the French Academy? That is an accolade which has thus far eluded him – lifetime membership of an elite council of forty men of letters known as "The Immortals", charged with maintaining literary standards for the nation. Most days, he puts the Academy high on his list of anxieties; but as he makes his way along the narrow path today, nettles occasionally snagging at his trousers and sunlight turning the Seine beside him to silver, he finds himself fixated on one item in this week's post.

In a letter from his English publisher, Vizetelly & Company, who paid three thousand francs for the rights in his last novel, *The Soil*, only two thousand is offered for the book he is presently completing. How is that fair? He sells them the English rights to all his existing works, and in return, they belittle him with a lower offer for the new one? The length is no different, and it is part of the larger whole of one family saga. To add insult to injury, he is still waiting for the final tranche of payment due for *The Soil*, even though it has already been published in England. He is not happy, not happy at all. He makes a mental note to write to his friend George Moore, the Irish writer who introduced him to the publisher. He will surely know what is amiss.

In order to dislodge the anxiety *du jour*, he counts his footsteps, a habit of his both here in Médan and on the streets of Paris. Sometimes he might choose to count mundane objects too – six street lamps, nine school children in blue coats, eight pigeons by the statue in the square. He takes a superstitious pleasure when they fall into multiples of four or seven, his lucky numbers. But his step counting is interrupted today by that other figure returning again to the forefront of his consciousness: two thousand francs. It is indeed an insult.

He is distracted from his fretful state by the sight of four white ducklings paddling out from the shore into the river, following their mother. There's a good sign. Reversing his path back to the house, he muses, what good news do you portend, little ducks? Will today bring a new sale abroad? That might allay the rawness he feels at the English affront.

His books are translated and sold around the world. Zola had amassed a considerable fortune from sales of his books in France, which is increasingly complemented by fees for translation rights in other countries. Prior to 1886, translation rights were subject to a haphazard set of bilateral treaties between France and various other nations, but the Berne Convention of that year ushered in a single international regime among several dozen countries, protecting the copyright of authors until at least fifty years after their death.

Zola admires the late great Victor Hugo, who, many years ago, instigated this campaign for authors' rights beyond their home countries; however, he feels he must dampen the general celebration in the artistic fraternity by pointing out that one of the best markets for European writers is America, a country that has thus far refused to join the Berne Convention, only recognising copyright in works written by American citizens and residents. He knows his novels have been translated for years in America, and are very popular – but he is told they are poorly rendered and sold without recompense to him. The same holds true for the works of British novelists, including those of Charles Dickens, whose novels are beloved of the American readership and reprinted there with impunity.

At least Zola can take comfort from the fact that there will be further stage versions from the Rougon-Macquart series in France soon – although his plays in Paris to date, including adaptations of *Nana*, *L'Assommoir* and *Germinal*, have never enjoyed anything like the success of his novels. Two fine composers, Massenet and Bruneau, have asked to create operas from other titles, which should bear some fruit.

He spends far more than he saves, above all on his beloved villa, adding not only buildings but land to his holding – including the acquisition of the little Isle of Médan in the middle of the river, on which he has built the structure he christened "The Charpentier Pavilion" in honour of his publisher, and which is used for soirées with friends: artists, journalists and men of letters flock here to see him.

Despite the abundance that surrounds him, Zola maintains that he has a poor child's ingrained respect for a buffer against future difficulty, should it arise. He tells friends, "I began life poor; poverty may return; I am not afraid of it." This is not strictly true – he began life in reasonable circumstances, living as a boy with his parents in Aix-en-Provence, the town that would become a model for the fictional Plassans, birthplace of the Rougon-Macquart family.

He has happy memories of playing in the fields with his best friends, among them Paul Cézanne, until circumstances turned for the worse with his father's early death, which left his mother without income. By the time he was twenty, living in a garret in Paris writing poetry that he could not sell, he knew real want. Often he took no food for a day or more, shivering without coal for the fire, his red fingers clutching the stump of a pencil. He recalls how he had to "play the Arab" and remain indoors for long periods, draped in a coverlet, when he was driven to trading his only coat and trousers for bread. It seems so remote now, like something he once read in a book he has mislaid or loaned to a friend.

Stopping in the ceramic-tiled kitchen on his return from the walk he has little for breakfast. On some days he eats a fried egg, prepared by the cook, who has been tutored by him on his preference. If she misjudges the cooking time, he chides her, saying, "My morning's work will be worth nothing!" He takes only a ripe apricot today. As he sinks his teeth into the soft flesh, the clock strikes nine in the hall, and he sees a blue dress and a white apron, a woman moving past a doorway with a pile of linen in her arms. He has an impression of height, dark hair, and a graceful figure – this must be the new housemaid his wife mentioned. No matter. He hurries upstairs to begin work.

Nulla dies sine linea: the golden engraving on the hood of a massive fireplace is the first thing his eye falls upon when entering the study. It is a cluttered, richly decorated refuge on a grand scale, nearly ten metres in length with a high ceiling. It looks more like an artist's studio than a writer's room, with floor to ceiling bay windows looking out over the river and the fields beyond. Pliny's "No day without a line" has superseded the boyhood motto "All or nothing" which he shared so fiercely with Cézanne, but it springs from the same well of total dedication to work. Unlike some writers he knows, he does not take it to mean covering a messy desk with scrawls and balls of rejected pages, as if the job of the writer were to engage in the act of writing anything, even if most of it is discarded; not for Zola the concept that a day is well spent if a few good sentences emerge.

He confines his work on his latest novel to the morning, writing three or four pages with an unwavering commitment that means he can calculate almost to the day when he will complete a book. After lunch he will take his siesta before turning to articles he must write. He provides a piece to a Marseilles paper every day, a weekly one to a Paris journal, and manages to also send a monthly contribution to a St Petersburg review. His dedication and consistency in work is shown by the magnitude of his output.

For Zola, Pliny's proverb is about putting down what a thing looks like, feels like, and how it tastes or smells – a record of well-researched truth set out in firm black ink, not merely a doodle or a scribble. He is quite sure of his trajectory before he leaps, although this was not the case in his early writings; now, at this mature point in his career, his manuscripts, like Mozart's scores, are for the most part free of crossings-out, and the basket for discarded paper by his desk is empty at the end of his morning's work. That is not to say he never makes corrections. He is meticulous about revision, and continues to make adjustments to everything from significant plot developments to tiny tweaks of spellings and names until the last hours before the final proofs go to the printer, much to his publisher's dismay. But his first drafts tend to be made of solid lines, the engineer's son's skill with a blueprint never more evident than at this stage of writing.

In contrast to the mythology surrounding Mozart, who was composing without amendment, some say, because he was taking dictation from God, there is a secular and earthbound reason for Zola's precision. For months, he has prepared for each stroke of the pen. He begins each novel with an outline, the preliminary sketch of an idea for his next novel sketched as notes to himself, concentrating on the themes he will investigate, and choosing which member of the Rougon-Macquart family it will feature as principal character. "This is how I do it," he once explained to his friend Paul Alexis, who was attempting to record his method for posterity, before correcting himself: "No, I can hardly be said to 'do it', rather, it does itself. I cannot invent facts, lacking that facility . . . if I sit down to my table to think out the plot of a story, I remain sitting for three days straight with my head in hand."

He makes a "primitive plan", as he terms it, first summoning his *dramatis personae* and giving them their main biographical, physical and psychological particulars. He researches locations for the story and records his findings in words and drawings, depending on "the class in which I have decided to place the protagonist's life". This is all-important; critics will condemn him for the extensive description of settings in his work, but he answers that "man cannot be separated from his milieu; he is shaped by his house, his town, his province".

The research stage can be longer than the time it takes to write the book, sometimes stretching over six months, with dozens of notebooks filled with sensory observations and anecdotes about real-life characters, be they miners, farmers, artists, doctors or prostitutes. Once all of this preparation is done, he uses his reason, like a scientist; his aim is to integrate science and literature. "Let us say so-and-so does this or that. What would be the natural result of such-and-such an act? Would such an act affect my personage? It is therefore logical that this other person would react in such-and-such a manner. Then some other character may intervene . . ." In this way, "threads knot themselves together" and it is then that he becomes clear about the story. When the results do not quite fit with his research, he also allows himself creative departures if necessary – after all, as he tells Alexis, "the human race is not predictable".

He then proceeds to make the "plan in detail", including descriptions of minor characters and even some snippets of dialogue, and he inserts his extensive research into each of the chapter outlines, like a chef filling so many fresh pastries with pre-prepared cream. Following this pattern, he has completed almost one novel per year since he first drew up the grand scheme for his proposed "family history". At that time, twenty years ago, towards the end of 1868, when he first set it down for his original publisher Lacroix, he proposed ten volumes. The interruption of the Franco-Prussian war in 1870 had decimated Lacroix, whose firm went bankrupt, and, much to Zola's dismay, the project came to a halt after only two books. He knocked on many doors as soon as the war was over, but such a large undertaking seemed impossible for anyone to take on in those dismal days. Fortunately, just when Zola was giving up hope, Georges Charpentier had stepped in with an offer. A decade later, after the tremendous sales of the seventh book in the saga, *L'Assommoir*, the plan was expanded to twenty books.

When he is working, his closest friends may not hear from him for weeks. "What has become of Zola?" they ask, though by this time they should know. He does reply to letters. Close to completion of an earlier book in the Rougon-Macquart saga, *The Ladies' Paradise*, he sent forth a pithy message. "What has become of me? Nothing, my good friend. I am in my hole and I am working . . ." To the same friend he would soon write, "I finished my novel on Thursday, and I am in the joy of this great relief. And now to work on the next."

The Médan workroom is furnished as he has chosen, leaving Alexandrine to see to the rest of the house, a role she relishes. Oriental carpets cover the study floor and tapestries adorn the walls. An enormous divan sits in an alcove near the windows, and there he will generally read and nap in the afternoons. Curios, pottery and images line shelves and side tables all around the room. There are framed photographs too, for he has a growing fascination with photography, and has recently acquired his first camera. One visitor and admirer of his work commented that his penchant for collecting is synonymous with his passion for research; compilation is his *modus vivendi*.

A wrought iron *jardinière* holds a large *fleur de lune* plant, meant to purify the air. His folders of research and books related to his current task are laid out on small tables within reach of his desk. A substantial library of books (in French, for he speaks no other language) is accessed by a spiral staircase, which leads to a gallery space and a roof terrace beyond. His desk sits in the centre of the room facing the windows with their view of the river. It is a long work-table of dark wood with thick and ornately carved legs. Underneath it, pushed to one side, is a chamber pot, which he keeps there in preference to leaving the room should he need to relieve himself in the midst of a working session. On his desk is his favourite green vase, filled in season by his wife with red and purple peonies from the garden below his windows. There is little else on the surface, for he dislikes clutter when he is writing.

Now he eases himself onto his high-backed padded chair and dons his pince-nez, bringing the scene before him into focus. Placed in the centre of the desk by his own hand the night before is a slim paper knife he uses to open his letters, set just so, parallel to his special J-pen in its thick ivory holder. That pen goes with him everywhere, despite the unwieldy weight of it, and why not? It has served him well. *The Dream* is the sixteenth novel in the Rougon-Macquart saga. In this episode, Zola had originally thought to tell the story of an older Rougon man, a scientist who falls in love with his young ward, but he has put that to one side for a later book, and is working on the story of an adopted girl, Angelique, who dreams of marrying a knight such as she has read about in *The Golden Legend*. It is a simple story, but the introduction of a girl abandoned by an amoral Rougon mother is central to his plan to conduct a scientific experiment with this series of novels; Angelique allows him to further test his theories about environment and heredity.

If we transplant a lovely, faithful, but passionate child away from her natural family, and raise her in a kind and protected household where there is no alcohol, no vice of any kind, surrounded only by care and morality, what will become of her? It has been a long and exacting work to write, and his heroine's tendency to daydream seems to have afflicted Zola on and off throughout the process. He reviews the last few pages he has written, set in the church that dominates the novel. He is not far from the end of his task – poor Angelique will achieve her dream, she will marry her handsome prince, but there will be no happy finale. Yet he is loath for her to arrive at the steps of the cathedral where she will lose her life on her wedding day; she is a lovely girl, dreamy yet rooted in the earth, curious and imaginative. Fatally over-imaginative, in fact. Her destiny is already fixed.

Zola dips the steel nib into black ink and begins to write. He loves this moment in his day, for it is only now that his anxieties fall away, and for the time that his pen is moving smoothly across the page, he feels calm and happy. It helps him to forget for a few hours that this saga can feel like a burden, despite his absolute devotion to it for the past two decades.

Though he has enjoyed success, he wonders sometimes if it has been worth it. He hints at this to a few close friends and his supportive wife: his eventful novels have overshadowed his real existence. In his twenties, when he was an art critic and a journalist, he wrote an essay about art and naturalism; in the process, he coined a nice phrase which has been oft quoted since. It haunts him now: "If you ask me what I came to do in this world, I, an artist, will answer you: I am here to live out loud." He does this with his writing, of course – but in his private life, he feels muffled and dull.

To combat this, he sets himself challenges through his work, and in the case of *The Dream* it has been, as he noted in the initial outline, "to make a book that is not expected of me". Some will say that the lyrical romance is a cynical bid to help his latest application to the French Academy; but this illogic suggests the adjudicators will be unaware of all the books preceding it, above all the last one, *The Soil*. Inspired in part by "King Lear", it tells the story of Fouan, an old farmer in the north of France who divides his holdings of twenty-five acres between his three children while still living, creating a whirlwind of jealousy and bitterness in the family, leading to a tragic and violent conclusion.

There was a frenzied outpouring of criticism for *The Soil* when it was first serialised in France last year, because he dared to write about the brutality of rural life and the bestial instincts within families in a context that was too visceral and primal for many readers to bear. When the first chapters appeared in the periodical *Gil Blas*, a group of five young French novelists who claimed to be former "disciples" of Zola (though he had never asked for disciples) decided to publish in *Le Figaro* a self-proclaimed "manifesto" accusing him of "preferring the profits of pornography over the fruits of serious literature". They went on to question his mental state, and even remarked on his inexperience with women as the rationale for his sordid choices.

Were he so inclined, he might show them, taking them page by page through the research notebooks on the shelf behind his desk, how *The Soil* is the result of painstaking investigations into the emotional and physical poverty of rural life. True, Zola may not come from that world; he is no more a rapacious farmer than he was a prostitute (or a client) when he wrote the story of the

Parisian courtesan *Nana*. Paul Alexis is fond of relating how his friend asked him one day, during the research phase of that novel (knowing Alexis to be a man of the world), whether one paid the girl before or after the sexual act. He had no concept of such things, and was anxious to get the details right.

As for the accusation that he is motivated by money, it is ludicrous. Money, Zola feels, is important to a writer only in that it emancipates him from protectors and patrons who would influence him. It allows truth to be told, and the novelist's task is to invent from truth. Zola has never flinched from the task. Are his critics saying that the miserable existence of the rural poor could never lead to events he describes in *The Soil* – infidelity, incest, rape and parricide? Prove him wrong then. He is unapologetic.

He knew even before the recent translations were published abroad that the Germans and the English in particular would react with even more vehemence than his compatriots, and news comes to him that there is a demand for the novel to be censored in those countries – but he is well accustomed to controversy and it does not worry him. He had another letter from Vizetelly & Company about this very matter, back in January. It was signed by a young man he had encountered on a few occasions years ago in Paris; Ernest Vizetelly is the son of Henry Vizetelly, the publisher he has never met. Ernest wrote to explain that he was undertaking the translation of *The Soil* himself, and that he had some "concerns", which he went on at length to explain in his prolix style. He regretted there would be a need to make considerable amendments within the body of the novel, averring that the company "tried as much as possible" to publish literal translations, "but we do sometimes have to alter texts . . . if some of the language might be too shocking for our readers."

Zola did not object. What would be the point? He knows about the English readership's prudery and has discussed it often with his friends there, including George Moore, who keeps him abreast of cultural matters across the Channel. Evidently, one must contend not only with conservative lending libraries, those self-appointed arbiters of literary success, but also with gangs of pursed-lipped English clergymen calling themselves "philan-thropists" and appealing for censorship "to protect our youth". The anecdotes Moore shares on his visits make them laugh together; Zola is not a libertine, quite the contrary, but he is amused by that desperate desire of the English to appear virtuous in all things and to dampen even the possibility of a sexual *double entendre* in print or conversation. Among other absurdities, they are careful to cover all of their tables with cloths, lest curved wooden legs provoke impure thoughts in the minds of men regarding the corresponding part in a woman.

Zola shakes his head. They make such fools of themselves. And yet, even though our table legs are generally left uncovered, we French have our zealots too – as Flaubert had found to his cost, thirty years earlier, when he and his publisher were tried for "insulting public morals" with *Madame Bovary*. They were acquit-ted in the end, on the basis that by exposing vice the author was promoting virtue. He was not the only author tried for immorality around that time in France; there was a rash of literary trials then

– and poor Baudelaire was convicted for "promoting immorality", paying a significant fine and seeing several of his finest poems banned. Times had changed since then; after the fall of the Second Empire, the cultural mood is more permissive here than in England, or indeed elsewhere on the Continent. In fact, if one buys an edition of *Madame Bovary* now in Paris, his lawyer Sénard's impassioned defence speech is included as an afterword, as Flaubert had insisted; it serves as a memento and celebration of his victory.

Zola thinks again, with a flare of irritation, of that "Manifesto" in *Le Figaro*. "A literature devoid of nobility," the group had said. "Our master has gone down to the very depths of uncleanliness." That had rankled for days while he was taking his morning walks. Their master. He knew only one of the men who styled themselves as his once-devoted followers, and him not well. To Zola, this was like a woman ending a love affair with a stranger. "I must leave you, my darling, for you no longer satisfy me," she cries, and he can only shrug, "Please yourself." He made no reply to the Five; he had enough to occupy him in the preparation for his next novel.

Ernest Vizetelly had also told him in his last letter, after apologising again for his expurgations, that the company's interest in the work was due in part to the parallels in the story with the current Irish land agitation, "making it all the more immediate and relevant here". He closed by saying that he and his father had high hopes for its sales. Zola approves of this way of thinking, though he cares little about Irish affairs and they were not at all on his mind when he wrote *The Soil*. His kind benefactor, Louis Hachette, who plucked him from a miserable existence when he was only twenty-two, taught him well.

A charity school boy himself, who had risen to great heights, Hachette gave the destitute young Zola a job packing books for delivery, and before long, sensing his talent, promoted him to writing copy for the publicity department. Hachette had been a wonderful mentor; without him there would be no Rougon-Macquart saga. "Write novels, not poems," Hachette counselled him, "and they will sell." Zola also learned from him that audiences look for similarities to themselves in fiction; they like to feel you are addressing them, that a work has some particular relevance to their own circumstances.

In Hachette's employ, Zola, who has been compared by the acerbic critic Pontmartin to the circus owner P. T. Barnum for his skill at drawing attention to his wares, also learned that "all publicity is good". He has never avoided controversy; in fact he has found ways to court it, sending his work to newspaper editors with a note saying, "I prefer a sincere slating to routine compliments or silence."

How the naysayers must be rubbing their hands together now, anticipating the next novel from the depraved creator of the Rougon-Macquart family. He will surprise them all with Angelique, tucked away in her pristine corner of a cathedral town; she is the cousin of the infamous Nana, but she bears no resemblance to her, beyond their mutual beauty. How she will vex the hypocrites who snatch the next book in its bright yellow binding from Charpentier's shelf, eager to read it in order to condemn it, only to discover this ethereal heroine bent over her embroidery, dreaming of a virtuous prince. This pleases him no end. Gazing at the high piles of quarto pages before him, the heavy paper covered with his flowing bold hand, he wonders if those four ducklings on the river this morning were a happy reminder that now, with this book soon done, there are only four to go.

2. *May 1888, House of Commons, Westminster*

"Mr Speaker, I rise today to call attention to the motion which stands in my name." Samuel Smith adjusts his wire spectacles to rest midway down his long nose, gathers his sheaf of notes, then looks out across the chamber. It is not the best turnout; a quick count of heads suggests at most forty-five M.P.s in attendance – thankfully they are still quorate. They have been in session for several hours, and, Smith tells himself, the crowd always thins at the dinner hour. Order papers are splayed across the central table; some have fallen to the floor.

In this chapel-like, neo-Gothic space, its seating arranged in opposing ranks of choir stalls, Smith looks like a provincial clergyman about to sermonise. He is a man with a lean frame and long black-grey beard, sporting a stiff collar and demeanour to match. Standing at his place on the Opposition's side, behind the empty ministerial row, he coughs to ensure he has the room's attention, and possibly to awaken two members nearby. The lesson begins:

"The motion reads as follows: 'That this House deplores the rapid spread of demoralising literature in this country, and is of the opinion that the law against obscene publications and indecent pictures and prints should be vigorously enforced, and, if necessary, strengthened.' I assure the House that nothing but an imperative sense of duty has led me to take up so painful and so disagreeable a subject. This and the knowledge that there has been an immense increase of vile literature in London and throughout the country, and that this literature is working terrible effects on the morals of the young. Such havoc—"

"Hear, hear!" He is endorsed by the customary echoes of

approval from the benches around him, and from a few men on the opposite benches. This is common ground. "Terrible!" "An outrage!"

The Home Secretary, Henry Matthews, the only cabinet minister present, remains impassive, arms folded, moving only to flick an imagined speck of dust off the sleeve of his black frock coat. Smith continues, his Scottish accent becoming more pronounced as he warms to his theme. His voice is by nature weak, and pitched high for a man of his stature, but as one supporter has said, it is "particularly suited to the expression of lamentation". He speaks as if the end of the world is nigh.

"Such havoc, I say, is it making, that I can only look on it as a gigantic national danger. Indeed, I question whether at the present moment the people of this country are suffering more from an excessive use of strong drink than they are from the more subtle poison of vile and obscene literature!"

A smattering of applause, and the Home Secretary whispers briefly to the M.P. behind him, who approaches the dispatch box when he is called. "Mr Speaker, can my honourable friend the M.P. for Flintshire provide any proof that there has been of late years a great development of this evil?"

Smith is happy to oblige, turning the pages of his notes again, unable to keep the satisfaction from his voice. Here is the nub of his argument, and he takes some pride that it was his own inspired idea to get his fellows in the National Vigilance Association to turn their attention to one particular instance of heinous literary activity. "I have here in my hand a public confession by the chief culprit, Mr Speaker. I refer to a Mr Henry Vizetelly, publisher of French novels, who in the *Pall Mall Gazette* a short time ago boasted that his house has been the means of translating and selling in the English market more than one hundred thousand copies of the worst class of French novels. And," he adds, smacking the page before him with his left hand as if it were Vizetelly's cheek, "without a word of reprobation. He boasts that he is, at the present time, selling in England one thousand copies a week of the writings of Mr Émile Zola." He holds up the paper as evidence, and reads from it. "'The success of this work,' Vizetelly writes, 'induced us to reproduce the whole of Zola's published novels to date, and purchase the English copyright of all his new ones.'"

Smith looks at the Speaker, upright on his throne, his eyes cast down – presumably in solemn contemplation. "The success of the work, Mr Speaker. In plainer words, he is suggesting that sales outweigh morality. I am told, though it fills me with sadness to report this, that such indecent literature – little better than penny dreadfuls and almost as cheap – is being supplied to young girls in low bookshops who are in league with houses of the worst class, to which – when the girls' minds are sufficiently polluted and depraved by this Zola's writing – they are consigned. It has become such a trade that I am told there is one street in London where ten shops are devoted to this purpose. How can we allow such abominations to continue? I myself," he adds hastily, before anyone can rise to enquire, "have not chosen to read this filth, but I have on good authority a summary of their content. Mr Speaker, I believe nothing more diabolical has been written by the pen of man."

Now he points theatrically in the direction of the Home Secretary, as if he were the author of the offending material. "I tell you, these novels are only fit for swine – and their constant perusal must turn the mind into something akin to a sty!" Huzzahs greet this last, from different corners of the chamber, in appreciation of his turn of phrase as much as for his larger purpose. Smith allows himself a small, gratified smirk.

The Home Secretary shifts on his leather bench, then extracts an ornate gold pocket watch from his waistcoat. Smith is a worthy man, to be sure, but it is not a pleasure to listen to him, particularly at this late hour. Above them, at the top of the Clock Tower, the Ayrton Light will be lit by now, the gas lantern flickering on high to indicate to the public and to their Queen, who can see the light from Buckingham Palace, that a number of her M.P.s are sitting after dark, diligently fulfilling their duty.

Smith is still on his feet. "Are we to stand still while the country is wholly corrupted by literature of this kind? Are we to wait until the moral fibre of the English race is eaten out, as that of the French is, almost? Look," he cries, eyes ablaze, "I pray you – look what such literature has done for France. It has overspread that country like a torrent, and its poison is destroying the whole national life. France today is rapidly approaching the condition of Rome in the time of the Caesars!"

If he were unobserved, the Home Secretary might roll his eyes at this last. Instead, looking at the scattering of Opposition M.P.s, most of whom seemed enthralled by the tirade, he crosses his arms again and gives a fine impression of being transfixed. Now

Smith riffles through his papers, dropping a few in his fervour, before extracting some recent newspaper articles hostile to the French, which he proceeds to read out to more fully prove his point.

Not one but five journals, the clerks sitting at the table before the Speaker note down carefully, have taken up the subject of the obliteration of the soul of Britain's imperial rivals by licentious reading material. *Plus ça change*; the French are more freethinking than the British, as Henry Matthews learned first-hand when he went to study in Paris in his youth. He loses himself in a memory of his university lodgings there some forty years ago – that view across the rooftops from his desk, the particular blue of the sky before night fell, reflected in the eyes of a lovely girl . . .

His reverie is interrupted by Smith reaching his peroration. "In short, my honourable friends, we are at risk of following the French – this garbage is simply death to our nation!" Several in the chamber applaud at this, some stamping their boots on the wooden floor. "Are we to wait until this deadly poison spreads itself over English soil and kills the life of this great and noble people?"

In the absence of an immediate answer, Smith's face reddens. "Where is the law? Where is the Public Prosecutor? I believe there is someone known by that title, but he seems to be asleep. Or perhaps he has had his wings clipped, as part of the current fashion for a false notion of liberty. Well, I believe in the liberty to do right, but not in the liberty to do wrong!"

The Home Secretary rises to his feet and in one movement is

at the dispatch box. He looks up, meeting Smith's eye, and frowns. Smith swallows hard, some of his bravura draining. "Mr Speaker." Matthews' voice is clipped and efficient, with all the command of the trial lawyer he once was.

"We are in sympathy with this sentiment. But the question is too general for me to express any opinion upon the propriety of suppressing the sale of the publications referred to. The State – in the person of the Public Prosecutor – is of the view that we do not act for private individuals. We have no argument with those who wish to institute proceedings, but it is not our duty to be moral police."

The Speaker turns back to Smith, nodding at him that he might respond.

"But Mr Speaker –" Smith's voice is shrill as a woman's now – "in other countries, Germany and Austria for example, the State undertakes this duty, and they have banned many of Zola's works from publication. This is the preferable way of dealing with this evil, in . . . in my opinion." He trails off.

"Mr Speaker," the Home Secretary responds, "it must be remembered that the law in this country is a tolerably effective weapon as it now stands, and that under the powers conferred by Lord Campbell's Obscene Publications Act of 1857, ample powers were given, which, if effectively used, can prevent the circulation of immoral literature. The reason this law is not put more frequently into force lies in the difficulty experienced in getting juries to draw a hard and fast line and to convict all cases that cross it. Juries are, in my own considerable experience in court, unpredictable. I have given careful attention to this and believe that public judgment is a safer guide than any official extension of power. However, the Honourable Member has done well tonight in directing attention to the insidious mischief resulting from publications which tremble on the verge of public taste."

Smith rises once again, hand held high as if in a schoolroom.

"Mr Speaker. There are, as it happens, many private individuals wishing to get a little encouragement to put the obscenity law in force in Great Britain today. I am happy to think that the Home Secretary thoroughly sympathises with me and I assure this House, I do not bring this matter forward in any opposition to the government. I hope the House will send forth such an expression of strong opinion tonight as would strengthen the hands of the officers of the law, in coping with the enormous evil of this pernicious literature. Thank you."

There is an immediate chorus of "Mr Speaker", "Mr Speaker", as first one and then several other M.P.s jump to their feet from different corners of the chamber. The motion to "vigorously enforce the law against obscene publications" is enthusiastically seconded by the M.P. for Tyrone South, Mr Russell. A moment later, the dapper Sir Robert Fowler, the former Lord Mayor of London, now representing the constituency of the City of London rises to speak. He thanks the M.P. for Flintshire "for doing a great service to the country by calling attention to this subject". Smith sinks back on his seat, dabbing with a handkerchief at his brow. Above the Palace of Westminster, Big Ben strikes ten.

Henry Vizetelly in his prime, circa 1863.   *Ernest Vizetelly, circa 1900.*

Henry Vizetelly is not in the mood for pie. He pushes the nuggets of beefsteak and kidney around his plate and reaches for his wineglass, but even this slight movement causes him to wince. Annie's keen eye falls on him immediately, her brows raised, as concerned as if she were his nurse rather than his daughter. Not wishing to interrupt his sons' conversation across the table, he gives her a surreptitious wink in reassurance. This might surprise a casual observer, for Henry makes a severe first impression; he has been described by a friend as looking "like an old engraving . . . or a character Dürer would have painted . . . truly gaunt and grey and yet with a strange vitality in his eyes."

The pain in his arm is an old shoulder injury, sustained in a carriage crash in Ireland while reporting on the Fenian strife some fifteen years past. It did not heal properly, for he neglected to take care of himself in those heady days, when there was always another challenge ahead and more national conflicts to report. Now and then, in cooler weather, he feels a twinge. Of greater concern to him is the effect the meal will have on his innards, for he suffers terribly from a stricture, which causes him much discomfort. He spends an hour sitting in a warm salt bath before bed each night, to ease the pain in his nether regions, in the vain hope of an uninterrupted sleep. It seems years since he has slept through the night.

What is Ernest grumbling about? Not that wretched article again. Henry drains the last of the fragrant Lafite in his glass, savouring it on his palate. It is an 1870 vintage, a good year.

". . . And the deuce of it is, Papa, Stead had no right to ask you what our sales figures were. What business is it of the *Pall Mall Gazette* if we are doing well or not? Surely our sales figures are only a matter for the Treasury and the taxman, and even they need not be enlightened."

"Ha! I like that, dear Eel!" Arthur, three years his junior, hoots with laughter. Together with his younger half-brother Frank, he is responsible for the business administration of their firm, and despite considerable success in the last few years they never have full coffers. Perhaps if Ernest, who earned his family nickname for an equivocal approach to practical matters, had returned home when they were first establishing the business, they would all be richer today, but Henry, as a writer and artist himself, takes pride in the proper treatment of their stable of authors and illustrators. Until recently, when they have been put under pressure from both their buyers and now the government, the company has always had a reputation in the trade for prompt payment and meticulous administration: they are a firm of gentlemen.

Ernest would not have troubled himself with accounts and contracts by choice; he is a reader, editor and translator – a creative contributor to the business. In his career over the last fifteen years as an author and journalist in France, he has styled himself as "England's youngest war correspondent", a reference to his school days, when he and his older brother were assisting Henry in Paris during the siege, at the height the Franco-Prussian war. Ernest's *nom de plume* when he writes books on French history is *"le petit homme rouge"*, a character in French folklore known for his uncanny skill in predicting calamity – a good choice, given his innate pessimism.

Lately this is much in evidence. Translation has eclipsed all other endeavour for Ernest since the cadre of established contributors at Vizetelly & Company had thrown up their hands at the end of last year over the proofs of Zola's new novel. *The Soil* had arrived from Paris in serial tranches, each one more alarming than the last. Ernest had stepped in with alacrity to take over the work, and brought to bear his superior knowledge of French idiom and custom; but he was gloomy about the material from the first.

His inclinations are more conservative than his father's, though he is half his age.

"Ernest," Henry sighs. "Let us labour this no further. I was caught by an old journalist's trick, and should have known better than to rise to Mr Stead's bait. When he wrote that editorial condemning our translations and querying our sales figures, I felt impelled to reply, to set matters straight, for the honour of our company."

"You mean, Papa, this was an act of ego?" Annie's soft voice has a smile in it, and the tilt of her chin reminds Henry with a pang of her poor mother, Elizabeth, when he first met her at a picnic at Broadstairs, so many years ago. Can it really be fourteen years since she was laid to rest, within a few months of Adrian, his beloved eldest son? What a terrible time.

Annie taps his arm. "Well?"

"What do you expect, my girl? We are a family of egoists, are we not?"

"Speak for yourself." Ernest has drunk the lion's share of the claret.

" Once and for all," Henry says, "I had to correct Stead when he suggested we did not expurgate the work of Zola. Of course we do – we throw a discreet veil over those aspects that might cause offence to our readers. It is common practice! He may require some judicious editing in translation, but I refuse to have Zola's work called pornography by those who have little grasp of literature and its trends. I have long said that he is the French Dickens, and I stand by this view."

Ernest shakes his head. "Your comparison falters in the face of the Bowdler test, Papa. Do you really think – or more to the point, will Stead in all his pompous Podsnappery ever believe – that Zola's works can 'be with propriety read aloud in the family'? Dickens can pass muster, but honestly, can *Nana* be read at the family table?"

Henry pauses for effect, then grins, his face crinkling like parchment. "At my table, certainly!" Annie laughs. The boys do not. "And remember, children, it was not my only subject in the letter to the *Gazette*; I also gave readers the context that you know is essential in good reportage." This is true enough; once he had answered the editor's points in the article, Henry had added a brief history of his distinguished time as a pioneer in the early days of the English illustrated press, making plain that even in the '50s, he was an innovator – for example, he published the first editions in England of Mr Poe's stories and of *Uncle Tom's Cabin*. He went on to share other "personal reminiscences" in the article, many of them beside the point, but a tendency to digress is, it must be said, characteristic of Henry's writing.

Ernest sighs. "And now you are vilified in Parliament. While I was living in Paris and you wrote to solicit my advice about bringing out the translation of *Nana*, I warned you of this."

Henry interrupts him, wagging a bony finger. "And I did not ignore you – in each Zola novel we have published I have included a preface, either from the pen of the author or from a learned colleague, which adds context and a certain literary imprimatur. And until now these seem to have satisfied my readers, and the regulators."

"But, Papa, the preface of *Nana* has Zola criticising the English for strangling their fiction with censorship! And preface or no preface, it remains a book about a professional cocotte. I told you; this country has not changed so much since the days when Mr Cleland and his publisher were arrested for writing *Fanny Hill*. You disregarded my advice that France has a greater degree of freedom of expression these days, while English journalism and publishing are still under the thumb of Mrs Grundy." Ernest references the figurative "judgmental neighbour" so popular in English discourse. "Her crusaders for purity see Zola's works as threats to the *status quo*, even to the Empire itself, as if such writing is an attack on all that is virtuous and English. And here you are boasting to the world, 'Zola sales: one thousand copies a week'!"

Now Arthur, who is as gloomy as Ernest about the whole affair, leans forward, his shirtfront dangerously close to the gravy pooling on his plate, his fork stabbing the air. "Papa, that devil Stead is Samuel Smith's close conspirator, and he has an uncanny knack for finding a few words amongst hundreds, isolating them from the text of an article, and making the phrase into a banner crossheading that is red as a toreador's cape to all detractors."

"Ah well, he twisted what I said," Henry shrugs. "What I meant was that we sell one thousand books a week by Monsieur Zola, which is not a great deal considering we have eighteen of his titles in print."

"That is precisely it," Ernest says. "Mr Stead warps any statement to suit his editorial aims. You might have said you abhorred Zola, Naturalism, the entire French nation for that matter, and he would have magically transformed your words into love poetry."

"What's done is done, my boy. We are not doomed just because a handful of politicians endured a windy speech in Parliament. This will pass when a more sensational or urgent story arises; it is always the way. Remember, I am a long-time contributor to the *Gazette*, not their target. Do you recall how we used to send dispatches to them by hot air balloon from Paris, eh, during—"

"During the Commune days, when the city was aflame and there was carnage in the street," intone his children, as one.

Henry has to laugh. Though they may be irreverent, a man could not ask for more loyal children. It is his own fault that they are independent thinkers – he had raised them to be so, exposing them to ideas, culture and experiences that few of their peers could match. His elder sons were forged in the excitement and danger of reporting alongside him in those war-torn Paris years and, with the assistance of their late lamented mothers, all of his children had had a liberal education, surrounded by books and the freethinking writers and artists who were dear family friends.

He is glad to share his home today, comfortably situated above the offices in Catherine Street, behind the Strand, with Frank and Annie, his youngest children, aged twenty-four and twenty-six respectively. He beams at them as they devour their desserts with gusto, racing to be the first to finish their French cook's colourful *macédoines*. He might be left a lonely widower yet, if they marry, but for now, his progeny surrounds him – those who remain. Tragically, the eleven children his two wives bore him over four decades have been reduced in number to five – the others dying in infancy or early adulthood, like poor Adrian. His eldest now is Edward, who has not been heard from for some time, though they understand he has been sent to Zanzibar for the *New York Herald*; he too is a war reporter, with his father's appetite for adventure and danger.

There is nothing Henry wishes for more than to leave his brood some fortune, and the legacy of a successful family business. This was something his own father failed to do for him and his brothers. He well remembers the anguish and shame that came from the failure of his father's printing firm when he was eighteen, and how he swore to himself then that he would make his family name respected once more in the trade.

It seemed likely, when he returned to publishing books after twenty-five years devoted to journalism, that he had found the answer: contemporary French novels in translation. He had observed for years that the novels he is now publishing were gaining steady and lasting popularity in France. His early ventures were not wholly successful, as he had also admitted in his recent *Gazette* article; Mérimée and Gréville did not sell. He moved on to popular mystery novels, and matters improved. At the same time he brought out a number of Russian novels, by Tolstoy, Dostoyevsky and Gogol, some of which sold well. Then, "after much hesitation", as he put it in that article (although privately he meant "after some concern about his company coffers"), he turned to Zola. Over half a million copies of Zola's Rougon-Macquart novels had been sold in France. His rival Tinsley and a few others had attempted to publish poor three-volume translations in England only to be thwarted by the moralistic circulating libraries, which would not stock them. How could the Vizetellys fail to succeed by selling them, direct to the public, as affordable one-volume editions? There was the brilliant idea.

Henry had always been an inspired thinker, as friends would be sure to say in his memory, when his time came. There was, for example, the *tour de force* of his own first book, an apparently eyewitness account of his adventures in the California Gold Rush, although at that time, he had never set foot out of England. *The Times* gave the book a fine review, remarking that the reader need not go west, as the author had done such a superb job of detailing his own experience – he had fooled everyone. It is equally true that some of his bold ideas could be fallible in execution.

Outside, the sounds of carriage and foot traffic come and go, as patrons depart the variety theatre in nearby Drury Lane. The laughter of a group of young men in high spirits, doubtless making their way to or from the Opera Tavern at Number 23, drifts upward in the night air. At the window there is a reflection of the deep red colouring from the gas jets of the streetlamps, vivid on this rare clear night. Enjoying a cigar after the ladies withdraw and stretching out his long legs by the fire, Henry is reminded of a long-ago trip to Bad Homburg before the war, when it was the Prussian Monte Carlo. Those were the best of times, he thinks – he had good health, a full head of hair, and the boundless energy of youth. He had travelled with his old friend Mayhew, he recalls, and that rogue Gus Sala, almost getting thrown out of the dining car at the border for their merrymaking and loud discourse, fuelled by French champagne.

At the spa, they had made for the roulette tables, confident of an infallible system he had devised. It was sure to make their fortunes. Within eleven days, the three of them were reduced to sharing a stale crust of bread for their tea, and made their way home red-faced, crushed beside the cargo at the back of the train. Infallible systems, Henry now knows, at the venerable age of sixty-eight, are doomed to fail. This is precisely why he had taken "the Zola risk", as Arthur dourly refers to it these days – it was a risk, albeit a calculated one, because he knows his audience.

234   PUNCH, OR THE LONDON CHARIVARI.   [November 14, 1885.

SANCTA SIMPLICITAS!

Mamma. "Don't stand idling there, Tommy! Why don't you read French sometimes! Look at dear Papa, he hasn't much time for Reading; but whenever he's got a spare moment or two, he takes a French Book out of his Pocket and reads it—just to keep up his French, you know!"   [*Dear Papa is much tickled, but keeps his amusement to himself.*

Henry Vizetelly has worked in the press and publishing world all his life; his father and grandfather before him were printers; he has ink in his blood. With a flair for artistry as well as for words, he began his career as an engraver, soon moving into printing and the publishing of illustrated books and periodicals with his elder brother James, before becoming an author, editor and journalist for various London papers. Along the way, he had also nurtured a thriving second career as a wine connoisseur, and became a respected author on the subject.

He might not be able to guess where a die would fall, or which card might next be turned, but he speaks with certainty about English readers. His success with Zola proves it: he predicted correctly that mass ranks of newly educated men, the first beneficiaries of the 1870 Education reforms to come of age, who were working their way out of the gutter with a few shillings to spare, would like to read about protagonists of their own background, preferably with the seductive promise of "realism" between the cardboard covers of affordable novels. Hang the dissenters, none of whom had spent a day of their life labouring in a mine, a factory or a washhouse, and whose soft hands deigned to hold only the French originals of the titles he published. As for the alchemy that they now claim he practises, converting fine literature into "pornography" by dint of an English translation – what utter nonsense.

"Nonsense," he says aloud. "These fools in Parliament and the press will lose their steam, and stutter to a stop at the next station, I warrant. I have told you before, Ernest, it seems to me the country is changing, her stays are loosening . . ."

Ernest is slumped over a decanter of Madeira in the corner, brown eyes dull under heavy lids. "I pray you are right, Papa." Henry knows that flat look. A few months earlier, Ernest had come into Henry's panelled office on the floor below, waiting until his father finished signing a letter before he spoke. Glancing up, Henry immediately knew by his son's face that something was amiss. "Tell me."

"Papa, I do not – I have no wish to worry you . . . but if *Nana* and *L'Assommoir* . . . were at the boundary edge of public taste, it seems to me that this new book, *The Soil,* is beyond that scale. What is more, it lacks the lesson that those tales of urban degradation carry. I can see how it was possible to argue that those stories were meant as warning bells, by a moralistic author, to dissuade his readers from emulating the sorry and desperate heroines. But I feel that option is not open to us here; frankly, I don't know where an apologist would begin with *The Soil.* I have been going over the final proofs today . . . there is more revision needed before we can print."

His father was irritated by this handwringing: much as he loved his son, the boy could be tiresome. They were in danger of losing as many pages in this new novel as they had eventually cut from Zola's *Piping Hot!* a year earlier. That was the tenth Rougon-Macquart novel, following the adventures of Octave Mouret, son of Marthe Rougon, a young salesman who moves into a Paris apartment building teeming with sexual intrigues. Its content was reduced by a third, once they had pruned away the potentially offending elements. Though Henry knew some reduction in length was inevitable in a translation from French to English, the latter being a more concise language, there had to be a limit.

"Ernest. I recognise that prudence is required, and I am keenly aware that my own sensibilities, honed outside the narrow confines of conventional society, are not naturally in line with the ordinary English reader. But we cannot continue to cut and cut. There will be nothing left."

This was not their first debate about *The Soil*; it began as soon as Ernest was given the French proofs. He was immediately struck by their boldness. To be fair, Henry does not have the same grasp or breadth of French vocabulary as his sons, and in fact he has relied on them over the years to make up for his deficiencies, even taking them along to meetings with French dignitaries as boys, in order to translate for him. Ernest has spent the majority of his life in France, living there since the age of twelve and educated at the Lycée Bonaparte, when Henry became foreign correspondent for the *Illustrated London Times*. He married a girl from the Haute-Savoie, Marie Tissot, who is now pregnant with their third child.

That wintry day in the office, he showed his father the letter Zola had sent about his intentions in writing *The Soil*: "He is very plain – he calls it a depiction of the human race at its worst. He says here: 'I wish to do for the peasant what I did in *L'Assommoir* for the Paris workman.' Think, Papa, what opprobrium was heaped on that work in England. Henry James, who counts himself amongst Zola's friends, even spoke against it. He said the book

70

was 'like an emanation from an open drain'. Have you forgotten?"

"That is Naturalism, dear boy," Henry had said. "And Mr James, a man known for being of two minds on many subjects, has gone on since then to say in public that the English novel is sorely constricted by its need to be kept wholesome for virgins and boys."

Yet Ernest protested further. Apparently, in France, this new addition to the Rougon-Macquart saga had excited widespread negative comment, more than ever before. Why, Zola's own disciples had denounced the author in the national press! Some critics, including the influential poet and journalist Anatole France, were hinting that Zola had abandoned his ideals and was turning to pornography for profit, "portraying peasants rolling about in the fields fornicating".

Henry dismissed all of this as more nonsense. It was as if everyone had forgotten that Zola had wealth and renown in abundance, and could have easily afforded to take a safer path at this stage. He remained confident of publishing the book, regardless of the amount of water his son must add to the brew to make it palatable to the English; he is also mindful of the significant advance he has given to Zola for English copyright in his works, which must be recouped. Henry indicated that it was for Ernest to apply the editorial principles he had established in the firm over the last four years for literature in translation, and which had sufficed to date. These were the basic rules:

¶ Soften bodily acts and sexual relations. Real abridging,
as far as Henry saw it, would mean deleting the fact of

those natural acts in the narrative; softening was trying to find another way to describe them. In *Nana*, "you slept with her" became "you knew her intimately"; "Nana was naked" became "Nana was next to naked". In *L'Assommoir*, when Gervaise Macquart finds her drunken husband slumped on the floor in a squalid room spattered with vomit, this became "Coupeau lay wallowing on the floor".

¶ Descriptions of "women's functions" had to be attenuated or cut if possible, insofar as they did not directly further the narrative – including references to pregnancy, labour, menstruation and women's experience of sex. For example, a passing reference to Gervaise's menstruation ("like women every month curdle milk") was excised, and the frequent rapes in Zola's novels were glossed over, so that the reader was dimly aware that intercourse had occurred but with none of the savage detail.

¶ Softening of Zola's frequent use of blasphemy and swearing with euphemism.

The Soil was duly purified. No longer was the character of Hyacinthe nicknamed "Jesus Christ" for his long hair and beard, and his habit of using explosive flatulence as a conversational gambit was much reduced. Scenes of rape and domestic violence had their careful emendations. The simultaneous experience of childbirth by Lise and her milk cow was restricted to a few lines.

And yet, the sense remained; it was impossible to quell the raw and erotic energy of the writing – the material was resistant.

What an irony. Henry established Vizetelly & Company as the publishers of inexpensive one-volume collections of European fiction alongside a number of English and Irish authors. At the same time he created the Mermaid Series, bringing out unabridged affordable editions of the Restoration dramatists and Shakespeare, which had met with success due to the firm's location in the heart of London's theatre district. *The Soil* tells the story of a man who divides his property between his children with disastrous results – Henry was merely offering an affordable French retelling of *King Lear*, was he not?

It does occur to Henry, of course, that the problem is political as much as prudish. Zola's interest in land rights and inheritance in *The Soil* does not describe a conflict amongst a royal family in a distant kingdom long ago – it is about contemporary peasant life. It is an uncomfortable mirror held up to nature for the British government, faced with the ongoing problem of agitation in Ireland over tenant farmers' desire for fair dealing and protection there. This could be the nub of it all, as Henry had discussed over a meal at the club in recent weeks with his young friend – and his firm's original conduit to Zola – the author George Moore. Two years earlier, Henry had published Moore's novel *A Drama in Muslin*, which dealt directly with the Irish land war.

Moore is born of Irish gentry – he inherited around twelve thousand acres of land in County Mayo on his father's death. He is an extrovert and enthusiast, a *bon viveur* with considerable writing flair who has been much inspired by Zola (he once proclaimed himself to be the "English ricochet" of the master). He made a friend of him while living in Paris during the '70s, and heartily recommended Vizetelly when Zola was looking to sell the English rights in *The Soil*.

Never in agreement with his own late father, an Irish M.P. and strict Catholic who did not approve of his career choices, Moore sees his publisher as a paternal figure. It has to be said, he is not so fortunate in his looks as his mentor and sons; the Vizetelly men are well made and handsome as a rule, with fine features and a natural élan in dress and bearing. G.M., as his friends call him, is forever hitching up his trousers on his gangling frame; he has a long pasty face, and dull reddish-flaxen hair that looks as if it has been pitchforked on to his head. A female acquaintance once remarked that he "looks like a codfish crossed with a satyr", and W. B. Yeats described Moore as appearing to be "carved from a turnip, looking out of astonished eyes".

When they last met, Henry told Moore that they had written to warn Zola there was a significant amount of necessary expurgation in *The Soil*, due to cultural differences between the two countries. He eyed the other man warily over the top of his glass as he spoke, for Moore had suffered much at the hands of censors at the start of his own career, before Vizetelly had agreed to publish his work. Would he think Zola must be outraged by this action? "Your esteemed friend did not resist, I must assure you, G.M., but I do not wish him to judge us harshly for it later," Henry hastened to add.

Moore clinked his glass with Henry's, the crystal chiming. "I am not surprised he was amenable. His English is even worse than your French, and he never looks back at the last novel when he is immersed in the next. Be assured, I will continue to vouch for you as the most courageous publisher in England, my dear friend. Remember, Zola is no stranger to the censor in France – think of *L'Assommoir*, which could not be sold at French railway stations for years – and the way the Minister of Arts demanded that he butcher the stage version of *Germinal*. My friend is practically inured to such responses, after a decade of constant *succès de scandale* at home, and he would expect no less. Nor would his readers, I imagine. Why, it has become a measure of popular appeal! When high-minded journalists and Catholic commentators squeal about pornography with each week's instalment of a new Zola serialisation, it is sure to sell out immediately in Paris."

The fanatics in England might do well to take note of this, Moore had said. If they were up in arms about the casual carnality described in the new novel, why, let the hypocrites wail and the sales rise! This crusade against Zola was becoming laughable, Moore observed, with all the relish of an inveterate gossip. Lowering his voice he had leaned over and asked Henry, "Did you hear the most ludicrous part of that M.P.'s tirade? One wonders at the time afforded him in the Commons. Evidently, within his wild ranting he let it be known that it was impossible for any young man to read two pages of Zola's writing 'without committing some form of outward sin within twenty-four hours'. Can you credit that?" Moore slapped his knee in delight. "And he has admitted, doubtless to forestall such a fate, that he himself has not ventured to read one page! What contempt without investigation!" Henry chuckled with him.

Another reason for the campaign against Zola occurs to Henry now, as he stares into the gloom, his cigar forgotten, the coals rustling and sighing as they crumble in the grate before him. Racism. His eyes fall on a favourite heirloom, a wooden mantel clock that has been in his family for generations, inlaid with Italian marquetry. Zola and Vizetelly's own Italian blood are suggested as cause for prosecution in certain tirades. What claptrap, Henry thinks; the Vizzetelli family first arrived on English shores from Venice three centuries ago, rapidly anglicising the spelling of their name and marrying into generations of good English stock. We are now more English than the men who despise us, including Smith, that finger-wagging Scottish M.P. with a voice like a reed whistle. He and his strait-laced cronies have no case. The whole furore is ludicrous. "Nonsense," Henry says aloud again, as if repetition will make it so. There is no response. Frank has gone to bed an hour since, and Arthur has slipped away home. Henry prods Ernest. His head lolls against the side of a velvet wingback chair. He is fast asleep.

4. *July 1888, Pall Mall*

W. T. Stead, editor of the Pall Mall Gazette *and a founding member of the National Vigilance Association, 1890.*

The meeting is brief and the committee expect their carriages by noon. "It is resolved then, gentlemen", the council's secretary, Mr William Coote, summarises. "We shall press home our advantage as soon as possible." His assistant, Mr Turnbull, scribbles notes at his elbow. "I shall speak to our solicitor, Mr Charles Colette, at my earliest opportunity and apply for a summons against Vizetelly & Company for publishing three obscene works, to wit . . . number one, *Nana*, number two, *The Soil*, and . . . er . . ."

"*Piping Hot!*" Turnbull says. "*Pot-Bouille*, that is. In French."

"Yes," his employer says, "Number three, *Piping Hot!*" Coote grimaces, as if forced to taste some bitter fruit. He is a prude, and even uttering these Zola titles makes him uneasy. A Londoner in his mid-forties, he is a solid fellow with large moustaches and a thick head of greying hair, with the broad hands of a labourer. He is the son of a poor widow, who left school at the age of twelve to become a printer's apprentice, and was "born again" at sixteen; he has been elevated to an important role on the National Vigilance Association's council due to his passionate dedication to the cause, and an appetite for hard work.

It is Coote who had volunteered, some months earlier, to step over enemy lines and enter Vizetelly & Company's offices, three streets away from the N.V.A. headquarters in the Strand. There, together with the group's accountant Mr Bloxham as his brave witness, he dared to acquire one of the Zola illustrated editions for consideration by the literary subcommittee. Though they took pains to affect nonchalance, it was clear that the bookseller suspected something, possibly due to Coote's agonised refusal when invited to look over the bawdy engravings within the book prior to purchase.

Coote's mentor is William Stead, host of today's gathering at the offices of the newspaper he edits. The *Pall Mall Gazette* is a name taken from a fictional journal conceived by the novelist Thackeray; founded a quarter of a century earlier, it is the leading London daily paper "by gentlemen, for gentlemen".

Stead unfolds his long limbs from his chair at the table's head and stands. He is approaching his fortieth year and is more than six feet tall. It would surprise no-one to learn that he is descended from a line of hardy Norsemen, with those sea blue eyes, that leonine head and the bearing of a prophet. He is renowned for his perfectionism, and does the work of ten men on every issue of the paper, controlling all aspects of its output. "May I make a few observations before we conclude?" He surveys the group before him and pauses for effect.

"Gentlemen. This is an auspicious day. My paper, and, it seems, virtually all the significant publications in Britain today are linking arms with the National Vigilance Association." He indicates the array of newsprint strewn across the long table, containing articles from the numerous publications reporting the recent Zola debate in the Commons, with many ringing endorsements of Samuel Smith's speech.

The article in the *Globe*, his biggest competitor, concludes, "Zola's books are characterised by a dangerous lubricity that saps the foundations of manhood and womanhood." The *Birmingham Daily Mail* has to concur: "Zola simply wallows in immorality." The *Western Morning News* says, "It is the shame of Zola that he has put an end to reticence." The *Standard*, the *Scotsman*, *Reynold's Newspaper*, the *Country Gentleman*, the *Methodist Times*, Catholic journal the *Tablet*, and many other papers join in the refrain.

It is a fine moment for the Association, the high point since their formation three years earlier. A successor to the Society for the Suppression of Vice (which had collapsed when its board was rocked by financial irregularity scandals), it had been established as a philanthropic society "for the enforcement and improvement of the laws for the repression of criminal vice and public immorality", and began with laudable campaigns to halt the trafficking of women and children. Like every group of its kind, they are fired with a profound sense of righteousness, and have a mission to swell their membership – but to do so, they must maintain a high profile and extend the scope of their interests. Hence the new focus on immoral "literature", a word invariably to be found in quotation marks in their newsletters and pamphlets.

"Yes, my fellow citizens," Stead sings out like a candidate on the stump, "we are linking arms against the sea of trouble which Vizetelly's catalogue represents for our country, and in particular for the youth of today. As a devoted father of six myself, I know that the curiosity of children is insatiable, and if we cannot get the government to protect the young from the kind of debasing material that is being published in the name of art, we are bound by our duty as Christians to proceed in this regard."

"Thank you, Mr Stead, this is noted," Coote says, reaching hopefully for his hat. There is still time to reach the midday meal with his mother, who despite her advancing years is still a deft hand in the kitchen. But Stead is not finished.

"As you know, I have shown, in my small way, that the power of the press can be greater than the power of government, and can influence real change in legislation by its ability to communicate directly with the people." He refers, of course, to his infamous campaign three years earlier, prosecuted from this office, when he

80

wrote a series of editorial articles titled "The Maiden Tribute of Modern Babylon". Through this bold and sensational investigation, he proved to doubters that there was a thriving sex trade in young children in London, and forced the government to take action.

Until then, the legislators had been sluggish when reformers had demanded change to the Criminal Act protecting children, and Stead, fired with the mixture of rashness, morality and zeal that had informed his whole life and career, had gone incognito into the depths of the Pimlico slums. He brought forth, with the assistance of a reformed brothel-keeper, a child called Eliza Armstrong – the twelve-year-old daughter of a woman addicted to alcohol and living in such depravity that she sold him her daughter as a sex slave: "A Virgin for a Fiver", as his cross-headline proclaimed.

As the story developed, Stead reported that he had kidnapped and drugged the girl and subjected her to a thorough medical exam to prove her virgin state (in order to demonstrate to the reader that corrupt doctors would certify such things for clients), before sending her to a life of lonely safety in the South of France, where she knew no-one and could not communicate. This was considered by his enemies to be as extreme as anything Zola might describe in his novels; some also remarked on his prurient interest in the sex trade and his "first-hand experience", an implied criticism of the proximity of vice and vigilance.

Stead maintained that the girl's so-called abduction was a brave rescue, stating in his defence that "the duty of a journalist is the duty of a watchman". He pointed out that his concerns had been shared for years by eminent literary and political leaders, including Charles Dickens and former Prime Minister Gladstone – and he scoffed at his enemies, including the editor and critic W. E. Henley, who put it about that his rival was henceforth to be nicknamed "Bed Stead". Not long after the success of the serialisation, Stead was in court, prosecuted by the Crown for abduction and for "revealing infamies under the very shadow of the home of our dear Queen". He stood by his intentions: one child suffered somewhat, and far less than she might otherwise have, that he might save a thousand more. The future depended on those who were prepared to make difficult choices for the greater good.

This episode was consistent with a lifetime of fanatical conviction. As a young man of just twenty-one, already taking an interest in the larger world of press and politics from his home village in Yorkshire, he read avidly about the Siege of Paris – possibly even in dispatches sent by Henry Vizetelly, who was trapped there with his young sons. During the one hundred and thirty days that the Prussians bombarded the city, attempting to starve out the Communards, it was reported that hungry Parisians eventually resorted to trapping and eating mice. Years later Stead would relate that he was so determined to live for himself the experience of those unfortunates that upon hearing of this, he trapped a mouse himself and ate it, "on toast".

Stead's account of his sojourn into "the Modern Babylon" was serialised over several weeks and provoked such public outcry that the statute was soon changed to raise the age of consent to sexual acts from thirteen to sixteen. He cared little that he had to pay for this moral success with a three-month prison term. Every year since that time, on the anniversary of his being incarcerated, he proudly donned his prison garb for the day to honour the memory of a small price paid for such a reward: he has made the world a better place.

Though he does not lack a sense of humour, Stead sees no irony in the fact that he is now campaigning against obscene books. His motives are and always have been pure; he strives to awake the public conscience, to serve the truth. Who could say the same of the profit-driven publisher? Small matter that the *Gazette* made plenty of money from the Eliza Armstrong story, which had whipped up such public demand for its next instalment that crowds of people had thronged the street outside their offices every morning, awaiting the latest edition. Unfortunately the paper's circulation figures have declined ever since, but let it not be said that they alone motivate Stead's interest in this new morality campaign. He is, once again, taking a stand against evil.

"Gentlemen." Stead is interrupted by the low voice of another council member, John Kensit, a former bookseller and now the publisher of the group's periodical, the *Vigilance Record*, as well as fliers and informational pamphlets. A militant Protestant campaigner, he has a habit of bringing matters back to earth when rhetoric is flying high at these meetings. "I am not confident we have satisfied ourselves on one point."

"And that is?" Mr Coote despairs of his lunch.

Crowds besiege the Gazette *office during the "Maiden Tribute" serialisation.*

"What are we to answer if they respond that the same works have long been published here in French with impunity?"

Coote starts to answer, but Stead pounces. "Indeed, my friend, you might well ask, for it is the logical avenue to take. Hundreds if not thousands of books by Émile Zola have been sold in French here. As you are aware, I have had the opportunity to peruse some of them, in the course of my work, with the advantage of a fair knowledge of that tongue. They are, to my eye, no better for being read in the original, save that the prose style is more refined, and the language and forms of speech befit the original setting.

"Do let us remember, gentlemen, that our intention here is not merely to silence a writer – and it essential that we are not seen to be so blunt. In fact, Monsieur Zola is an accomplished man, I can admit, and a capable journalist who had a fine critical career before he wrote these novels. My objection is that he now presents vile invention as if it were real, in the form of so-called "naturalistic stories", for his private gain. In short, he may write what he will, and his native audience may take action if they wish, or do nothing and weep for the degradation that may follow. But we are Englishmen!" He thumps the table for emphasis, causing one of their group, Miss Beswick, the only female of their mixed membership to join the subcommittee today, to blanch.

"And women," Stead goes on, with a kindly nod in her direction, "which is why we are seeking to stop the material this Frenchman writes from falling into the wrong hands in our country. I do not speak only of our youth, or of the gloved hands of an educated reader; we must keep this pernicious filth out of the bare hands – and minds – of the masses! These people, literate but barely educated, have no filters, and no deeply bred training that will save them from the potentially dire affects which have been so vividly outlined by our friend Mr Smith here, in the Commons."

Mr Coote nods thoughtfully, in full accord. Though he is not what anyone might call an educated reader, and began his life amongst the so-called masses, he considers himself made in a new mould now, having been blessed by God to rise from the gutter and improve his life. "They", those masses, are so vulnerable. They must be protected, and he is pleased to be dedicated to a movement that will do so.

Samuel Smith, M.P., at the opposite end of the table, acknowledges Stead's compliment with a modest smile, while privately thanking the dear Lord that he will never have occasion to fight for his electoral seat against Stead. He is also glad of his lack of French, as he would not wish to waste an hour of his life reading pages of the putrid material in question, but he has to admit, it is helpful that Stead has done so. The man had been able to apprise the committee of the contents of the work, in the broadest outline, from the moment that Smith had suggested "literature" as a focus for their campaign. At first, they were wary of the idea, on the grounds that by bringing certain books to prominence they might increase the public's appetite for reading them, thereby causing greater damage to the country's moral fabric – especially if they lost the case against Vizetelly. But Stead had stepped in, arm around Smith's shoulders, and signalled such unqualified support that the proposal was carried.

Smith and Stead do not always agree. The Scotsman does not approve of Stead's support for the expansion of certain women's rights – why, Stead even goes so far as to employ some women on his newspaper as journalists. Smith is dedicated to halting of the spread of suffrage, and to keeping women in their rightful place by the hearthside. The two men also have divergent views about the reporting of divorce cases, an increasing practice in the English press that Smith finds unsavoury, and liable to incite yet more marital breakdown. Stead, as pragmatic as he is moralistic, understands his public's keen appetite for such matters and his journalists continue to report from the divorce courts. What can you expect, Smith's wife wants to know, from the man who had invented a column called "Tittle-tattle at Teatime"?

During his tenure as editor of the *Gazette*, Stead has also initiated a practice of giving column space to interviews with celebrated figures in the news, often-controversial characters in the world of arts and letters – including the subject of their meeting today, Monsieur Zola. Four years earlier, on the eve of publication of the novel *Germinal* in England, the author was interviewed about the book, which had caused a sensation in Paris with its socialist message and vivid scenes of striking miners and mob violence. Smith still remembers how that interview had stirred quite a response in the drawing rooms and corridors of Whitehall, with its stark concluding note from Zola: "My book is a warning to those who think the future is safe."

It may be that publishing such invidious material is Stead's way of showing balance, or simply increasing circulation. He is adept at walking the tightrope between commercialism and morality, that much is certain – and his "New Journalism" devices sell papers. Smith, Coote, Kensit and others in the council hold their tongues, recognising the import of having one of England's most influential and ingenious editors among their ranks; it is rightly said that his paper "leads the leaders of public opinion". But they are in regular discussion about the thorny question of the power of the press, when Stead is not present; it can be a force for justice and morality, but equally it can be an engine of corruption. There is a constant ethical calculation to be made about how a group espousing purity should utilise to best advantage those associated with the impure.

Stead is coming to a close at last. "Protection of the innocent is the essence of Lord Campbell's original obscenity Act, and our golden opportunity, gentlemen, is to add power to the original ruling by defining what actually constitutes obscenity, widening the definition from obvious pornography to pernicious literature."

"Hear, hear!" Miss Beswick bursts out, and Turnbull suppresses a smile. She blushes prettily and looks down at her hands.

"Thank you for your enthusiasm; it is a valuable asset to our cause." Stead gives her a bow before taking his seat. "Gentlemen?"

"We will reconvene on the fourth of next month, for a report on our progress," Coote says. "I am sure we all thank you for your valuable insights, Mr Stead." And he leads a round of polite applause, in the face of which Stead bows his handsome head again; he is the picture of humility.

Chairs are pushed back, goodbyes said, hats donned, and the

men disperse. Miss Beswick makes much of tidying the papers scattered across the mahogany table. She is the last to the door. She turns back. "Mr Stead? You are . . . that is, I mean to say, I am so pleased we are taking this important action."

"Everything wrong in the world is a divine call to use your life in righting it, Miss Beswick. That is my motto." His passion is genuine. His blue eyes shine, as if he is on the brink of tears.

"My!" She cannot think of a better response, suffused as she is with admiration for him. Mortified, she feels her face grow hot again – she must look like a beetroot.

"A divine call," he says again, with a winning smile, and now he is by her side. Does she imagine it or does his hand touch the small of her back, as if to guide her from the room?

PART II:
ON TRIAL

5. *August 1888, Bow Street*

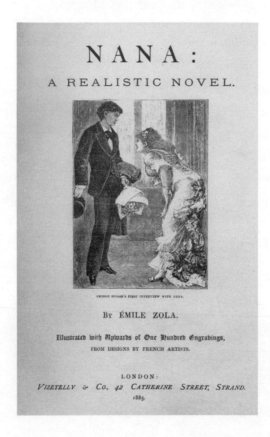

NANA:

A REALISTIC NOVEL.

GEORGE HUGON'S FIRST INTERVIEW WITH NANA.

By ÉMILE ZOLA.

Illustrated with Upwards of One Hundred Engravings,
FROM DESIGNS BY FRENCH ARTISTS.

LONDON:
VIZETELLY & CO., 42 CATHERINE STREET, STRAND.
1885.

The court is not yet in session. Mr Lickfold is bent over a slim volume, turning the pages. Ernest, sketching the solicitor in the margins of his notes in an attempt to allay his nerves, catches the man's double chin and the stray hairs escaping from his wig in a few swift strokes of his pen. He shifts forward to get a better view of the book. It is no legal tome; the binding is too delicate. Is he reading poetry as a kind of ritual, like the athlete who prays before the race? Unlikely, for Lickfold. Ah, he can see now, it is Byron's "Don Juan", which forms part of their defence.

Now the solicitor makes a careful dot in the margin of the left page and then turns down the corner – a practice Ernest loathes. He tries to catch his father's eye to share his disapproval, for that heedless mutilation of books is his *bête noire* too. But Henry is perched on the edge of his chair, his eyes cast down as if the buttons on his boots are the most interesting objects in the world. Focusing on something mundane is one way to cope with the acute pain he experiences more or less constantly these days. Thankfully, his son thinks, Papa will not have to stand like a common criminal in that hideous wooden dock; he is not under arrest, he is simply answering a summons.

Ernest has walked past the impressive Portland stone building many times; it is not ten minutes from the Vizetelly office. It stands facing the front entrance of the Royal Italian Opera House, at the northern end of "Bow Street" – so named because it runs in the shape of a bent bow on one side. The courtroom was purpose-built not long ago and it still has a newness to it, he fancies, combined with the faint scent of perspiration. There is also a whiff of beer in the air, given the nature of the earlier sessions. The mornings at Bow Street are set aside for applications for summons and night charges (generally drunken men and women); today's session thankfully adjourned soon after their arrival. A different type of defendant has replaced the morning's motley crew, men dressed in frock coats and hats, clutching bulky files. They are accompanied by their lawyers, some already wearing wigs while others opt to carry them until the last moment – the heavy hairpieces are prickly and hot in the summer heat. A few police officers stand by to keep order.

Ernest's eyes come to rest on the prosecutor's table. Their counsel is also studying a leather-bound volume. Ernest looks up at the wooden clock, high on the wall near the door. We were scheduled to begin at eleven, he thinks irritably – but of course, the courts keep their own time, and all you can hope for is to not be left in limbo for several hours, rather than for the mere twenty-five minutes that they have been sitting patiently, awaiting the magistrates' return.

The prosecution's solicitor is Henry Herbert Asquith; he is around the same age as Ernest, in his late thirties, and of similarly slim build. His long legs stretch out before him and are crossed at the ankle. Evident under his wig is a fine head of hair and he is blessed with the good looks of an actor. He is quite ruddy in the cheek, however, like some who are overfond of their porter. During his recent campaign to be elected as Liberal M.P. for East Fife, there was sly comment in the press about his nickname: it seems his friends from school days call him "Squiffy".

H. H. Asquith, M.P.

The case is being made in the name of the Secretary of the National Vigilance Association committee, Mr William Coote, who sits alongside Asquith at the table. He looks a miserable sort, Ernest thinks. I wonder if he has a father he loves? There are three others present, staring straight ahead. With their dour expressions, long whiskers and high collars, they resemble a team of undertakers. Asquith takes a cream-coloured visiting card from his pocket and uses it to mark a page. He is of another class of reader to Lickfold, you have to grant him that.

The book in his hands is one of the firm's fully illustrated quarto editions. Which one? The green cover with ornate gold and red engraving is hard to read at this distance. Was it *Piping Hot!*, *The Soil*, or *Nana*? All three titles were cited in the summons. It is *Nana* – Ernest can discern Bellenger's engraving of the voluptuous girl on the cover, leaning forward to greet an awe-struck suitor. Ranged before Asquith and his clients are several other books from the series. It appears they have brought the complete works of Zola with them today, but plainly they will lead with the most notorious, the story of the *mangeuse d'hommes* who captivated Paris.

Now the senior clerk calls the court to order and announces the arrival of the judges, and both Ernest and Arthur move to help their father to his feet. Henry waves them away, standing on his own with a little grunt of effort, facing the bench, hands clasped behind his back. He often takes this stance on public occasions; it makes him look important – and with his chest out and head held high, he seems ready for anything. Ernest knows this is also a way to hide the involuntary tremors in Henry's hands that accompany his spasms of pain. His pride will not let him play the feeble old man, particularly in front of the reporters in their box and the gawpers in the public gallery. Bow Street, situated in the middle of the theatre district, has become a sort of entertainment of its own over the years, with dedicated regulars, male and female, who laugh and chat together now as they take their seats, looking as if they were about to enjoy the latest programme at Drury Lane.

As ever, Ernest is impressed by his father's sheer effort of will; he is not sure that he would stand so tall in his place, though he and his brothers had been sincere in their offers to do so. Frank had begged his father again last night to allow him to take his place as the representative of the firm, arguing he was the youngest and therefore the most resilient. "Resilience, Francis, is earned with age, I assure you," Henry had replied fondly, and would hear no more about it.

"Mr John Bridge," intones the clerk in his nasal voice.

The man who will determine whether this case will proceed to a jury trial walks in briskly and drops into his carved wooden chair, facing the solicitors' tables. A second magistrate in the same long robe and wig sits down at his side. In addition there are two clerks taking their seats, followed by a subordinate staff of ushers and a small group of police officers in uniform, attached for duty to the court as gaolers or process servers. They take up their posts at various desks and doorways. Mr Bridge begins to speak, directing his remarks at the solicitors.

"We begin with an examination of the sufficiency of evidence in the case of Mr Henry Vizetelly of Vizetelly & Company, 16 Henrietta Street, Covent Garden, as regards the publication of works of an author by the name of . . ." He squints down at his notes before continuing, "Mr Émile Zola." He pronounces the name carefully – it emerges as "Zoolah". Who represents Mr Vizetelly here today?"

There is a pause, then Lickfold stutters enthusiastically, "I do, Your Worship, I do. Mr Lickfold, from the firm of Lewis and Lewis."

"And for Mr William Coote today, we have . . . Mr Asquith?"

"If it please you, my Lord," Asquith says, in a tone so familiar that Ernest concludes with a pang that the two men are old friends.

"I should note, gentlemen, that our time is short, and we must proceed without embellishment or delay."

Is that good or bad for us? Ernest cannot guess.

"H.H. – Mr Asquith, you may begin."

You see, he knows him, Ernest thinks; they probably dine together every week at the same club.

Everyone is seated, and after a moment of paper shuffling, throat clearing, and a brief whispered conference with his assisting counsel, the prosecutor rises to his feet. He is taller than he looked when seated, but less elegant when standing – his coat is quite rumpled, and his collar is not well fitted at the back.

"We ask Your Worship today for the committal of the aforesaid Mr Henry Vizetelly following recent discussion at the highest level in the land regarding the urgent need to take action to stem the moral decay that is a danger not only to our youth, but to the very roots of our empire. This publisher has lately boasted in print of the profits he has made from selling impure and corrupting literature of the most pernicious kind. His company has benefitted from selling the worst and most offensive works of the French author, Mr Émile Zola." Asquith pronounces the name like a French native.

Lickfold jumps up. "My Lord, my client is not just selling the worst of Mr Zola's works, he is selling all of them. And has been for four years, unchallenged."

Arthur Vizetelly can barely contain his dismay at this eruption. He was against the choice of Messrs Lewis and Lewis when the firm was first suggested by a family friend. The rationale, on the face of it, is ingenious. Their man Mr Lickfold defended W. T. Stead during the Maiden Tribute scandal, when he was expressly tried for abduction, but in substance, everyone recognised, for obscene libel. "And the rascal was sent to prison!" Arthur had exclaimed in the conference with his father and brothers. "How can this choice be sound?"

Henry had, as usual, managed to calm him. "Arthur, Mr Lickfold defended a man who now sits on the general council of the N.V.A., and who attempts to blacken our firm in the pages of his newspaper each day. I believe the judge will see the irony in this and it will help our case." The brothers grudgingly agreed, but between themselves, Ernest and Arthur remained dubious. Lickfold is an unprepossessing figure, with no knowledge of French literature. Moreover, although Ernest had been living in Paris at the time, he did recall reading that W. T. Stead had effectively defended himself when he stood in court three years earlier, with great brio and skill, much to the delight of those reporting the trial.

Asquith is in full flow, making a sweeping gesture towards the series of books arrayed on his table. "Looking at the works of Monsieur Zola as a whole, no decent-minded person would say they are not detrimental to public morals. I shall begin with this one." He picks up the book he held earlier, clearing his throat before he reads out the title. "*Nana: A 'Realistic' Novel*. This work, named in the summons before you, tells the story of an actress, though she is in fact a society prostitute. Set during the Second Empire in Paris, this tale of moral contagion begins as it continues, finding Nana on a public stage, in a certain state . . ." He pauses, and turns to the page marked with his card, then reads out a brief passage: "'Then scarcely was Diana alone on stage, than Venus made her appearance. A shiver of delight ran round the house. Nana was nude. With quiet audacity, she appeared in her nakedness—'"

A similar expression of delight arises from Bow Street's gallery, as if the audience here is in thrall to the actress too. The magistrate calls for silence in the court and addresses Asquith. "Are you planning to read to us from all of those?" He juts his chin at the volumes set out on the long table. Asquith falters a moment – deflected from his script, he finds himself momentarily at a loss.

Henry shoots a quick sidelong glance at his sons, dark eyes glimmering with mirth.

"It will be sufficient," Bridge goes on ponderously, "to confine your argument to a single book." He consults the papers in his hand. "Yes – here it is. This one."

Please, God, Ernest prays. Do not let him choose . . .

"The Soil", the judge says.

"Of course, Your Worship," Asquith says smoothly. At his side, William Coote silently passes him another book and the prosecutor barely misses a beat, as if it had always been his intention to begin his case as the judge has now directed.

"A novel worse than filth, and aptly titled in its English translation. *The Soil.*" He inflates the word with sarcasm and lets it hover in the air a moment – several members of the public titter, exactly as he intends. Mr Bridge frowns, signalling silence once more, and nods for Asquith to continue.

"Evidently this work, the fifteenth in a series of similar novels, has a high moral object," the prosecutor goes on, "to bring about reform for the oppressed French peasantry – or so says the publisher's preface. But the content of the novel is another matter. The manifest depravity of the work you have so wisely identified, Your Worship, is exacerbated by the fact that this volume and others by its author are sold by Vizetelly & Company in one volume, despite their length, for a mere six shillings, making them widely available to a common market, including the most vulnerable readers."

What a wretched law, Ernest thinks. Preposterous. The court wishes to prosecute on account of Henry's possible customers, rather than defining with any precision the meaning of "obscenity". This is patently unjust. But precedents define English common law, and the few cases prosecuted using the Obscene Publications Act of 1857 have eschewed the opportunity to discuss a work's inherent value. The intended reader is all.

Asquith is saying, "Lord Chief Justice Campbell laid it down that the best test of obscenity was whether the tendency of a work was to deprave and corrupt those into whose hands it was likely to fall. The book is readily available in shops around London and beyond, as my colleague Mr Coote, who purchased it with ease, a mere two hundred yards from this building, will confirm. I will now set before the court certain passages from the Vizetelly translation of *The Soil* which demonstrate our case in this regard."

Oh, why had the judge chosen this book? Others in the series, even the sensational *L'Assommoir*, the seventh book, which Henry had presented to his readership as "the prelude to *Nana*", would have been so much easier to defend, despite the low city slang and the relentless squalor, drunkenness and violence. It was *L'Assommoir* that had made Zola's name known to the British, and promoted the idea that his realism was a tool used to decry immorality – though Ernest knows that was not his intent; Zola is an observer, not a moralist, laying out the truths he sees, and allowing the reader to decide what to make of them.

First published in France in 1877 to a tremendous response, *L'Assommoir* began its life in Britain as a play in 1879. Like many of Zola's novels, it was dramatised on the Paris stage after the book was published, and it enjoyed more success than his other theatrical works. In the wake of this, leading English dramatist Charles Reade translated and adapted it for a Victorian audience. Certain details of the plot were changed, however – for example the heroine, the drunken washerwoman Gervaise Macquart, did not have a daughter called Anna who grew up to become the prostitute Nana; her child simply died young so as to avoid such a vulgar fate. Incredibly, in the English stage version the drunken lout Coupeau, who dies a dramatic and hideous death in the novel, is persuaded to sign a temperance pledge before the curtain falls.

The title had given English theatres pause, just as it had Henry, who ultimately left the novel's title untranslated when he published it. If anyone had consulted me, Ernest thinks, I might have suggested something like *The Dram Shop*. The Parisian slang word "*l'assommoir*" (from the verb *assommer*, to bludgeon), references a blunt tool used to stun farm animals before slaughter in the abattoir; Ernest knows that in street parlance it means a shop selling cheap liquor. English theatres finally adopted the title "The Drink", and the play had become a favourite of temperance groups, revived in over forty productions around the country after a long and successful London run.

Ernest brings himself back to the courtroom. Asquith has come to the crux of his case, reading from a sheaf of notes. "I refer to pages 11, 13, page 72, page 79, page 202, and pages 206 to 210 from this edition of *The Soil*, published by Mr Vizetelly's firm, as particularly bestial examples of Monsieur Zola's writings."

Ernest knows the book backwards, having spent so many long hours reworking the text; he alone at the defence table understands quite how damning are these particular extracts. He tries to clear his throat, but this sets him off on a fit of coughing, attracting looks of irritation from the table opposite, as the noise threatens to drown out Asquith's summation. The prosecution counsel simply raises his mellifluous voice.

"I am certain, the court having perused these pages, that we must all agree: the publisher must be brought to account at the Central Criminal Court for obscene libel."

Obscene Libel. That is the charge as it was described on the summons to appear at Bow Street and delivered to the offices of Vizetelly & Company a few weeks earlier. Annie had studied the document, which lay open before them all on the table like an unsavoury dish, and was bemused. "Who do we defame, father, by printing these fictional stories?" Ernest had stepped in to explain the matter to his sister, who was not, as a woman, to be expected to know about such things.

"There are four sub-crimes associated with the crime of libel," he set out, counting them one by one on his fingers for her. "Seditious, blasphemous and defamation libel, as well as obscene libel, this last generally relating to books or published material – though it could be found in private correspondence or an article in a daily paper. The word 'libel' is taken from the Latin for a small book or petition – *libellus*."

"But surely, dear brother, is that not a matter to be discussed at liberty among private individuals, rather than something for a criminal court, where they try people for robbery and murder?" Ernest raised his eyebrows at this. Had she been reading John Stuart Mill? Britain's pre-eminent philosopher was a proponent of free speech who had coined the expression "liberty of discussion". Ernest had not spent a great deal of time with his much younger half-sister over the years; she was a clever one. He was beginning to see why his father encouraged her to undertake some simple translations and assist him in his editing. He explained to her, in a warmer tone, "The prosecution argues that the publishers of this alleged obscenity are, unfortunately, seen to be partaking of a criminal act, though I agree it is hard to conscience."

"And does the author have to answer for his work as well?" Annie said, worrying the point, like a dog at a soup bone. Henry put a gentle hand on hers. "Only in France, Annie, where he is often challenged, though never prosecuted. It is our choice to publish Zola here, *my* choice. That is all that is of interest to the English courts. We stand by our decision and we will defend it to the last." With that, Annie threw her arms around him, ever the demonstrative one in the family. Now she sits stiff-backed in the gallery, side by side with Ernest's dainty, dark-browed wife Marie, watching intently.

The clerk scuttles from his desk to the prosecution table, taking the book from Asquith and ferrying it back to the magistrate. He turns to his colleague, who moves closer to his side, and the two men slowly turn over the pages together in silence. The clock ticks loudly on the wall. Henry looks across to Lickfold, who is gathering his own papers and books in preparation for his response to Asquith. The man holds out the volume of Byron towards Henry as if it is some kind of talisman, smiling his gummy smile in what he probably thinks is reassurance. Henry nods briefly and resumes his earlier study of his boots.

Ernest eyes the magistrates, watching them read the pages they have been given. At one point Mr Bridge utters a choking sound, a cross between a cough and an "ah-hah". Then he looks to his colleague to see if he is ready to turn the page, and thus they continue to the final marked extract. They finish at the same time – and it is impossible to say from their impassive faces what they have made of their introduction to France's greatest living novelist.

"Mr Lickfold. What have you to offer in defence of . . . this?" Bridge holds up the book in his hand by pinching the top corner and holding it at arm's length – as if it is a cloth soiled with ordure. Ernest's heart sinks. Beside him, Arthur plucks at his sleeve, but he shakes him off.

Lickfold bounds to his feet, eager as a puppy.

"Mr Bridge, sir, distinguished gentlemen. Our contention will be that we have a perfect right to publish these works under English law. Let us consider for the moment the wider vista. I beg the court to understand, first and foremost, that many of the novels of Monsieur Zola, including those cited in the summons today, have been and continue to be available in our country in the original French, widely circulated for many years. Anyone – well, anyone who knew French that is, could read these works well before the commencement of their publication in English some four years ago, when they were translated and edited with appropriate expurgations, by my client."

He takes a triumphant breath and plunges on.

"I repeat, these novels have been sold and read in this country in the original French for over a decade. I respectfully ask, what sense is there now in the National Vigilance Association – a fine body, I will add, one of whose founders I have had the privilege to serve – what sense is there in suddenly bringing Mr Vizetelly to account at this moment in time?"

Mr Bridge looks down at him, unimpressed. "Is that all?"

"All, sir?" Lickfold recovers himself. He had forgotten the most important part of the defence. "Byron!" he cries. "Lord Byron's 'Don Juan'." He waves the slim volume of poetry towards Asquith like a newsboy hawking his wares, then in his other hand he holds aloft a much bigger volume. "The complete works of William Shakespeare!" he trills. He looks across at Asquith, who is regarding him with mild surprise. "Perhaps my learned friend is not familiar with 'The Merry Wives of Windsor', but surely he will know Byron's poem – I beseech the court to peruse just three pages of this venerated work, and tell me if Émile Zola's writings could possibly be deemed more base?

"Mark this, my Lords, from Lord Byron." Lickfold starts to declaim from the book, unbidden, and with some relish: "'A little she strove, and much repented, / And whispering, "I will ne'er consent" – consented.'" There is a silence as the court waits for him to continue, but he clearly thinks this is enough, and stops.

The judge prompts him. "And?"

Lickfold goes on. "And ... well, Mr Asquith appears to indicate that his client's case before a jury will be predicated on the idea that these novels of Mr Zola are the most immoral books ever published. Now, I do not pretend myself to have read the whole of

English literature, but there are certainly many works within the cognisance of all men of education which are more offensive than those now under discussion. Again, I offer you Lord Byron – and William Shakespeare."

Bridge signals to the assistant clerk to bring up Lord Byron's poetry and the fat volume of Shakespeare's works to the bench. The magistrates turn away and engage in hushed discussion. They look up once or twice at Henry, and then to Asquith and his stone-faced employers. They do not consult Lickfold's books. After a few minutes, they rise, standing shoulder to shoulder. The assembly stands to face them.

"Henry Richard Vizetelly, of Vizetelly & Company, Covent Garden. We hereby deem that there is a case to answer before a jury and you will appear at the Central Criminal Court in their September session to answer the charge of publishing matter that constitutes an obscene libel. The clerks will draw up indictments for your signature. Mr Asquith, please submit the three novels named in the summons. The court will retain these as evidence. Good day." An excited buzz of conversation begins as soon as he finishes speaking; several reporters make quickly for the door.

And with that, it is time for the next summons to be heard. The Vizetelly men move out of the courtroom, while Lickfold lags behind, busying himself stuffing paper and books into a voluminous leather case, not looking at his clients. Henry pauses on a bench in the anteroom, flanked by his sons, as they wait for the women to join them.

"Not a bad outcome, I would say." The boys look at him in

amazement. Was he doing this to keep their spirits up?

Arthur speaks quietly. "How can you, Papa? An Old Bailey trial. We have committed all our capital to the printing of these novels. There are piles and piles of printed pages as high as you are tall, teetering in the warehouse waiting to be bound . . ."

"And how are we to pay for our defence?'" Ernest whispers urgently.

"By selling more books!" Henry slaps his leg for emphasis, and smiles for the first time that day. "By God, we have not been prohibited from doing anything yet. And as you say, Arthur, we have thousands of books to sell."

"But—"

"No buts, dear boy. We have our case and it is a good one."

They watch as Asquith and his cohort move towards the door without a look in their direction. Unable to resist, Henry calls out, "Good day gentlemen!" as a parting shot, and William Coote turns, startled. "Good day," he responds gruffly through his large moustaches, before he hurries out to join his fellows in the white August sunshine.

6. September 1888, Henrietta Street, Covent Garden

George Moore.

For gentlemen in London at this time, writing a letter to a newspaper editor is the equivalent of tribal leaders in the jungle using drumbeats to telegraph their messages. Henry loses no time in composing a plucky missive to the *Bookseller*, upon his return from Bow Street, in order to reassure his clients.

A week later, George Moore appears at the Vizetelly door unannounced, not long before teatime, as is his wont. "Greetings, gentlemen! I have just returned from the most trying visit to Dublin and . . . I trust I do not disturb?" A quick reader of faces, he understands that he has stepped into the midst of a row. This does not deter him for a moment. He unbuttons his coat and settles into a wide leather armchair next to Henry.

"You may have inherited your mother's gift for languages and you certainly know more ways than I do to conjugate a French verb, my boy," the old man is saying to a grim-faced Ernest, "but you are not privileged in your understanding of English booksellers and readers. This is my area of expertise." For all his increasing physical frailty, Henry's voice is still strong.

Ernest looks to his brothers for support, but both Frank and Arthur, charged with keeping the firm solvent in difficult conditions, can hardly go against their father. Arthur is, as ever, fixated on the mountains of paper in the adjacent warehouse, awaiting binding and delivery. He spends hours arranging, counting and rearranging the stock as if this might have any effect on their dwindling clientele, who have been made nervous by the court proceedings. If his father's letter to the trade makes even a handful of buyers willing to hand over cash for books, Arthur will not complain. Their list of creditors is growing. He feels his responsibility to them keenly, and although he would not let his older brother know it, he admires his father's boldness and ability to maintain a positive view of the future.

"Can I offer some assistance, my friends?" Moore asks quietly.

Ernest turns on his heel and goes to stand at the window, arms crossed over his chest. Arthur puts his head in his hands, and Frank, sitting at his desk against the far wall, tilts back in his chair like a schoolboy, eyes to the ceiling as if the answer to all their problems might be inscribed there. Henry simply hands Moore the *Bookseller* in silence.

Moore opens it and soon finds Henry's letter, raking his thick hair with his fingers as he reads it aloud. His slight Irish lilt and the almost comical appearance of his outsize silk necktie and drooping trousers somehow lighten the mood. "The trade is informed that there are no legal restrictions in the sale of *Nana*, *Piping Hot!* or *The Soil* and that none can be imposed until a jury has pronounced adversely against these books, which the publishers continue to supply."

"I have always admired your willingness to fly in the face of difficulty, Henry," Moore says sincerely, when he finishes reading.

"A man is innocent until tried, eh?" Henry says.

"Look at these before you congratulate him further," says Ernest. He thrusts a pile of newspapers at Moore, whose hair is standing on end now, making him look more than ever like Yeats' "astonished turnip". Ernest has never liked Moore much, not when he had encountered him in Paris from time to time over the years, nor here in his father's home where he is too familiar and too filial. Ernest is at one with some of his French friends, who perceive the man as a self-seeking self-publicist, forever mingling with artists and writers both in Paris and in London, as if their talent might rub off on him. This privileged gentleman, who had first paraded himself about the Paris salons as a would-be bohemian artist before "recreating himself as a man of letters", as one critic had so tartly put it, styles himself as "the English Zola". Ernest has read some of his work and it is not without merit, but he does not rival Zola.

Moore studies the press response, not only to Henry's announcement but also to the impending trial. There are numerous articles. For the most part, they speak with one voice: Vizetelly & Company must pay the price for their folly. A number of letters and a few journals express concern about the meaning a censorship trial might have for English authors and their publishers, but these are eclipsed by a righteous clamour for the quashing of reprehensible French fiction.

The men are gathered in Vizetelly & Company's new, larger premises at Henrietta Street, a short walk from the old site. Their move had gone ahead in June, regardless of the legal challenge and the uncertain future they faced; Henry is convinced their troubles will soon recede and he would not hear of a postponement. A serving maid slips into the room to light the lamps – their only servant now, Frank thinks ruefully; he has been obliged to find savings in their office and household running costs. Dusk is falling, and the clatter of the carts from the market rolling over the cobblestones mingles with the shouts of newsboys hawking the evening papers.

Despite Henry's bold proclamation, the trade response to the news of an imminent trial has been to put off further purchases from the firm. Booksellers do not wish to be saddled with goods they might suddenly be forbidden to sell. Just this week, the matter had been complicated by a further summons for obscene libel issued by the N.V.A. to another publisher, William Mathieson Thompson of the Temple Publishing Company in Holywell Street – an unfortunate location for a man who seeks to defend his good name, as it has long been home to pornographers and their clientele.

Thompson is issuing low-cost abridged translations featuring the most salacious stories from Boccaccio's *Decameron*, and the self-proclaimed crusaders have pounced on this as another high profile example of "literary cheapjacks" selling translations "in a direct appeal to the worst passions". As with Zola, they do not object to the work in the author's original language, but in the words of one of their council, "a translation can only feebly plead the privilege of Art". The press is delighted to quote such pronouncements.

Moore sets down the last of the articles Ernest has collected. "Good Lord, do they not know the rule of *sub judice*? Henry, you are being tried before you set foot inside the court!"

"True enough," Ernest says stiffly. "But that is the habit of our press."

Moore picks up the *Pall Mall Gazette* again. "I see Stead is still leading the charge." He reads in a pompous voice, nicely tinged with Stead's Yorkshire cadence: "Émile Zola has flooded French literature with a prurient and loathly realism in the prostituted name of Art." He waves the paper as if to banish a foul odour. "All this shouting from the rooftops about Art, Art, Art – and that cretin Smith continuing to rage about corruption of the masses, both in *The Times* and in the Commons – it all seems so excessive, do you not agree? It makes me wonder if there is something else afoot."

"What do you mean?" Arthur pipes up, his thin face pale.

Moore shakes his head, his brow furrowing. "I cannot tell you, it is only a feeling I have . . ." He looks at Henry's anxious face and jumps to his feet, eager to banish the sombre mood. "And therefore I suggest we refuse to speculate, and retire to the Crown immediately! What say you, gentlemen?"

* * *

The trial at the Central Criminal Court, long known as the Old Bailey for the street in which it stands, is set for September 18. Numerous friends, and even a few acquaintances and strangers who are sympathetic to the Vizetelly cause, had urged Henry to replace his lacklustre legal counsel before that date, but with all that had to be attended to at the office, and with the many days that passed when Henry was indisposed due to poor health, the matter had not been addressed. Mr Lickfold of Messrs Lewis and Lewis may be uncertain of his position after the result of the Bow Street proceedings, or perhaps there has been some miscommunication, and this gives rise to confusion on the day.

That morning, Henry dons his best suit of clothes, which seem to hang from his thin frame as if borrowed from a larger brother, and together with his four children and several friends, including George Moore, arrives at the court only to find that the policeman guarding the door will not admit them. "Not on my list, gentlemen, not on my list," Moore parrots the officious man beautifully at a later date, for a group of friends at his club, to uproarious laughter.

Henry thought he was prepared for anything on this day. "But I am to be tried today!" he bursts out, as Ernest and young Frank attempt to talk quietly with the officer, in hopes of avoiding a scene. Already a crowd of those usual onlookers that hang about the entrance of a criminal court is drawing near: many of them will be reporters.

The policeman asks them to wait, like dustmen at a servants' entrance, or so Ernest mutters to Frank under his breath. Henry consults his watch. "The time is correct. The day is correct. Where is Lickfold? He was to meet us here on the hour!"

"I shall go immediately to his chambers and enquire, Papa," Arthur says, eager to absent himself.

Despite this unhappy development, the family mood has lifted today. They have learned that Thomson, the publisher of the *Decameron*, has had his case dismissed at Bow Street, and word has it that the N.V.A. are demoralised by this failure. The magistrate ruled that because Boccaccio's book had been in print for four centuries, and copies were held in the British Museum as valuable artefacts, he could not allow it to be considered an obscene libel. He even said in his summation that he had read the work himself in the original Italian, and had no quarrel with its content. This gives new hope to all who hope to slow the march of the puritanical campaigners.

After long minutes of standing in the mizzling rain under the poor shelter of the entrance door's narrow arch, as one of London's dank yellow fogs begins to blanket the city, the Vizetellys are enlightened. It seems that Mr Poland Q.C. has applied to postpone the proceedings "for the convenience of counsel", until the next Sessions, at the end of October. "Defending counsel," explains the bespectacled clerk who emerges with the police officer to speak with them, "failed to be present today. A Mr Lickfold, of Lewis and Lewis, I believe. The postponement was decided without him."

"But . . . I instructed the firm vigorously to oppose any request for delay!" Henry is nonplussed.

"Sir, with the greatest respect, your counsel cannot do so if he is not at court."

Ernest wants to leap forward and strangle the man, and struggles to contain himself, while the unstoppable Moore blurts out at the top of his voice, "Outrageous!" One of the men in the group of onlookers takes out a notebook and a pencil. Quickly, Henry reaches out and puts a hand on his friend's arm to silence him. One has to control Moore – he thinks little of striking a man for obstructing his wishes either with his fists or the nearest blunt object – most recently a champagne bottle in a restaurant fracas. Turning to the clerk and assuming a mild manner, Henry asks, "And, with all due respect, sir, do I have no right to object, given it is my case?"

"I am afraid the matter is settled. It is out of my hands."

It soon becomes apparent what has transpired. The case is postponed because the prosecution is changing. Sir Henry Bodkin Poland Q.C. acts for the government as a legal advisor and counsel in the Treasury. The clamour in the press, beautifully orchestrated by its conductor W. T. Stead and aided by a continued outcry in the Commons led by Samuel Smith, has at last caused the government to intervene. The Public Prosecutor will now take up the case. This is what G.M. suspected, Henry realises now – all those vitriolic articles, the sheer verbosity of the operation, was calculated to force the government to take responsibility "as moral guardians of the nation". Make enough noise and they will have to act – this is Stead's approach, to prove once more that journalism has more power than politics.

It is a great victory for the N.V.A., who must be relieved by the financial implications too, since their resources have been depleted by the *Decameron* fiasco. They will not now be funding the criminal prosecution; the Treasury will shoulder the costs. Henry's response to this news is swift: he returns to his office and composes another energetic tattoo before luncheon, this one addressed to the editor of *The Times*, noting what has taken place outside the court, and concluding on an acerbic note:

> . . . It would appear, therefore, that unless defendants are actually in custody, they have no right to be present when their cases are under consideration. Your obedient servant, Henry Vizetelly, *et cetera, et cetera.*

He insists that the message be delivered to the paper at once. As night falls, the gaslights flickering feebly outside in the fog, the Vizetelly family gather in silence, oppressed by their various thoughts. They are sitting in the book-lined drawing room above the office. Six weeks' delay, thinks Arthur. How can we hold off our creditors, now clamouring for payment of their overdue invoices, for six more weeks? Annie bites her lip, a nervous habit she has acquired, and eyes her father, who is reading a book as the mantel clock chimes the hour. His hands are shaking. Ernest meets her eye – he sees it too.

Once again, George Moore is the one to break the mood. He makes his usual flurried, noisy entrance holding the evening edition of *The Times*. Gone is his earlier laudatory tone. "Henry. I feel that I must say this to you, in the presence of your loving family. You are not helping your cause with these volleys to the press. I may – in fact, I will – write to *The Times* myself on your behalf tomorrow, but you must desist. It pre-empts your case and will only fan the flames of antagonism against you, when what is demanded here is a large bucket of water."

Moore plunged them into this mess, Ernest thinks, by introducing Zola to them and by urging Henry to publish *The Soil*. I should like to see how he can dig us out. What possible remedy can there be? Annie moves close to her father's side, setting her hand lightly on his shoulder. He lowers his head, his bravado fading.

At that moment, Moore bursts out laughing. His mirth is so uncontrolled that tears spring from his eyes and the tips of his protruding ears turn red. "Forgive me, my good friends, but I have just been struck by a great irony." He holds up the newspaper, showing them a page with a bold cross-headline: "THE WHITE-CHAPEL MURDERS".

"Even as we speak," Moore says, "a violent madman is stalking the streets of East London mutilating and murdering defenceless women at his whim, eluding capture for months, and yet . . . Her Majesty's government have decided they will devote their energy to prosecuting an elderly man for publishing a mere book. A mutilated book, to be fair, Ernest, for you've ripped out the innards of the text, I believe."

Ernest, red-faced, makes to speak, but Moore holds up his hand. "I mean no criticism. I only decry the ludicrous fact that law and good governance have been reduced to the sport of a gang of philistines who attempt to censor invented stories which might, or might not, corrupt the young and the female, rather than making our streets safe for those very innocents. Moreover, the daily papers report the murders in such glaring detail that one might call it, dare I say, a pornography of violence. And yet, the same publications pursue you as a pornographer. It baffles me. The English – they baffle me."

Young Frank, who has secret literary hopes of his own and much admires the Irishman, raises his hand for leave to speak. "May I suggest, sir – is there some argument we can make to the court for Papa, as regards his health?"

"No!" Henry roars. "I won't hear of it." He looks around at the small assembly of anxious faces. "We shall go up against Her

Majesty's government or a pack of hypocritical zealots – it is all the same to me. We will fight not for the name of Vizetelly, or for a mere book, as you call it, G.M., but for the principles at stake. We fight for the future of publishing! This is England, children – not some far off despotic state; it is a democracy, and we shall exercise our rights as free men to argue for the importance of literature in our culture, as generations of good men have done before us. Think on it: this trial is not a burden, but an opportunity to change the law of the land. We are lucky enough to be the test case for a defence of free speech – and we shall not be defeated!"

He is exhausted by this valiant speech, and sinks back in his chair. Moore stares as Annie fusses around him, loosening his collar and offering him a sip of sherry. Then, to everyone's amazement, their guest bursts into applause.

"Henry, you devil, you have solved it. It is all about the principles of the thing. We must appeal to the Solicitor General and the tax-paying public immediately, to halt the trial before it begins, as a waste of time and public money."

"And how do you propose to do this, with neither time nor money on our side?" Ernest says.

Moore ignores the question, turning his bright blue eyes on Henry, who is intrigued by his friend's sudden animation. "Do you remember when we published my piece about the libraries, four years since? I came to you in a lather, eager to return the blows that blasted Charles Mudie had dealt me."

"I remember, of course," says Henry.

They are referring to a pamphlet penned by Moore after Mudie's, one of the country's most powerful circulating libraries, effectively blacklisted him. These thriving businesses, which had operated in Britain for more than a hundred and fifty years, were launched to provide books to the middle and upper classes via subscription. They charge an annual fee to members, approximately the purchase price of one three-volume novel – half a guinea. The "triple-decker", which tended to run to an average of a thousand pages, and which the libraries themselves have cultivated for commercial reasons, has become the accepted format for novels: if customers enjoy Part I, it creates an appetite for the subsequent volumes, and income from the first volume might even be applied to printing costs of subsequent parts. From the customer's point of view, the economic argument for subscribing to a library is persuasive: it allows them to read dozens of volumes for the price of one. In addition, the libraries provide an editorial service, by choosing "appropriate" books to lend.

Since 1860, Mudie's Select Library and W. H. Smith & Sons have become the largest circulating libraries in Britain, and, in the face of the rising tide of conservatism which has come with the era's social reforms, they preserve their status by a conspicuous display of prudence. Novels must "entertain in an innocent fashion", they decree, and "provide spiritual and ethical models". As a result, most publishers go so far as to ensure the libraries approve of their list of titles before accepting them for publication.

Five years earlier, in 1883, Moore had fallen foul of this system with his first novel, *A Modern Lover*. Mudie's judgment of the novel as "an immoral publication" damned its chances, and Moore then wrote open letters in the press, lamenting the lack of freedom of speech for authors (or "freedom from the illiterate censorship of a librarian"). He provoked considerable debate in the literary world and this in turn led him to Vizetelly, fuming about the libraries' "pulseless, invertebrate jellyfish-like novels".

Vizetelly published Moore's book and his next novel, *The Mummer's Wife*, in single-volume six-shilling editions. The delighted author also convinced his new publisher to issue a pamphlet denouncing the libraries, called *Literature at Nurse or Circulating Morals*, since he was no longer at their mercy. Henry was happy to do so, adding advertisements for Moore's and other novels inside the covers, to make the most of the opportunity.

The Mummer's Wife was a critical and commercial success, reprinting twenty times, and Moore felt vindicated as a result, suggesting in another letter to the press that Mudie's must "pass defeated from the Bar of public opinion". Ernest had read the pamphlet in Paris and thought there was a flaw in Moore's logic: the problem was not the librarians, but the prudery of their subscribers – and therein lay the danger to his father now. Zola's novels were outside the ambit of Mudie's, but not beyond reach of the purity fanatics.

Now Moore jumps up and pulls the wooden library steps from the corner with a loud clatter, and to the astonishment of all, he begins pulling down volumes and throwing them through the air to the others as if playing a game of ball. Frank catches one with both hands, then another, clasping them to his chest, laughing in spite of himself. Moore's energy is infectious. "Arthur, my boy!" Arthur reaches up just in time to catch a thick volume. "Ernest!" Ernest does not want to play, but nor can he stand by and see the delicate volume that George has plucked from the highest shelf fall to the floor. He catches it and looks at the engraved cover: *Shakespeare's Sonnets.*

"What does this signify?" Annie cries, delighted by the diversion. "You are throwing poetry in our defence?"

"Precisely, Miss V.," Moore says gallantly, jumping down from the ladder. "I am proposing exactly that – that we rain down on the prosecution a storm of literary evidence that is so persuasive they cannot fault our argument."

"Which is?" Ernest has had enough of this game.

Moore kneels before Henry in his chair. The old man is holding a volume of Swinburne's poems that Annie has caught and handed to him. Moore looks into his eyes, speaking quietly and clearly. "A storm of books, Henry. You said it yourself a moment ago – we are fighting for all of literature. If the government now feel it is a matter of prime importance to ban the works of Émile Zola, they have also to ban works by Shakespeare, by Congreve, by Defoe—"

"And Swift!" Frank shouts, holding one of his catches up in the air like a trophy.

Moore smiles. "That fool Lickfold attempted to raise this line of defence at the committal hearing at Bow Street, did he not?"

Arthur holds up a volume of "Don Juan" – imitating the hapless solicitor's nasal voice to perfection. "Surely you have read Lord

Byron's filthy poem, Your Worship?" Frank bursts out laughing. Even Ernest cannot help but smile.

The ebullient Moore continues. "The prosecution's case at the Old Bailey will rest on Zola's concentration on sex in his writing, and the need to protect vulnerable women and children – although why anyone assumes that all fiction is intended for young girls and widows is a mystery to me. These self-appointed regulators of reading will make much of the fact that you dared to publish Zola's works in English at an affordable price – meaning you indulge the lower classes, whose reading habits they wish to control."

Henry is leaning forward now, gripping the sides of his chair, rapt, as are the others. Moore can be mesmerising when he wishes, and this is for him a matter of utmost import, of artistic life or death. "Now: there are countless examples of bawdy fiction that are widely available to a mass audience by virtue of being deemed 'classic'. Dozens of instances, maybe even hundreds, right here", he goes on, making a sweeping gesture at the shelves that line the room. "Ban all of these, if you ban Zola! That shall be our battle cry and we'll take it to the government, by direct appeal, in a new pamphlet you will also offer to the general public, containing choice extracts from all of these classic texts. Will the Treasury squander public resources reconsidering the best if bawdiest of the entire English canon as libel? They cannot ignore our logic! What do you say?"

"I am very tired," Henry says. "But I am grateful to you, G.M. And I should like to try it. Ernest, please will you assist in the preparation of this pamphlet in every way possible. I shall compose a letter to go with it, to Sir Augustus Stephenson, Solicitor to the Treasury, whom I know a little. He is the effective director of prosecutions for the Crown, and may be our best hope for entertaining the literary argument."

With that, he rises, leaning on Annie, who throws an encouraging smile back over her shoulder to her brothers as she helps their father from the room. Ernest paces on the hearthrug without saying anything for a few moments, and then bursts out, "It is a damned excellent idea, Moore, excellent. And I should like to suggest we include a preface by Zola himself."

"Do you think the government wish to hear more from him?" Moore's tone is not unkind.

"If we mount a defence on the basis of artistic quality, by placing Zola in such company," Ernest says, gesturing at the array of books Moore has chosen, "then the artist should speak to this argument as well, and explain his *raison d'être*. You know it well: Zola defines the Rougon-Macquart series as a grand experiment, a social investigation into heredity and environment – he can persuade anyone of the scientific and reforming motives behind his novels."

"A superb addition!" Moore thumps him on the back. They all help to stack the chosen books in a tall pile, while Ernest, fired with an energy and optimism no-one has seen in him for months, clambers up the ladder himself and selects other useful volumes to add – works by Fielding, Dryden and Sterne. "Here! Here!" cry his younger brothers, swooping to catch them as fast as he locates the titles he seeks. It is the most entertainment they have had in weeks.

Ernest feels positively warm towards Moore, and pumps his hand when he bids him goodnight, both men promising to make a start on the project early the next morning. In such adverse times, facing the full might of the Crown, there is no time for internal division. If he has any qualms later that night, as he pulls on his nightcap and prepares to join his snoring wife in bed, Ernest ignores them. He knows that his family needs this public appeal like a tonic – if nothing else, it will allow them to move forward, and keep hope alive until the trial.

7. October 1888, Médan

Médan is a small village on the Oise, a tributary of the
Seine, about twenty miles from Paris. Were it not for the
great novelist's house, it would be totally unknown. As it
is, you are sure to be told at the Gare Saint-Lazare that
the place you want is Meudon not Médan. Even when you
have secured your ticket and have arrived, your difficulties
are not at an end. There you are told that a couple of miles
of a country walk lies before you. And the lanes are of the
most complex nature; but the peasants are obliging, and

after a climb up a steep incline, after passing an old parish church with its adjoining collection of hamlets, you find yourself at the door of a handsome modern house. It stands on the extreme verge of the hill, and is surrounded by a high wall. Below lie the wide French meadows, with their everlasting curtains of poplar trees.

George Crawford has read and re-read this description of today's journey on his way, between anxious glances at his pocket watch; he must not be late for the interview, which is of the utmost importance to his editor. This is a chance to prove himself. He is the son of two esteemed journalists – his late father was an associate editor for the *London Daily News*, and his mother Emily is one of the few successful women in her trade, highly regarded as "the Queen of Journalists". For many years she has been the Paris correspondent of the *Daily News*; she also writes for the *New York Tribune* and other newspapers. Now her son, who has recently gained his degree (and his gold watch), has landed the opportunity to interview Émile Zola about this week's censorship trial at the Old Bailey – a plum debut. The old journalists' maxim, "preparation is all", has been drilled into him since boyhood, and he was pleased to find George Moore's article about a visit to Zola's country house in a back issue of the *Gazette*, while he was readying himself for this assignment.

"Médan, not Meudon," he says to the guard at the station, who makes no reply, but gives him a liverish look with his ticket, as if he hears this too often. Now the young man puffs up the steep hill towards the house, pulling off the silk scarf at his neck as he goes. Past the old church, and there, that must be it . . . he can see the wall, beyond which lies the white villa, sandwiched between its two proud towers of brick and cement. He stops outside to smooth his curly hair and wipe his brow; he is more used to spending days at his desk than on country walks, and his overcoat is heavy after the exertion.

He knows he is here largely due to his mother's recommendation of him to W. T. Stead, the *Gazette*'s illustrious editor. She dotes on her son, like any Irish mother, and is enormously proud that he is following in his parents' footsteps, while his brother pursues an alternative career in mathematics. "These are the elements of any good interview: observe, reflect and be genuine," his mother reminded him the night before, wishing him luck and admonishing him to set out early. He has transcribed her words on the first page of his pristine black notebook, underscoring them twice for good measure: *Observe. Reflect. Genuine.*

He rings the bell at the gate, and immediately jumps back, alarmed by the histrionic barking of a dog – he is afraid of the creatures, having been bitten on the leg as a boy. An impassive servant appears, followed by a mud-coloured terrier so diminutive that Crawford blushes at his faint-heartedness, and stutters effusive apologies and thanks.

What does he observe, upon entry to the house? He notes how dark and cool it is inside, which is a relief after his walk – and admires how the coloured light from the splendid stained-glass window and door panes makes pretty patterns on the floor. He gasps aloud when he looks into the magnificent billiard room, which he has read is M. Zola's pride and joy, noting the ornate carved ceiling decorated with the Zola family coat of arms. He sees Madame Zola too, though they do not meet – as he passes a half-open door, he glimpses her ample figure seated by a window, staring outside, a book lying unread in her lap. There is fine lace at the collar of her dark dress, and her neatly coiffed dark hair is touched here and there with white. Crawford has a fleeting impression of melancholy, and wonders if she is in mourning for a friend or relative.

He follows the servant up a series of staircases, through a warren of highly decorated rooms, much as Moore's article also described, "hung with Japanese tapestries and filled with heavy medieval furniture", until he arrives at the door of the man Moore called "the author of the great social studies of our time". He knows what to expect in terms of Zola's appearance – he is a familiar figure in the illustrated press: a short, portly man with a round beard and piercing eyes. Crawford imagines him as a ball of energy and intellect, possibly with something of the satyr about him.

The servant melts away, closing the door. ("The heavy door, flanked with richly carved pillars in dark brown oak", Crawford hastily makes a mental note, hoping he will retain this detail until he is able to transcribe it into his notebook.) Sitting at the large desk in the middle of the room is a spare, dark figure, muscular of build and lean of face. ("A strangely interesting face, but that of a man who is tired, and suffers permanent discomfort," Crawford composes.) But can this be Zola? There is the famous high forehead, pince-nez and black hair combed back in the style of an artist. This is the great man – but *sans* at least two stone. What has happened? Crawford wisely resolves not to ask.

Zola ushers his young visitor to the large divan by the window, and takes his place in the armchair opposite, (". . . crouching, with his legs crossed, his long, nervous fingers twining around each other.") They talk of the weather, of Crawford's mother, whom Zola knows and admires, and of his late father, whom Zola met years before. After a decent interval, Crawford takes out his notebook, pencil at the ready, and looks at Zola expectantly, as if it is for his subject to begin the interview. "What would you like to discuss?" the author smiles. The young man starts, consults his notes briefly, then blurts out, "Vizetelly, why not? Shall we discuss the impending prosecution? I assume you must be concerned for your publisher at this difficult time?"

Never assume, he hears his mother's voice say in his head, but it is too late. Sure enough, Zola surprises him with his answer. "Oh, it doesn't ruffle my happiness and contentment – not one particle. Not so much as a feather grazing the surface of a lake." He waits patiently while the young man captures this graceful simile on paper, then leans forward, as if taking him into his confidence. "I have heard that thousands of translations of my books have been sold in England – I believe your paper reported this fact. I was astounded to hear it. Do you know what profit these great sales have brought me? Very little. Well, *Nana, L'Assommoir* and *Piping Hot!* brought me nothing, not a *sou*. I neither gave leave nor got thanks."

"That must have been before Berne?" Crawford says. "But subsequently . . ."

"Yes subsequently, with *The Soil* – I will tell you what happened. My publisher offered me three thousand francs for the right of translation in England forever. I accepted. At the moment of publication he wrote to say that the risks were great and enclosed only two thousands francs, delaying the final sum due. I understood that there was risk – and this prosecution proves it – so I wrote back to accept. But I told Mr Vizetelly if this was the English way of doing business, I thought it was a very queer one."

"But do you not feel the English prosecutions injure your name as an author?" Crawford asks. Surely Zola must be concerned – all writers have egos, and are protective of their reputation, are they not? Once again, he is taken aback by the reply.

"As to what injury it may do me in England I don't care. As you see, it cannot hurt my pocket, and as to the effect on my reputation there, I frankly assure you, I care even less. You know we French are – not exactly vain . . ." The author pauses to find the right word. "*Suffisants*. We are sufficient for ourselves. We care no more than the man in the moon for what goes on elsewhere. I am not saying this to boast, but I state a fact. It is a fault, a great fault, I admit, but so it is." And with that, he gives a perfect Gallic shrug.

Crawford notes it all down; then a thought strikes him. "You say, 'we French' – but Monsieur Zola, are you not Italian?" Stead had asked him to mention this in the interview, and he is pleased to have got it into the conversation so early.

Zola smiles. "Ah! I have an Italian name, from an Italian

134

father, and yet I know not one word of Italian and was never in Italy. Understand me, young man; I don't speak of scientists and engineers and their kind, but authors and artists as '*suffisants*'. Which of the masters of French literature, of yesterday or today, knew a language besides their own? Neither Hugo, Lamartine, Dumas, nor, coming to contemporaries, Daudet, Guy de Maupassant, nor the younger Dumas."

Crawford wants to disagree – from his studies, he knows this isn't true. Hugo was trilingual, Mérimée translated Pushkin from the Russian, and Lamartine had an English wife and family. But he can feel his grasp of the thread of discussion slipping away, as often happened with far more experienced interviewers and M. Zola. From his reading of a large archive of interviews, it is plain that the author's innate skill at self-publicity and self-justification make him past master at manipulating his interrogators, twisting their questions to his own purpose and diverting them onto his chosen conversational path. To forestall a debate on the linguistic limitations of the French literary pantheon, the young man steers the conversation back to the headline he envisions above his eventual article: M. ZOLA ON THE RECENT PROSECUTION.

"Then you will not be sorry, Monsieur Zola, if the prosecution against Vizetelly & Company succeeds?"

"On the contrary, I shall be pleased. I had much rather the educated public in England read my books in French, than sell thousands of wretchedly done translations to the uneducated, who cannot comprehend me."

Crawford can barely contain his delight as he writes this down word for word – such copy will thrill Mr Stead. Zola is throwing his publisher to the dogs, vilifying the translations Stead despises and advocating the editor's argument that literature should be read in the original language! This is golden. Zola will denounce the licentiousness of the publishing world next, and make a perfect paragraph.

Once again, Zola does not conform to expectations. He is up from his chair, pacing to and fro in front of the windows facing the gardens below. Crawford uses the pause to scrawl another observation: "Garden prettily arranged. Model of formal French garden. Less grass."

"Tell me," Zola turns suddenly. "Who in the world started these prosecutions – can you tell me that? It doesn't vex me, but I cannot account for it; it seems so absurd."

Crawford stammers an answer. "Well, sir, there are societies in England that make this sort of – of work their business, campaigning against corrupting influences in society, particularly of the young."

Zola throws up his hands in a most Italianate gesture. "I don't understand you. I am truly puzzled. What can be corrupting in a book?"

Be genuine, Crawford hears his mother whisper in his ear. He must give his own answer now, not the one that Mr Stead would like him to offer. Taking a deep breath, he replies that English youth of both sexes, in his personal observation, are brought up with such freedom that some reserve had to be exercised by writers and their publishers. He had learned during his school years in England, when it was too dangerous to live with his parents abroad, that boys (and even some girls) there – unlike their French contemporaries – could read almost whatever they liked, and the time for keeping one set of books on the drawing-room table and the other out of reach on the top-most shelves of the bookcase was past. Or so it seemed to him.

"I am more puzzled than ever!" Zola exclaims. (Crawford scribbles, "He screwed up his face as if anxious to grapple with a hard problem.") "You speak of the freedom of your English boys and girls. I suppose you mean they are not confined under lock and key as in France, nor obliged to give an exact account of every moment of their time."

"Precisely!" Crawford feels, for the first time, that they are peers, or at least that he has some expertise to offer. "Why, I knew an English boy," (he is speaking of himself), "only ten years old, who began crossing from London to Paris twice a year by himself. Imagine that! And a young man in England may escort a girl from a tennis party without harm or impropriety, while here . . ." He trails off, thinking of his own dismay in the face of the strict rules that bind polite French society, and his failure to gain access to the young French beauties he meets in Paris. Zola's response is scathing.

"And that is your English prescription for keeping your youth pure – to let them wander freely through the streets! But, good heavens! Is it not the street that infects, and not a book? It must be the same in London as in Paris, I imagine – I have never been to London. Vice flaunts itself in the streets here, and is seen and touched. Its contact is corruption. Place a basket of apples in a cellar; the first one that rots spreads the rot to the whole basket. Just so: the school, the convent, the barracks, the factory, the ship in motion, are all centres of human putrefaction. I can only tell you what I know in France – *bien entendu*. Is it different elsewhere?"

"Well, Monsieur Zola," Crawford says, his voice quavering a little, "we do not think that in England, at any rate, things are as bad as you describe."

"Ah, I admit I cannot understand your English girl. And yet as far as the French one goes, I know every bit of her composition. She's . . ." At this, he breaks off. What was he going to say? His eyes have a far-off look, almost as if he can see a particular French girl before him now. Perhaps he is suggesting that the typical French girl is "rotten to the core", like a bad apple. That must be it, Crawford decides, finishing the sentence for him in his notes, and goes on to offer the renowned student of human nature a few more home truths about the English. Zola leans against the desk, gazing down at him, rapt.

Social relations could be quite unrestricted, without bad consequences, Crawford explains. The daughters of the well-to-do have always been protected by strong public opinion, and latterly their poorer sisters, when it was found they required it more, have been further defended by a stringent obscenity law. Fortunately the English Court, with the exception of Charles II's, never was flauntingly immoral. In France, since the time of the

Valois at least, there has been a court very brilliant—

"And also," Zola interrupts him, anticipating where he is going, "very naughty." He adds ("with a sad look"), "It was the example of that court that infiltrated down into all classes – a court brilliant outside but rotten within, a nest of elegant lechery." How did we come to the Valois dynasty, Crawford wonders, when I had supposed we were talking about the Vizetelly case?

Later, on the train back to Paris, scribbling his reflections on the meeting, the young journalist notes: "Upon vice, M. Zola looks neither with pleasure nor aversion, but with passive indifference." A good sentence, though he is not sure it is true. It is challenging to reconcile the writer's ambivalence with his obviously passionate nature, and he cannot think how properly to express this. He decides to leave that line as it is – it will form part of his conclusion.

"Vice is the only thing M. Zola's analysis in his novels reveals at the bottom of human nature. With his wonderful Italian faculty for imitative reproduction, he is driven to paint what he sees – and he has the skill of the great artist, without the soul of the greatest. The realistic note he strikes, one should never forget, is not French, but Italian. The unvarying characteristics of French literature are sobriety, balance and delicacy; all of these are wanting in M. Zola's works." There. That should please Mr Stead, and, he hopes, his dear Mamma.

It is not that Crawford lacks admiration for Zola's writing; on the contrary, he has enjoyed reading his novels, particularly *Nana*. But now that he has met the author, he considers that the man is

139

more self-involved than is suggested by the humanitarian face he likes to present to the world. How dismissive he was of the elderly publisher! True, he is not a personal friend, nor has Zola lost great earnings, but he had a sense – well, Monsieur Zola must have more pressing matters on his mind. There was something in his manner, a kind of dreamy, distracted air – but he stops himself there. *Never assume.*

Zola watches from the window as Crawford lopes off down the long drive, enthusiastically waving a long arm back towards the house, and sighs. He has no great hopes for the lad in his field – it is plain that he had wanted him to conform to an idea rather than to express the truth of his feelings and his experience, and he has scant faith that the article will accurately convey his attitude.

Was he too harsh on Vizetelly? The young man's face suggested he was. Well, he has never met the man, and after all, his firm has profited handsomely from selling Zola's novels, both before and after they purchased the English rights. He assumes that they have ample resources to pay some court-imposed fine, if that is the outcome of this farcical prosecution; after all, it is not as if publishers are imprisoned for such matters these days. They must allow for prosecutions and fines as part of their business arrangements; this is common enough in France, a form of insurance. It is not Vizetelly that deserves reproach, of course; it is the ridiculous English judges. Anglo-Saxon hypocrisy is intolerable, as are the vigilantes who raise their eyes in holy horror when any mention is made of what they insist on calling "French vices".

They would have the world believe that all the evils of their social system are imported from ours.

And why am I considered the incarnation of all that is worst in France? He mutters to himself, as he turns back to his desk. The irony is that Paris has recently honoured Shakespeare with a statue in the city; he feels like calling across the Channel now, "Let those who condemn my writings read what *he* has written!" Let them say if they can find in the whole range of French literature, let alone in my novels, anything more coarse and indelicate than you might find in *his* collected works, or those of Smollett, Jonson or Lord Byron for that matter. But he understands this argument has been shouted from the rooftops already, by Vizetelly, Moore and others. Justice is not blind in England, she is deaf.

A haphazard London jury is incapable of deciding whether I write with a base and mercenary aim or whether my ambition is towards what is truthful and right, he thinks. Happily, there is only one judge who may discriminate between good and bad, and that judge is Time. A good line – Zola makes a mental note to use it in his next interview.

He turns to his desk and begins the pleasurable task of writing his daily letter to the woman he loves: Jeanne Rozerot. She is the flower of his middle age; how she has surprised him, arriving in mid-life like an unwarranted gift, waking his dormant passion and instilling in him a profound desire for a family. His love for her is infusing his life, like the sunlight that has gradually spread across his writing desk in the course of the afternoon, making every white page brighter and every detail clear. Jeanne has become his consort, though they are not yet lovers; each of them is inching in that direction, out of mutual timidity and respect.

Their romance was born during the summer at Royan: the Zolas travel there for a seaside holiday each year with his publisher Georges Charpentier and his family. Unbeknownst to her, Alexandrine, who is in poor health of late, was partly to blame. She complained of "flushes" of heat that left her breathless and red in the face; she was forgetful and moody, sometimes inexplicably fatigued. The bright sun reflecting off the Atlantic gave her headaches, and her increasing weight made afternoon strolls onerous. She urged her husband, who expressed a desire to lose weight, to go cycling and take walks with the agile young housemaid.

Zola's first interaction with Jeanne was through photography, which had become a pleasurable hobby. Another of Charpentier's guests, the editor Victor Billaud, had given him instruction, and Zola had been an apt pupil. Now he could not stop photographing everything – a plant, a humble cottage, a winding coast road; he planned to install a darkroom at home, as soon as they returned. "You cannot claim to have seen something until you have photographed it," he wrote with great excitement to a friend. He took a photograph of the young housemaid in the act of threading a needle, a study in serenity that captured her uncommon beauty, "her milky skin like white silk", and a particular quality she had: "the freshness of the provinces". His wife's cousin Amelie, who joined them mid-way through the holiday, observed this, and warned Alexandrine of a flirtation, but Alexandrine laughed at her. Her dear husband had never so much as looked at another woman and was most unlikely to start straying now.

In contrast to his wife, Zola appeared to be filled with energy during the holiday. He began a new diet, whereby he ate no bread and drank neither water nor wine with his meals. A friend had recommended it, and, thanks to this and the fresh air and exercise he took, the wieght fell away. With his paunch went much of his shyness, and after some weeks he ventured to declare his feelings to the housemaid. Jeanne was a good Christian girl, and demurred at first, though she was flattered by his attentions. Cautiously, he wooed and won her heart. It is his guilty secret now, this sober, profound love he feels.

On their return to Médan, they agreed she must leave his wife's employ. Jeanne resigned her position, much to Alexandrine's irritation, for the girl was useful with needle and thread, and she had only been with them for a few months. Now Zola has secretly installed her in her own apartment in the rue Saint-Lazare, just by the church of Saint-Trinité. He tries to visit her often, using the excuse of conducting research at the Saint-Lazare railway station nearby, an important setting in his next novel. On his last visit to her there, he counted the steps he took, which quickened as he approached, until he was almost running. One thousand, two hundred and thirty-nine steps exactly. Less than fifteen minutes from door to door, but not so close to his apartment that she might cross paths with Alexandrine in the street; he shudders at the thought.

He cannot be at ease with the arrangement, despite the joy of falling in love at nearly fifty. He wakes each day worried, filled with guilt and remorse – and these are also the main themes in his new novel. The affair has distracted him; it makes him restless in company, irritable with his wife and the dogs, and, he admits, it has greatly slowed his usual writing process. Having written one book a year for the last decade, he realises he may now take at least eighteen months to finish the next, for he has not even properly begun the research phase. But his love for Jeanne also makes him feel young again, and time spent in her company is worth any delay. His night terrors are gone, too, a remarkable release after so many years captive to them.

The new novel does not have a title yet – he has put down a

few ideas, but so far, he has not found the right one. It will come in the end, as titles always do. Sometimes one tries out dozens, a hundred or more, before the perfect solution arises. His plan has it that a book about the banking world, which thankfully merits a simple title, will follow this one: *Money*. When he moves on to the realm of the soldier in the nineteenth and penultimate novel, he will describe the French defeat in the Franco-Prussian War. That too has a plain title already in place: *The Downfall*.

The seventeenth novel he is planning now was meant to be "the legal novel" in the series – an opportunity to show the bureaucracy and corruption of the court system under the Second Empire. Once they came to live at Médan, with the Paris–Rouen railway line running past the bottom of the garden, a further concept came to him; he would write about the law, about murder, its perpetrators and its victims, but set the story in the context of France's burgeoning railway network. He has been collecting news cuttings about railway trains and murders in the course of the last decade, and now has a bulging file. It seems that in France – and further afield – killing people on trains is not uncommon. This makes sense to Zola, who often finds it useful to think his way into a story by imagining the sounds involved. Perhaps the loudest screams are swallowed up by the roar of the engine, and the rattle and roll of the wheels.

This and the visit of the young Englishman today put him in mind of the murderer who fascinates him most at this point, the killer who has been terrorising women in London's East End. He opens his cuttings file and looks again at a recent story in

Le Figaro, which describes an extraordinary development in the case. A month ago, a letter was delivered to the Central News Agency in London, boasting of the author's exploits ("Grand work the last job was, I gave the lady no time to squeal") and threatening to continue apace, crowing, "I am down on whores and I shan't quit ripping them till I do get buckled." He signed himself "Yours truly, Jack the Ripper", adding a cheery postscript, "Don't mind me giving the trade name." Zola is of a mind to call his homicidal protagonist Jacques.

Enough of this. He will write to his beloved now, amusing her with the story of the foolish boy reporter, and describing the colour of the river in the fading sun, and the profusion of *orpin pourpre* flowers below his windows, which have matured from summer's pink to a coppery red through the autumn. He takes up his pen, and opens with his now-customary greeting. "Chére femme . . ."

8. October 1888, The Old Bailey

The Old Bailey's Number Two Court in session, circa 1888:
judges to the right, counsel tables in foreground.

"If only" is not a phrase Henry Vizetelly allows himself. For a journalist, there is fact and interpretation, action, reaction and analysis, but no wistful maybes. On the short journey in the hansom cab down the Strand, he does not waste time considering faster routes they might have taken, perhaps circling round

Holborn through Fleet Street or travelling along the Victoria Embankment. All roads lead to the same destination: the Old Bailey.

Annie, sitting beside him with her small, gloved hand tucked in his and her eyes closed, might be day-dreaming that if her mother were still alive, none of this would be happening, for Elizabeth always had a steadying effect on her husband. For his part, Henry misses his late wife sorely, but he is certain he would not have heeded her warnings if she had attempted to dissuade him from this fight.

Ernest, sitting on his other side, mouth set in a grim line, bracing himself as the cab bounces and jars along the rutted thoroughfare, is probably lambasting himself (again) for not demanding Lickfold's dismissal the moment they left Bow Street in August – or better still, before they ever arrived there. Henry is grateful that they have found a good barrister for the jury trial, even if he is not the most renowned Q.C. in the land. This is not only a question of funds, though these are stretched to the limit. The best advocates are simply not available; most of the great men of the Bar are occupied with the pending Parnell Commission, the most talked about matter of the moment – an inquiry into the alleged capital crimes of the Irish parliamentarian, which began in September and threatens to continue indefinitely.

The Vizetellys approached various chambers, taking advice from friends, and were refused by the first quite bluntly; the leading counsel there said he could not defend the case "because then he would have to read the book". Another Q.C. regretted that it would be impossible for him to defend the case "because no-one could say what one had a right to put in a book"; the law was too ill-defined. Just as they were beginning to despair, they were urged to consider looking beyond the London set. Soon enough, Mr Francis Williams, Recorder of Cardiff, expressed himself willing to take the case.

Far from being the "least worst" option, Williams looks to be an able man, assisted by an excellent lieutenant, Mr Cluer, a young solicitor whom the Vizetellys liked immediately. He is an admirer of Zola, and a student of the Naturalist movement. This has added some confidence to their preparation, alongside the staunch support of Moore and several other friends who will be in attendance today.

Frank and Arthur, perched together like two birds on a branch in the cab following behind them, are most likely still fretting about Moore's "Pamphlet Defence", an exercise which had cost them considerable time and a little money they could ill afford to invest. It did not even earn a letter of acknowledgement from Sir Augustus Stephenson at the Treasury, and seemingly has made no impact at all, except to alert the prosecution of their defence in advance of the trial.

Vizetelly & Company had issued the eighty-seven-page pamphlet earlier this month. "Our most affordable publication ever," Henry teased Arthur: they had offered it for sale to the general public for the price of a stamp. It was a bold effort, even if it did not have the desired effect. Henry spent considerable time helping to craft the document. He is pleased with the result, titled *Extracts Principally from English Classics: Showing that the*

Legal Suppression of M. Zola's novels would Logically Involve the Bowdlerising of some of the greatest Works in English Literature. Henry ended the appeal thus:

Time we are told brings round its revenges, and the books burnt by the common hangman in one age come to be honoured in the next. England may render itself ridiculous in the eyes of Europe by visiting the works of M. Zola with the same kind of condemnation which the civilised world has accorded to the writings of the degraded Marquis de Sade; still it requires no foresight to predict that a couple of generations hence, when the tribe of prejudiced scribes – who, ignorant for the most part of their own country's literature, now join in the hue and cry against M. Zola – are relegated to their proper obscurity, the works of the author of the Rougon-Macquart family saga, spite of their admitted coarseness, will take ranks as classics among the productions of the great writers of the past.

They are arriving at their destination. The cab eases past the seventeenth-century church of St Sepulchre, and draws up at the impressive edifice at the corner of Newgate Street and Old Bailey Street. Henry can see a small crowd of onlookers outside the court, though whether they have come for his trial or for one of several others to be heard today, he does not know. At least the general public no longer throngs to the street to see the aftermath of certain criminal prosecutions – the ones that resulted in hangings. These had taken place on portable gallows, set up outside Debtors' Door at Old Newgate, the prison next door. In Henry's younger years, it was not unusual to hear people, both men and women, confess that they "liked a good hanging". He himself has never attended one, though he had reported on an execution or two in France during the war, where the preferred method was not the rope but the guillotine. There too, crowds of people came out, bringing picnics, and rugs to sit on, as if it were a country fair.

Thankfully the barbaric and popular practice (there had been at least four hundred executions by public hanging during Henry's lifetime, most of them for murder) had ceased, some twenty years ago; now the condemned were hung behind the walls of the prison. This was due in no small part to the diligent campaigning of some of England's literary greats, including Henry's late friend, William Makepeace Thackeray, and Charles Dickens, the social crusader with the mighty pen.

The Vizetelly family approaches the court entrance, clustered around Henry to support him, though he appears as well as he has in days, and prefers to walk without aid if he can. There is a bit of warmth yet in the thin October sun, and he takes off his hat briefly as they wait to be given leave to pass indoors. In that moment, a rogue thought darts into his mind; he wonders whether he might end the day in the cells of Newgate. What if this is the last time he feels the sun on his forehead as an innocent man? He shakes himself out of this fancy; only a second-rate journalist or a third-rate novelist would indulge in such melodramatic speculation;

after all, as G. M. said, he is on trial for "a mere book", not bloody murder.

He also knows full well that Newgate, that ghoulish place of childhood nightmares, is today chiefly a holding prison for those awaiting trial – defendants who are sentenced to prison terms are generally taken to London's Pentonville or Holloway Prisons, and only those convicted of capital offences stay on at Newgate, awaiting execution. Enough morbid thinking, Henry admonishes himself. This is not the end of the story; it is the beginning of your defence, and the clearing of your name. He straightens his back and replaces his hat firmly on his head. Ernest is speaking to the officer at the door, thankfully not the same officious man who had barred their entrance a month earlier. This time there is no delay, and they are waved inside.

Sessions are held at least twelve times a year in the three different courts within the building. A throng of people mill this way and that inside the lobby, and the Vizetellys are soon hailed by a cluster of friends and well-wishers, joined by Mr Williams and Mr Cluer. The latter is weighed down with two large leather cases of law books and documents. He maintains his usual positive demeanour, calling out "A fine day, Messieurs!" when they approach.

"This way," Williams says, steering Henry towards the ill-lit, dark wooden staircase up to the courts. Henry does not like to admit that climbing a flight of stairs is daunting, and clenches his teeth against the pain of each jarring step. As he reaches the third, he wavers and fears he might tip backwards, but there is Annie by his side, gripping his hand fiercely and taking his weight on her slim arm without allowing him to lose his dignity. Ernest flanks him on the left, and together, without a word, the two children virtually carry their father into the courtroom.

It is not as Henry imagined. Everyone knows that the Old Bailey and Newgate are under review for demolition, and have been for several years – a fire in the gaol in 1877 had prompted proposals to pull down both buildings (built two centuries earlier) and erect a grand new one, and works are expected to commence soon, but the process has been fraught with bureaucratic and financial delays. The old building itself, seen from without, is so massive it gives the impression that the internal rooms will have high ceilings and rooms of great dimension, but Number Two Court is narrow and dingy, and not much more spacious than a large drawing room.

At one end is the judge's seat, with the Sword of Justice hanging on the wall above it – somewhat tarnished, Henry notices. Immediately below the judge sits the clerk's table, so that his Lordship might give whispered instructions or be handed up information and papers pertaining to the case. And beside that is the large dock, though in view of his age and health, Henry has been given permission in advance to sit with his lawyers at their table. This is an advantage for their side; he is sure there is something about the placing of a man in the dock before a jury that already begins to whittle away the presumption of innocence.

There are no steps from the dock directly down to the cells below – if a man is given a gaol sentence he must have to pass back through the well of the court and make his way to a little low door

Henry can see, off to the left. This connects the courtroom with "Dead Man's Walk", the exterior corridor that leads to the prison next door.

Ranged along the right wall are the jury seats, and facing the bench are tables and long wooden benches for the defence and prosecution teams. At the back of the room, accessed by another staircase, is a mezzanine gallery for the public. This is filling rapidly. Henry twists around and sees Annie with Ernest's wife's Marie, flanked by Arthur and Frank, taking seats in the front row – Ernest will stay below with him. In the reporters' box there is a crush of people; something in the cacophony of voices suggests there are Frenchmen among the crowd. Henry can make out the inflection rather than any particular words, the music of spoken French being so markedly different from the sedate drone of the Queen's English.

When Mr Williams was first engaged as his counsel, Henry had taken him to one side to ask what would happen if he were to plead guilty, assuming he also offered to withdraw the three offending translations cited in the original summons. It was simply to measure the land; he intends to fight the charge, but it is always useful to understand every possible outcome. If there were a way to stave off a prison sentence as well as a heavy fine, they would be wise to discover it early. Williams had gone to meet with the prosecution a week earlier. He came back to report that he had been told Henry could, if convicted, only hope to avoid gaol if every one of Zola's works in circulation by the publisher were immediately withdrawn, and if a stiff fine were paid. All of their

Zola stock sacrificed on the puritan altar? This was impossible to contemplate, both morally and financially. They would fight on.

The crowded court buzzes now with the arrival of the Recorder, Sir Thomas Chambers, a former Liberal party politician of advanced years – older than me, Henry guesses, well past seventy. This may or may not make him sympathetic, he supposes. Age does not always mellow a man; it can also render him inflexible, irritable and forgetful.

The prosecutor for the Crown is the Solicitor General Sir Edward Clarke, assisted by Mr Henry Bodkin Poland Q.C. and by H. H. Asquith, who has been drawn into the government's team given his foreknowledge of the case. The three men represent a formidable array of legal artillery. Clarke, not yet in his fiftieth year, is one of the leading members of the Bar and recently knighted. Henry thinks he remembers him in his youth as a law reporter; the man is recognisable by his long side-whiskers and that high forehead, which bulges as if overstuffed with brain matter. Mr Poland, who applied for the case's postponement a month earlier, is Counsel to the Treasury and advisor to the Home Office. He is older than Clarke, sixty or so, and is known as "the sleuth hound of the Treasury" for his ingenuity in proving evidence. He has a large, curved beak of a nose, dominating his long, gaunt face with its neat grey beard; Henry thinks he has the look of an eagle, or better still a vulture, for at the moment, he is standing with his arms spreading his robes in such a way that he appears to have long black wings.

Sir Edward Clarke Q.C. for the prosecution.

Asquith is somewhat diminished in this company, now that the Crown has taken over from the N.V.A. Still, he wears the smug look of a top student who is singled out by his professors to join them in their study for sherry. All three men are well known to the press, who are whispering amongst themselves in their box now, trying to discover who the unknown defence counsel is. "From Cardiff, did you say? Why Cardiff?"

The jury files in, a group of nondescript men who, as Ernest would say later, "appeared to be of the usual petty trading class". Would that the case were being tried in the countryside with a jury of farmers, Henry thinks – if any person familiar with rural life were to read *The Soil*, they would recognise the familiar themes and find little to shock them.

The Senior Clerk calls suddenly for silence, which takes several seconds to achieve. He stands at his table and reads out the first indictment in a monotone, which may be intended to subtract drama from the proceedings, for the sake of harmony in the courtroom. "The Jurors of our Lady the Queen upon their Oath present that Henry Vizetelly, Publisher and Bookseller of number 16 Henrietta Street, Covent Garden, in the County of Middlesex, being a person of a wicked and depraved mind and disposition . . ."

Henry keeps his face and body immobile. He does not look down but focuses on a long crack he can make out on the wall, curved like the penned emphasis under a signature. The pain starts up again, thrumming through his muscles and his lower organs in a familiar refrain of torture. He feels that if he moves an inch now he might simply give in, and slide down to curl in a foetal position on the cool marble floor.

". . . intending to corrupt the morals of all the subjects of our present Sovereign Lady the Queen and to debauch, poison and infect the minds of the youth in this Kingdom and to bring them into a state of wickedness, lewdness and debauchery . . ."

A mere book, Henry thinks.

". . . and did lawfully, wickedly and wilfully sell and utter and cause and procure to be published, sold and uttered a certain lewd, wicked, bawdy and obscene libel in the form of a book titled

The Soil, a "Realistic" novel by Émile Zola, in which said libel are contained among other things diverse wicked lewd impure and obscene matters . . ." The clerk drones on, reading out the other two indictments next, which repeat the same charges verbatim, against *Piping Hot!* and *Nana*.

Clarke now opens for the prosecution. His voice is patient and conversational, giving an instant impression of reasonableness. The jurors look at him with reverence and awe, like obedient children in front of a new schoolmaster. "Gentlemen. I believe you will find this case to be of great interest to the community at large. The charges against Mr Vizetelly, are, as stated, that in publishing books by a well-known French writer, Émile Zola, he has committed an offence the law calls obscene libel. Mr Vizetelly has already admitted he did publish the works, and contends that they are not obscene. I am glad to say that there are but a few previous cases of this unsavoury nature which can be mentioned as precedent, and I will only cite the most important for your benefit."

He goes on, in plain and persuasive language, explaining that the first obscenity law had been proposed by the then Lord Chief Justice Campbell, who put forward a bill that allowed for seizure and destruction of obscene materials. The language of the law, drafted in 1857, stated that a work contained obscene passages if it was calculated to produce a deleterious effect on those into whose hands it might come.

Henry knows well that Campbell's target at the time was crude pornography – a word that was in those days widely defined as "writing about or having to do with prostitutes". He specifically excluded "serious literature", even holding up before the Commons a copy of Dumas' tragic tale of a courtesan, *La Dame aux camélias*, and saying that while it was not to his taste, he "had not the most distant contemplation" that the Act would proscribe against such works. Clarke does not enlarge upon that point.

Now the Solicitor General briefly outlines the ruling in the case of Hicklin v. Regina in 1868, "which is of utmost importance, my friends". It was a turning point, because this judgment provided a "test" for obscenity. The bookseller Henry Scott was convicted by the lower court of selling lurid anti-Catholic propaganda ("shewing the depravity of the Roman priesthood" and "the iniquity of the Confessional"). He mounted an appeal on the grounds of his moral aims as a Protestant, rather than any desire for titillation or corruption of readers. The appeal judge, one Benjamin Hicklin, agreed that his intention was innocent, because he was seeking to expose problems in the Catholic Church.

But the new Chief Justice, Alexander Cockburn, soon reversed that opinion in the Court of the Queen's Bench. He held that Scott's *intention* did not matter; the publication was "obscene", regardless of the author, publisher or bookseller's aims – it was on sale to an impressionable audience. Obscenity was defined in the Act as material intended "to deprave and corrupt those whose minds are open to such influences, and into whose hands a publication of this sort may fall". In short, context and intention had no relevance.

It is an excellent and logical introduction to the case – and now Clarke caps his effort by proceeding to dismantle the

Vizetelly case for "artistic merit" so nicely laid out in the pamphlet that was recently disregarded by his employers at the Treasury, though he never makes direct reference to it.

"You may hear today, my good men, about certain classic works which contain objectionable extracts here and there, but enjoy wide circulation in our libraries and bookshops. Why, you may be asked, should they pass unpunished if the works of Mr Zola are banned? I will explain. An isolated passage in a work otherwise unobjectionable would not subject it to this judicial process. There are in all languages, and in our own classics, especially those dating from some centuries ago, segments which conflict with our current ideas. This has nothing to do with the case. Simply because some old works have not been indicted, a modern publication cannot be free from scrutiny and prosecution."

As if on cue, Asquith leans forward and hands him a book – an illustrated quarto edition of *The Soil*. "Thank you," Clarke says. He holds up the book towards the jury. "Turning to this filthy book in my hand, we have twenty-one extracts, some of them extending over several pages, such as no writer with pure motives ever put into a literary work." Why, Henry wonders, is he bothering about motives if Hicklin deemed them immaterial? Sometimes Clarke is too pleased with his own logic to see that it is becoming tangled. Obscenity is not so much a category as a confusion, it seems.

The prosecutor is speaking about *The Soil*, his voice becoming more urgent. "I cannot mention one character of a woman in this book that is a decent woman – not a single scene which is free from vicious suggestions and obscene terrors. I assure you, this is not a prosecution in connection with certain passages picked out here and there. It is that of a filthy book from end to end, published here to pander to the worst passions."

As he opens the book's green covers, the entire courtroom seems to lean forward in their chairs to see what may emerge – as if foul smoke will pour forth, or the pages spontaneously combust. Even the bailiffs lounging at the back, Henry notes, who have so far demonstrated scant interest in the proceedings, are spellbound. After a quick summary of the plot, Clarke makes to read Zola's words aloud.

But first, he takes a theatrical pause. "I will not call what I am about to read literature. There can be no question of literature with regard to this garbage." He commences at last, starting with the first scene, in which Jean Macquart, a single man in his thirties working on a farm, encounters Françoise, a girl of fourteen, assisting a recalcitrant bull in impregnating a cow. Henry looks at Ernest, but he has an elbow propped on the table and a hand over his forehead, as if unable to watch. They worked together on this scene for some hours, but it is difficult to "soften" the fact that this nubile young girl is masturbating a bull to allow it to mount a cow.

After some lead-in, emphasising the physical description of the girl "with her ruby red lips half open", Clarke comes to the nub of the scene. '"Raising her arm with a sweep, she aided the animal in his efforts, and he, gathering up his strength, speedily accomplished his purpose. It was done. Firmly, with the impassive fertility of land which is sown with seed, the cow had unflinchingly received the fruitful stream of the male . . . Françoise, having withdrawn her hand, remained with her arm in the air. Finally she lowered it, saying, "That's alright." "Yes, and neatly done," replied Jean.'"

Laughter rises from the reporters' box where several Frenchmen are mimicking Clarke's poor pronunciation of "Jean", which, to their amusement, he has made rhyme with "keen". Clarke ignores them, turning to the next marked pages.

Henry watches the jury. As a seasoned reporter, he knows that the temptation is to let the rhetoric of an experienced barrister dominate the room and draw the eye only to him – but it is the faces of the jury that are all-important. The twelve men do not much alter their expressions as Clarke reads, but Henry can see that there is movement among them, elbows nudging, silent signals being passed along from one to the next until like a ripple in water it spreads as far as the jury foreman who jumps to his feet of a sudden, interrupting Clarke in mid-sentence, blurting out, "Is it necessary for you read them all?"

Judge Chambers leans forward and peers at the man, his lined face further wrinkled in dismay. "These passages are charged in the first indictment as being the substance and essence of the case. They are revolting to a degree, but they are charged in the indictment, and must be proved."

Ernest's head is up now – he meets Henry's eye. It does not take much to understand that if judge and jury are this much offended by only a few pages of Zola, they are not going to accept a defence of artistic merit. Ernest dreaded this from the outset, but Henry has cloaked himself in optimism from the day he received the summons to Bow Street, refusing to be daunted; he has always had great reserves of confidence and courage, allowing him to surmount many obstacles in life, from the tragic loss of loved ones to reversals of financial fortune to the threat of a marauding army or two. But now he feels that cloak falling away, leaving him naked and vulnerable.

It is all he can do to stay upright as the scene plays out over the next and longest minute of his life. The agony is exacerbated by the prosecution counsel's expert display of politeness and humility. Clarke defers to the jury, full of care for their wellbeing, while reiterating the Recorder's admonishment about correct procedure. "I regret that these extracts are charged in the indictment and must be proved."

A stout fellow with not one hair on his shining pate, sitting behind the jury foreman, prods him in the back, as if to drive him forward like a mule.

"But is it necessary to read them all?" The foreman asks again, plaintively.

"The Solicitor General will exercise his own discretion," Judge Chambers decides.

Clarke bows to him and turns again to the jury. "Gentlemen. I hope you will understand that it is at least as unpleasant to me to read them as it to you to listen to them. If you think, subject to my learned friend on the part of the defence, that these passages are obscene, why, I will stop reading them at once." At this, there is a noisy reaction in the courtroom, a mixture of laughter and dismay at the irregularity of it all. "Have you ever seen the like?" A woman's coarse voice is heard to ask above the din.

Mr Williams and Mr Cluer beg the Recorder for a pause to consult with their client, which is granted. Henry and Ernest lean close to them and they speak in whispers. "I think you have no choice . . . then it will not go well for you . . . you can see they are against you, sir, it is plain . . . we cannot simply . . . I regret, sir . . ."

The conference soon ends. Mr Williams stands and faces the bench. "Your honour, my Lords, I have had the opportunity of speaking with my client, and acting on my advice, he desires to withdraw his plea of not guilty, and to plead guilty as charged."

From the gallery comes a stifled cry of protest, but in Henry's ringing ears it is impossible to tell if that is Annie or one of the boys – it may even have been G.M., who will be incensed at the turn of events. It is a wonder he has not vaulted down from the gallery with a dagger drawn.

"My client, Mr Vizetelly, realises that the book in question contains passages which the jury had intimated were very disgusting and unpleasant even in the discharge of a public duty to have to listen to."

A fine choice of words, Henry thinks, ever the editor, despite the pain that was now assailing him, from his roiling stomach to his throbbing shoulder and the shooting pains in his bladder; it is not that *I* think the book is disgusting or unpleasant, but I appreciate that *they* do.

Williams is now pleading for diminishment of the sentence, in light of the changed plea and the literary stature of the offending work. Henry stipulated this in their hurried conference – Zola's merit as an author must be included in the court records, even if they are unable to go on to fight the case on that basis now.

"These are the works of a great French writer . . ." Williams is saying.

"Oh no," Clarke interrupts sharply. "A voluminous French writer, if you like."

The clerk, taking all of this down in shorthand, looks from man to man as they speak, a spectator at a tennis match, his pen moving rapidly across the page all the while. Judge Chambers proposes a compromise, for the record.

"A popular French writer, I might suggest."

Williams is eager to reply. "A writer whose work certainly stands high amongst the literature of France."

Good man, thinks Henry – now mention Zola's Legion of Honour award, do not neglect that! It was only awarded last month; its lustre might have some small impact.

Sir Edward Clarke will not allow Williams any ground. His voice rises. "Oh no, Mr Williams. Do not malign the literature of France!" At this, many in the courtroom laugh – the distinguished gentlemen's battle of words is turning into the stuff of child's play: "Yes, you did" and "No, I did not!"

The ushers call for order once more, and Williams continues. "My client has pleaded guilty, and therefore it is not open to me to contend what he so firmly believes, namely that the works are not obscene." Clarke opens his mouth, but this time Williams will not allow him room to speak. "That being so, Mr Vizetelly undertakes to withdraw these translations from circulation and I understand that my learned friend does not ask that Mr Vizetelly be imprisoned. I leave it to your Lordship to deal with the matter." With that, he bows to the bench and takes his seat.

Clarke briefly consults his team and his clients, and then addresses the judge. "I am glad that a course has been taken which will not only stop from circulation the three books contained in these indictments, but which carries with it an undertaking by Mr Vizetelly that he will be no party to the circulation of any other of the class of works which Monsieur Zola has produced – that is, any other of which are at least as objectionable as those that are indicted before your Lordship today." There is also the implication from Clarke that if anyone else is to publish translations of Zola's work in England, or even works of a similar character, he will do so at his peril, and cannot escape as lightly as Mr Vizetelly.

This is the first time such a judgment has been made against a literary work this century; it is momentous. But Henry and his family cling, in those final dreadful minutes of the trial and well beyond that day, to one phrase: Vizetelly & Company can "be no party to the circulation of any other works which are at least as objectionable". This offers the possibility that Zola novels beyond the three indicted here today – and they have a further fifteen in their catalogue – might be cleansed of objectionable material and sold. All is not lost.

Now all that remains is to mitigate the punishment. Henry rises to his feet, hand gripping the table for support.

"Am I correct in saying a few words?"

"You may," Chambers nods curtly.

"I merely wish to ask that witnesses to my character who have known me for nearly half a century may be called, before sentence is passed."

Chambers does not pause. "What difference would it make? I am not going to punish you because your character is not good, but only for having published an obscene libel, which you admit to. These works have been published for the sake of gain. I am quite prepared to believe your character is good, which makes this all the more surprising."

Williams attempts to help his client to be seated – the last thing he wants now is an irritable judge. Henry stands his ground, head high, the picture of dignity. "My Lord, I have been guilty of a fault I quite admit, but I was unaware it was a crime."

The judge thanks him for his comments, saying they will be duly entered in the record, and turns away to confer with a colleague. After a few minutes, the ruling is handed down from the bench. The sentence is a fine of one hundred pounds. At this, Ernest presses his father's hand under the defence table, as if to say, it is a considerable sum, but we will raise it. It is less than he imagined, and nothing compared to what they will lose by not selling the three books. A moment later, matters turn for the worse. It seems Henry will also be bound over for a two-hundred-pound bond to his own recognisance, which is to be forfeit "if he fails to keep the peace and be of good behaviour for twelve months". Mr Williams responds immediately, lest Henry try to plead further. "The fine will be paid to the Sheriff by Saturday, Your Worship."

"On that undertaking, he may go," Chambers says, and gets to his feet. The whole court rises with him – except Henry. He is so depleted that he is unable fully to comprehend the chatter that begins around him, and he does not respond when Williams leans in to say something. The man's lips are moving but Henry is damned if he can understand a word. Is the fellow speaking in Welsh? If only he could shut his eyes and be carried home in a blink of an eye to the blessed relief of a warm bath. If only he could then be laid in his bed for one night's unencumbered sleep, then he would have the strength to address this on the morrow. There it is: "if only". He has succumbed.

PART III:
CONSEQUENCES

9. December 1888, Henrietta Street, Covent Garden

"Ah . . . choo!" Ernest sneezes for the fifth time since he arrived early this morning in the dusty warehouse. It is crammed nearly to the roof timbers with printed stacks of paper and piles of bound books, arranged in seemingly random order, though Arthur insists he knows where to find every volume. But Arthur is detained in the office upstairs just now, warding off increasingly angry creditors who, ever since the trial, have been appearing at all hours, demanding to know how and when they will be paid. Ernest is on his own.

"It has to be here somewhere," Ernest mutters. He is looking in vain for illustrated copies of the first Rougon-Macquart novel,

The Fortune of the Rougons, which he was told could be found in the northwest corner. So far all he has unearthed are a stack of scarlet-covered editions of du Boisgobey's popular crime novels, which, he notes, might be sold on to generate a little revenue, and several leather-bound illustrated editions of Daudet's *Sappho*. There's a title that would generate some income, though it would be impolitic to sell it now. Wincing, he recalls how his father announced the book. "A glowing picture of Parisian life, with all its special immorality." He tosses Daudet back on the pile.

Henry has constantly promoted Zola's novels as "realistic", a popular euphemism for "salacious". It is not just the N.V.A. and their ilk that are eroding the boundary between art and pornography, Ernest realises; publishers are responsible for the way their books are promoted. He should have returned from Paris earlier; he might have averted this disaster if he could have tempered the firm's sales approach.

It is not the first time that Ernest wonders whether his father might have escaped his fate by using subtler methods to market his more contentious wares. Henry's method smacks of "intentionality", that vexed legal concept on which they had tripped and fallen at the Old Bailey: Henry was in effect convicted of deliberately seeking to attract a particular kind of reader, and appealing to their baser instincts.

Advertising, it strikes him now, may have brought the novels to the attention of their enemies in the first place, for it is unlikely that members of the N.V.A. had read the books in either French or English, but anyone could see an advertisement and take offence.

In fact, even as they celebrate their victory over "pernicious literature" at the Old Bailey, the group are turning their eye to other
assaults on Britain's moral fabric. The Indecent Advertisements
Act, aimed at limiting explicit medical advertisements, and spon-
sored by the N.V.A. advocates in Parliament, is gaining much
attention in the press. Doubtless they will win this battle too,
having proven that if they can convince the public that they are
victims, they can change the law of the land.

Their reach is expanding. Ernest has just learned that the
Home Office, not content with prosecutions in London, is taking
the unprecedented step of notifying the mayors of all major
cities in England of Henry's trial outcome, urging them to initiate
local proceedings against booksellers who continue to offer the
banned works. The national newspapers have abetted this with
an outpouring of articles even more damning than those that
encouraged the government to take action in the first instance,
suggesting that one trial was not enough, and that this action is
only the beginning of a vital cleansing of the nation's bookshops.
Ernest is reminded of something Victor Hugo wrote, half a century ago in France, but never more true than today in England:
"The peculiarity of prudery is that it multiplies the guards in
proportion as the fortress is less threatened." The moral militia
are out in force in the English press.

"Mr Vizetelly may consider that he has done very well to have
escaped from an English court with only a moderate fine," the
Star wrote; "He is rightly punished," echoed the *Globe*, while the
Saturday Review sniffed, "Better late than never." The *Standard*

included Zola in their vitriol after the trial: "It was an outrage to write such books, an offence to translate them, and it makes the matter all the worse to issue them in cheap and popular form." It seems they damn Henry most for daring to make reading affordable for the working classes. Ernest loathes them all for their lack of humanity, let alone any skill whatsoever at literary judgment.

Of course, a few journals objected to the verdict, here and there, mainly via anonymous letters from Henry's supporters, and there were articles from some worried members of the trade, speculating on the impact for their own businesses. The *Publishers' Circular*, for example, had written of Henry's fine, "We hardly know whether to congratulate Mr Vizetelly or sympathise with him." Congratulations are in order, they infer, for escaping a prison term. The *Telegraph* had phrased their comment with similar caution, falling in line with the prevailing views on protecting the reader while refusing to damn Zola by saying, "There are competent critics among us who regard Zola as a man of genius, but were he ten times as great a writer as he is . . . we should still deny the right of any English publisher to scatter translations indiscriminately among the public."

The highlight of all the rejoinders came from the controversial author and journalist Robert Buchanan, even if he has never met Henry and has often professed dislike of Zola's work. A few days after the trial, he published a defiant poem, as if to prove that the pen is mightier than the Old Bailey's Sword of Justice. It opened with a defiant thrust:

ZOLA

A lifelong task to paint the woes of men
With lurid flashes here and there of light.
    Spurner of life, he scorns the silky pen
That glosses shameful ills, and calls wrong right
    To suit the prudish ears of rich and sleek.

The matter had excited debate for a few weeks, but that was all. Soon enough, other matters occupied the editorial and letters pages. The N.V.A., determined to bring the controversy back to public attention while they roam around Britain in search of new victims, are publishing a victorious pamphlet, titled *Pernicious Literature*. This will detail the court case, with not only a full transcription of the proceedings but including the entire text of Samuel Smith's original speech in the Commons, as well as numerous editorials from London and national newspapers. "The wreckers", as Ernest has branded them, intend to circulate more than a hundred thousand copies of this pamphlet in the New Year.

With a deep sigh, Ernest gazes around the ill-lit room. Herein lies the family fortune, such as it is, and he has taken it upon himself to rescue what he can; he feels like a diver circling a shipwreck, hoping to extract a little gold. It is impossible to salvage the entire stack of novels lining the wall opposite, of course – those are the three Zola titles which were cited in the trial; they were the most sought after by the public and therefore the most abundantly printed by the firm. Hundreds of bound, gilt-embossed copies of each book, and they will never see the light of day, nor earn a penny. It is a devastating blow. Again and again, how he wishes his father had listened to him with regard to *The Soil*, a book he knew the English audience could not accept. "I warned you" has no value now, but Ernest cannot help feeling like Cassandra, his cautions all ignored.

There is no use going over mistakes past; the family must look forward now, and recover as best they may. In this room are hundreds of copies, bound or waiting to be bound, of many Zola titles besides the offending three, as well as a few by popular French authors other than Zola, such as Flaubert and Maupassant. Ernest has a plan. The verdict was that no other novels could be published by Vizetelly & Company that were "at least as offensive" as *Nana, Piping Hot!* and *The Soil*. Those three were banned. But if further titles in stock can be sanitised and therefore rendered inoffensive, what is the harm in selling them? The judge had definitely not said, "None of Zola's books can be sold in any form." Releasing a new catalogue within weeks, announcing revised "clean" editions of Zola and others, will make the most of the high public interest and generate much-needed income.

What is the alternative? Henry had agreed to this plan, and had even, without his sons' prior knowledge, issued what would be his final fervent letter to a London editor on the matter. This time he addressed himself to the *Publishers' Circular*, insisting, "The undertaking made in court does not apply to the whole of M. Zola's works." So far, no-one has taken him to task for this in public, but Ernest feels sure that the N.V.A. have seen it and are circling silently, like sharks in the water, ever a menace.

The first thing we will do, he resolves now, is remove some wording from the front pages of every book we re-issue. He holds up a copy of *Nana* to the light, dust motes dancing over the engraved cover, and turns to the frontispiece. TRANSLATED WITH-OUT ABRIDGEMENT FROM THE 127TH FRENCH EDITION. That will go from every book we re-issue – and we shall drop the price, cut-ting it from six shillings to three and sixpence; that will move the stock. A page falls open, and there is Nana in all her buxom glory: he recognises it as a drawing by André Gill, which he is familiar with from the French edition. Nana stands in a transparent *pei-gnoir*, admiring herself in a mirror. Peering closer at the image, Ernest realises the original has been altered; the gown has been made opaque over Nana's nakedness, revealing her body only from knees to feet – thereby protecting her modesty, even if she will not. Too little, Papa, he thinks, and too late.

He rummages further through the piles and unearths a stack of company catalogues. He recognises them on sight, for his father dispatched a copy of each and every one to him when he was living in Paris, and often sought his ideas about future acquisitions. The first catalogue he opens, from 1884, is a slim example, at only sixteen pages. There is George Moore's *A Modern Lover*, also promoted as a "realistic" work, like *Nana*, advertised on the facing page. Although the ninth book in the Rougon-Macquart saga, *Nana* was the first to be translated by Vizetelly, followed soon after by the seventh book, *L'Assommoir*. Ernest knows that Zola's series was meant to be read in order, but each book stands on its own, and though a sequential reading may deepen the reader's

Nana in the French edition, before her attire was rendered acceptably opaque for an English audience.

understanding, it is not essential. In fact, Zola himself has recently set out a recommended reading order of the books that differs significantly from their order of publication.

Also in this catalogue, Ernest discovers advance notice that the tenth book in the series, *Piping Hot!*, is coming soon. Why the exclamation mark, he thinks peevishly, what does that add? The French title, *Pot-Bouille,* a slang term for "stew pot", needed no such addition. I suppose Papa believes this little touch sells books, and he may be right.

In a similar vein, Ernest knows the American editions alter Zola's titles to make them sound as enticing as possible. After the tremendous success of *Nana* there five years ago, scarcely a month goes by without a new Zola in translation being issued by one American publisher or another. Until the country becomes signatory to the Berne Convention, the books are there for the taking. *The Conquest of Plassans*, the fourth Rougon-Macquart novel, has been published in Philadelphia recently as *A Mad Love*, of all things; and the fourteenth novel, *His Masterpiece*, a sensitive story of a Parisian artist who fails to live up to his potential, has been published for an American audience as *Christine the Model*.

How Ernest grimaced to hear of this from a friend recently returned from New York. Whatever next? How will the Americans christen *The Soil*, he wonders – perhaps as *Love on the Farm*? Some publishers there are even bringing out novels set in France which are not written by Zola at all, and putting his name on the cover because it guarantees sales, especially in the cheap paper-covered volumes which they sell for twenty or thirty cents each.

Evidently his notoriety is not confined to the common people – in American literary circles, he is (for good and for ill) the most discussed writer of the decade.

He pulls another catalogue from the pile, this one from 1886 – by then, Vizetelly's output had doubled. It trumpets the firm's acquisition of du Boisgobey's detective novels, as well as announcing publication of Thackeray's *Shabby-Genteel Story*, and more translations of Zola. Over time, the firm's offerings were growing broader, becoming a collection including English fiction, travel books and histories, as well as the translations that formed by then at least half of their output.

As a matter of course, the books were grouped into series, a device used in publishing both here and on the Continent; in fact, Zola's publisher Charpentier had pioneered this idea in France years before, with relatively inexpensive collections of contemporary novels grouped under the heading "modern classic authors". Henry had always favoured this approach. The prettily illustrated catalogues and covers testify to Henry's origins as an artist and engraver. Titles are arranged under series headings such as 'The Mermaid Series" (of Restoration and Shakespeare's plays), "Celebrated Russian Novels" and "Popular French Fiction", or by price, such as the "Half-a-Crown Series" and the "Sixpenny Series of Amusing and Entertaining Books". Best-selling authors also had their own series, like the mystery novelists Gaboriau and du Boisgobey – as well as, of course, Moore and Zola.

Most of the Vizetelly's titles were offered in various formats, illustrated or otherwise, with cloth or paper bindings, from cheaper pocket books to illustrated octavo editions to folio editions with lavish illustrations. To keep prices down, Henry, like many other publishers of the day, inserted advertisements at the front and back of his books, alongside news of future publications, and in the Zola series the reader would see notices for sewing machines, hair dyes, a French jewellery company, and "Rimmel's Choice Perfumery". Thumbing through these, Ernest can't help but think that such female-orientated advertising further bolstered their enemies' belief in Henry's corrupting intentions. Then again, everyone knows that in the main it is women who read novels – what sense would there be in not trying to please them?

All in all, it appears that the firm went from publishing eight or nine titles in its first year in 1880 to as many as eighty-five in 1887; last year ten of them were by Zola. This year, the overall figure had dropped to nearer seventy, but Ernest shudders to think what will be achieved in the year ahead – they might be lucky to publish a third of that number. He can hardly bear to look at the most recent catalogue, in which Henry has inserted his battle cry after the first trial, the same paragraph he insisted on sending to the *Bookseller* after the hearing at Bow Street. "The trade is informed that there are no legal restrictions on the sale of *Nana, Piping Hot!* and *The Soil* by Émile Zola and that none can be imposed until a jury has pronounced adversely . . ." Ernest drops the catalogue like a hot coal and renews his search for such nuggets as can be sold; there is no use wasting more time on the wreckage of the past.

Ah, there it is. Hidden under a low bench, Ernest locates a box of illustrated editions of *The Fortune of the Rougons*. There is a foldout family tree inside, which Zola himself has drawn. Each "leaf" bears a character's name and his or her key inherited physical and mental characteristics, so that the reader can trace the progress of the Rougon-Macquart defects and proclivities as they move through the generations. It is a shame these books are already bound, Ernest thinks, tucking the drawing carefully back inside the covers, but it should be possible to replace the offending sections with revised versions, then re-use the covers.

This book launches all of the major characters that appear in the subsequent books in a story that rivals Hugo's epic romances, setting the stage for the rich and multi-layered series to come. Written when Zola was thirty years old, it is a tremendous accomplishment in itself, let alone in the context of what follows. Ernest pauses to read the author's introductory note, which culminates: "This work, which will comprise several episodes, is therefore, in my mind, the natural and social history of a family under the Second Empire. And the first episode, here called *The Fortune of the Rougons*, should scientifically be titled *The Origin*." It is signed Émile Zola, Paris, 1 July, 1871. A significant date, Ernest knows full well: at the moment that he and his father watched the Second Empire fall, Zola had launched its monumental literary post-mortem.

Ernest will start his rescue mission here; why not begin where Zola did? This first book seems, from his recent investigations, to have made the least impression on their antagonists compared to the rest of the series. Therefore, once he has read through and decided on necessary changes (and he will be "more than cautious", he has assured his anxious wife), this, along with selected other titles from their warehouse stock, will go to the printers for revision as soon as possible, so that the firm may re-issue new editions. Their regular printers in Whitefriars will work seven days a week, with the promise that the consequent sales will allow them to recover all overdue payments.

What of Henry in this process? No-one in the family is as deft an editor, nor more suited to an assignment requiring such mental alacrity. But the old man has deferred to Ernest and his brothers now, and taken to his bed. Nothing could be more alarming to his children; not illness, anger, nor Henry's pride, or his "tilting at windmills", as Ernest privately calls it, his penchant for writing letters to the daily press. There is none of that now – only silence. Henry is wrapped in it, spending long days abed, or in a bath, unable or unwilling to discuss in detail the next strategy for saving the firm.

Annie has done all she can to draw him out, sitting with him for hours on end, reading to him from his favourite Walter Scott novels, preparing him special drinks and broths that might ease the pain he suffers, but there is little relief. Some nights, as she watches him fall asleep, his expressive face twitching and unhappy even in repose, Annie fears that the judgment at the Old Bailey is killing her father, and one morning soon she will not be able to wake him. But he lives on, with odd moments of clarity and humour, particularly when Moore comes to visit, as he does often – bursting with ideas and schemes to reverse his friend's situation. Henry waves these away with a weary, "Talk to the boys, please, and tell me the news of the day instead."

* * *

Two months later, Ernest is at the printers in Bouverie Street, also home to the popular journal *Punch*. Trade gossip has it that the *Punch* compositors never smile at the cartoons. They are a serious and industrious lot, treating type, plates and paper with the dedication and single-mindedness of miners bringing up coal. The composing room is at the top of the tall brick building, half under glass to profit from the maximum natural light, though the sun is already fading fast on this chill winter afternoon. Ernest stands in the doorway, winded by the climb up four flights of stone stairs. Gas lamps as well as candles, the latter set in small metal holders affixed to wooden composing frames, further illuminate the work of the dozen or more men who are concentrating on the effort at hand. It is an impressive operation.

In order to prepare the amended pages, now totalling three hundred and twenty-five across fifteen different novels, Ernest has worked night and day for weeks, with some assistance from his brothers and a little oversight from Henry. He is exhausted. But at least he is reaching the summit of the chore, and the prospect below is hopeful. Buyers are clamouring for more Zola, even cut to ribbons. There is nothing like a censorship trial for whetting public appetite.

It has been one of the leanest Christmastides he can remember – almost unmarked at Henrietta Street, although Annie did her best with a festive currant cake, made by her own hands now that they have let both the housemaid and the cook go. His children are too young to notice the change, but Marie, his beloved wife, who is used to far better from her privileged childhood, is not happy. It is for her and the little ones that he labours now, Ernest thinks, and of course for his father, who has mostly stayed in his room all winter, swathed in heavy blankets like a newborn. Only on Christmas Day could Annie tempt him downstairs to the parlour to taste a morsel of her modest cake. With a flash of his old spirit, he had toasted her with a small glass of very ordinary wine, savouring it as if it were vintage champagne, and pronounced her cake the best he had ever tasted. Annie, who has overnight developed a permanent furrow on her smooth brow, toasted him in return, bravely holding back tears.

She'll soon be brighter, Ernest thinks. He looks around with some satisfaction at the aproned men and dogged apprentice boys working at full capacity. Most of the compositors wear caps, for it is cold in this unheated, high-ceilinged space, despite the bustle of activity. The noise and the level of concentration are acute; the men's nailed boots echo on the boarded floor and the boys rattle carriage trays to and fro carrying frames of set type.

The compositors are herded by their "clickers", a group of managers who each command a small team; they hand out the tasks assigned by the overseer. The work then starts at sloping tables near the windows, crested by rows of divided wooden frames containing individual upper and lower case letters, from which the type is set by hand. Each page is then moved to one of the individual steel topped tables, known as "stones". There the compositors assemble carefully numbered "formes", or blocks of pages, which are set in groups of four, eight or sixteen, and secured with wooden blocks. Clever planning of the room affords easy access for the apprentices and compositors as they move smoothly from station to station in practised movements. When the formes are ready, they are rolled with ink and a "proof" page is test-printed on the hand-operated Albion presses.

After that, they peel off each page and set it in front of a proof-reader, who checks it and gives it to the client for final approval. Proofreading could involve finding spelling errors or a missed word or phrase, but today they are also looking for any slight un-evenness in the printed lines, which sometimes happens when a single word has been expurgated from an existing plate; this makes it more difficult to re-align. Once the client is satisfied, the pages are sent down to the floor below to be printed on large rotary machines; then down again to the finishing and binding room where books are cut, collated and bound, ready to go to the warehouse at ground level, where they will eventually roll out of the street doors for transport to buyers.

Ernest tugs his coat around him. He cannot imagine what it must be like to sleep in this cold, filthy room at night, as many of the apprentices do – he spies their ragged blankets under the long table at the centre of the room, with tin cups for milk set beside each sorry pallet; he knows there is a convention in the trade that drinking milk will "settle the lead" in the ink dust that coats the surfaces in the room, and blackens the nostrils of every man and boy. As it happens, Ernest would be glad of some milk himself right now, or even a glass of something stronger – he is in need of some fortification, after barely three hours' sleep last night, finishing the final pages.

This process of expurgation has been like assembling the most complex puzzle. It would be too costly in time and money to reset so many pages by hand; Ernest has therefore chosen offending passages and written replacements for them that fit exactly to the space left by the excisions. He has struggled sometimes to invent something suitably anodyne, "a version of events", in order to preserve the integrity of the page if not the integrity of authorship. Of course it is also possible to leave blank spaces and printers commonly insert a line of dashes in place of objectionable wording, but Ernest has sought to avoid this ugly solution. It is impressive that he has managed to achieve this in such a short time, though his labours will leave a lasting false impression on the English reader that Zola is a leaden, elliptical writer.

The compositors work from the original stereotype plates, plaster cast when the books were first printed: these produce a perfect reproduction of handset type. Using this method, rather than setting the type letter by letter and printing one page, before removing all the letters and starting over again with the next page, they free up their letters; it is by far the quickest way to print in volume and most books and journals intended for wide circulation have adopted this method.

To create the stereotypes for a book in the first instance, each page's plaster cast was pressed in hot metal and mounted on a block of wood, then secured in place with pins at each corner.

When the metal plate needs amendment for a new print run, as now, the pins are removed, the plate is lifted off the wooden mount, and the selected phrases or paragraphs are cut away with a fine fret saw, or, in the case of an individual word being lifted out, the compositor uses a small drill to extract it from the middle of a line like a bad tooth.

Ernest cannot bear to think what the author would say about it all. Imagine if Zola walked in here now, to see a wizened little man in a flat cap bent over his precious text, wielding a saw or drill, extracting the word "breast" or "nude" or "ecstasy" as directed, and reducing the violent expressions of primitive natures to discreet exchanges with all the fervour of a limp handshake.

He watches the saw's sharp teeth biting into the opening of a chapter, mesmerised. As the drill is applied to the next plate, its operator grimacing as he turns the handle to puncture the cold metal, Ernest cannot bear to look any longer, and gets up from the table to go outside. Downstairs, he strides past two apprentice boys sharing a quick pipe in the alley by Lombard Street, and fishes in his pocket for the slim flask he carries, to temper the winter wind. Taking a deep drink, he leans his weight against the wall, gazing up at the slate sky, and indulges in a morose reverie; this round of expurgations, which took matters so much further than any earlier "edited translation", feels tantamount to slashing at the Mona Lisa, or hacking a limb from Michelangelo's David. But of course it has to be done. He only hopes he lives to see the day when this sorry deed can be reversed.

10. *April 1889, Henrietta Street, Covent Garden*

Frank Harris, author, publisher, editor and man about town

What is it about Henry Vizetelly and the Celts? The gentleman author from Mayo, George Moore, has been a staunch ally since the outset of his difficulties, and now it seems that his latest champion is an Irish-born Welshman.

The family fortunes are at their lowest ebb when this new player makes his entrance into their on-going drama. Their debts are escalating, and their landlord has lately told them they will need to find new premises. Now their solicitor, Mr Cluer, arrives at Henrietta Street with a long face and further bad news.

They invite him to sit when he appears unexpectedly during their midday meal. It is a poor affair; Annie is scrimping in the kitchen and there is only half a carafe of wine today and no meat at all. Cluer, whose coat is wet from the steady downpour without, declines to join the group at table, apologising for the interruption as he leans his umbrella against the iron stand by the door.

He struggles to mask his alarm at the sight of Henry, who, though seated in his old chair at the head of the table today, is eating nothing from the plate before him, nor even pretending to hold his fork. A napkin is tucked under his chin, as if he might drool or drop his food like a baby, should he attempt to partake of any. His already slim frame has become emaciated, and he looks barely half alive. The decline is stark, even in the few months since Cluer saw him last.

"Gentlemen. I will not keep you from your repast. I simply had to come immediately." He withdraws from his jacket a parchment document. "I am sorry to say that we have this morning received a new summons to court."

"What? Whatever for?" Ernest bursts out, spittle and red wine flecking the tablecloth before him. "It cannot be!" Cluer hands him the notice and he tears it open, lips moving silently as he reads.

"What is . . ." Henry's voice is faint. He trails off and looks down at his hands in his lap, as if surprised to find them there.

"The N.V.A. is on the warpath again, Papa – those wretched, preening, preaching, parasites. When will they cease to torment us?"

"Pound . . . pound . . ."

"What do you say, Papa?" Annie leans close to Henry, who is making a feeble gesture with his hand towards the summons document.

"Pound of flesh."

"Precisely! They've had that," Ernest says. "And now, it seems, they are coming for our hides as well."

The document accuses the firm of further dissemination of obscene libel since the Central Court's ruling of October last, naming the Zola novels they have re-issued as well as Gustave Flaubert's *Madame Bovary* and Guy de Maupassant's *A Ladies' Man*. Sales of these new and severely pruned editions, many of them close to half their original length in French, have kept the family business alive, as it limped through the winter months and into the wet spring. Today's summons specifies that Henry is in breach of his bond conditions for continuing to publish obscene material in defiance of the court.

Cluer and his colleagues are not entirely surprised by this. They cautioned the Vizetellys after Henry's letter in November to the *Publishers' Circular*, in which he declared that he would publish more Zola, and others of his ilk. The re-issued books might well be "new versions", but it was the lawyers' duty to remind Henry that he gave his word to keep the peace for twelve months, and therefore utmost care was required. "Utmost care is being taken," Ernest had responded grimly to this entreaty, on behalf of his father, "but we must feed our family." There was no choice – they could not bury the company's vital remaining assets.

The summons document passes between the brothers at the table, who consider it in silence. Annie bites her lip and reaches across to take her father's limp hand. "We cannot afford another trial," Arthur says, pushing the page away from him as if it were contaminated. "In truth we can scarce afford to be speaking with you now, Mr Cluer. Please do not bill us for your time spent coming here in person, when you might have sent the summons by post."

Cluer clears his throat. "Ah. Yes. To that end . . . I bring some positive news, at least. You are familiar with Mr Frank Harris?" He detects the slightest upturn of Henry's mouth at the mention of the name; most people of an enlightened attitude have that reaction. Frank Harris, a self-made, self-aggrandising publisher, born in Ireland but of Welsh parentage, is a London society character, a legend of his own making; he is also a prolific editor who shares Henry's journalistic background and taste in literature. He is either loved or hated, depending on the political bent of his audience – and whether or not he has made love to one's wife, for he is a renowned Lothario.

* * *

Henry is not among Harris' *intimes* – but he does know and like the man, who was the first to publish Zola's good friend Maupassant in English, in the pages of his periodical, the *Fortnightly*

Review. Ernest on the other hand does not find Harris' antics at all charming, though he can admire the man's career and his excellent literary relationships. He is wary.

"What of him?"

"Mr Frank Harris has made it known to our firm that he would like to fund your further legal battles, to whatsoever may be their conclusion."

"We cannot accept!" Ernest's pride speaks before he can think. "That is out of the question."

"We must accept," says a low voice beside him. Annie gets to her feet, and faces the group of men, hands clasped in front of her. "I do not know this Mr Harris, nor should I wish to share a room with him from what one understands of his reputation, but if his principles as a fellow publisher drive him to help us, and he has the funds to offer, why, we should be thankful. What other options do we have, Ernest?"

"Frank Harris." Ernest pushes his chair away from the table. "What will we owe him in return, eh, Mr Cluer?"

"Not a thing, Mr Vizetelly. This is not a loan, there is no *quid pro quo*; he simply wishes to support your family and the firm in its time of need, and is not short of the resources to do so. He has written your father a letter, which I have on my person, as he is aware that you are not receiving visitors at this time."

He passes a letter over the table to Henry, who inclines his head towards Annie. She breaks the ornate seal and opens it, carefully smoothing the creases to read it aloud. After a brief and cordial greeting, Harris outlines his offer, calling it "a contribution to the cause of freedom" and wishing his friend and colleague good health and success against the odious, dangerous N.V.A.

This is in character. Harris loves using flamboyant gestures to underscore his ideals. Only a few months earlier, aggravated by the fact that certain famous literary figures seemed blind to the dangers of censorship, he had published a passionate statement of his position on the matter of literary suppression, not long after Tennyson was quoted in the *Contemporary Review* as saying "the name of Zola is synonymous with sewage".

Harris wrote, "There is far less freedom of speech in England and America than anywhere else in Christendom, and this Anglo-Saxon prudery is hardly more than a century old . . . It is manifestly founded on Puritanism and is supported by the middle classes . . . In France, and indeed in every country of Europe, the man of letters today can treat sexual facts as freely as the painter or the sculptor treats the nude . . . Since this prudery has come into power, English literature has lost its pride of place."

Ernest cannot object for long to the offer of assistance. It will be necessary to retain a new Q.C. as a matter of urgency. Their previous man, Williams, is not available. The Vizetellys would like to use Mr Cluer, for he has been both advocate and friend to them, and shares their love of literature. Apparently, Frank Harris also approves of him, and expressly states this in his letter to Henry, saying he would choose him for counsel. But the young man is not yet a Q.C, and it is held by his colleagues that it would be wiser to pit someone senior and more eminent against the Solicitor General, who will again be acting for the prosecution.

There is a man of great experience whom several friends recommend, by the name of Mr Alfred Cock. His reputation is not entirely orthodox, but it is suited to this instance. In the words of Tommy Bowles, *Vanity Fair*'s all-seeing editor, "He drives witnesses to desperation by loud and persistent badgering . . . and believes in the supreme importance of getting facts to come out on his own side." "Is that what we want?" Ernest, for one, is unsettled by the description. But he is persuaded that they must fight fire with fire. Mr Cock will be approached and briefed, while Cluer will deal immediately with the committal hearing at Bow Street and go on to act as Cock's junior counsel if the matter proceeds to trial. Evidently, Mr Cock's fees are not the lowest, given his reputation for success, but this is irrelevant now that their Welsh "angel" has appeared.

* * *

The hearing at Bow Street on Wednesday, May 1, reveals the sheer scale of the N.V.A.'s renewed campaign. They have summoned four other publishers and booksellers on the same day, including two London merchants who have been caught selling banned editions of *Nana* and *Piping Hot!* There is also William Thompson of Holywell Street, who was spared a trial for publishing *The Decameron* last year. Not content with that ruling, the N.V.A. are now trying to prosecute him for publishing a sixteenth-century text, the *Heptameron*, Queen Marguerite of Navarre's short story collection, which was inspired by Boccaccio's work.

The prosecution have counted out and dissected all the pages in the named Vizetelly & Company publications that, to their minds, remain offensive to the public. This includes a full nineteen titles within the new catalogue, issued after the Old Bailey trial last autumn. All of the actions are brought once again by Mr Coote, Secretary of the N.V.A., who has mustered a crowd of messenger boys as his witnesses; he has sent them out on a mass errand over the last several months, to attempt to buy copies of banned or suspect novels around Britain, leaving no stone (or filthy book cover) unturned; the summons have been issued as a result of these diligent labours.

Coote's mentor, the *Gazette*'s editor W. T. Stead, appeared to have softened in recent months towards Zola; he had even published a positive review soon after the trial praising his latest novel, *The Dream*, greatly preferring it to the author's earlier "garbage". In a piece titled "M. Zola in a New Character", he rhapsodises:

> In the new volume which M. Zola has just added to his library of "natural and social history", he very literally turns over a new leaf. From the brutalities of the gin-shop and the slough of the cow-shed we pass in *The Dream* to the peaceful quiet of the cloister and dim religious light of the cathedral aisle . . . If no novelist has ever put before the public such moral garbage as is to be found in *The Soil*, neither has any ever presented prettier flowers of idyllic innocence than bloom in the pages of *The Dream*.

But it would be a mistake to see this as forgiveness of Vizetelly & Company. Stead is far from placated in that regard. He is regularly heard on the topic of "pernicious literature" through his editorial columns, and on the day of the committal hearings at Bow Street, Henry and Ernest see that he is among the first journalists to arrive. He takes a prominent place, sitting tall in the reporters' box, heedless of the noise and scramble around him. He watches the proceedings through narrowed eyes, taking no notes, and later, he does not report many details from the actual hearing itself, but editorialises on the folly of it being necessary at all: "What possessed Mr Vizetelly, having placed his head in the lion's jaws, to allow his son to twist the noble animal's tail is one of those things which pass ordinary human comprehension."

An objective reader might think he regrets the matter has come to this. Ernest, who bans the *Gazette* from his house, thinks otherwise; he fervently believes Stead is the architect of their downfall. The man has fomented press agitation from the start and has been instrumental in keeping the matter alive since the sentence last autumn. Stead is the ruination of the house of Vizetelly, and Ernest will despise the man forever.

* * *

It is the night after the Bow Street hearing: as expected, the magistrate has sent the case against Henry for a new trial by jury at the Old Bailey. Ernest, Arthur and Cluer are reviewing the day's events and plotting new stratagems in the room below, while Henry lies in his bed. But he does not sleep. Annie leans over him, arranging the blankets. "Papa, may I bring you something? A drop of your port still remains in the decanter – I have hidden it from the boys, just for you." He loves port wine; he once wrote a whole book on the subject. Surely this will lift his spirits.

"Annie." His voice is low but surprisingly strong. "I need you to write something for me."

"Of course." She goes to the writing table in the corner, and takes out pen and ink, setting some paper ready. "A letter?"

"Yes, please." He clears his throat. 'I, Henry Richard Vizetelly, do certify to all whom it may concern . . .'"

She writes swiftly, then pauses as he stops to take a sip of water before he continues. "On this first day of May in the Year of our Lord 1889, in the presence of my daughter, Anne Elizabeth Vize-telly, I hereby assign all assets, chattels, currency and goods held in my name, to remain in trust for the benefit of my creditors, in order that my publishing company, Vizetelly & Company of 16 Henrietta Street Covent Garden, London, may be liquidated. I assign all responsibility for this to my son Ernest Alfred Vizetelly and his brothers, Arthur and Francis, to sign in my name as appropriate and otherwise act in accordance with our principles to honour any and all creditors that may be due payment upon my sentencing and imprisonment."

At this last, Annie, whose hand has been moving smoothly across the page, gives an involuntary squeak of dismay. Her father holds up his hand and concludes the letter with the assurance that he is of sound mind at the point of writing, *et cetera, et cetera*.

Annie blots the ink, and hands the letter to her father to read and sign. His signature is quavering and lacks its characteristic flourish, but it is clearly his own. "There." She takes it back, and sets it in the middle of the table. Then she moves to his bedside, head bowed, unwilling to meet his eye. He reaches over, gently taking her hand in both of his, as if to warm it.

"It is essential, my girl. It would be foolish to pretend otherwise."

"But – what will become of us? You cannot go to prison, look at you!"

"I can, and I will, if the court decrees it. I see no clemency in prospect, Annie, in these strange, bitter days. But remember what I said when I wrote to Lord Stephenson before the last trial? Time will bring round its revenges. Zola's books may be vilified and burnt today, but they will return to glory – of this I am certain."

"Hang the books!" Annie explodes, unable to restrain herself. "I care nothing for them. My only concern is for you, dear Papa. I cannot bear to see you sent to prison. You will not survive it, in body or in spirit."

"Annie. We are not at the prison gates yet. We will fight on. It is not definite that we shall lose our case, and we have many supporters who will speak for us in court. We also have, apparently, a bull terrier for a defence counsel, thanks to the generosity of Frank Harris. We have paid our debt to Her Majesty already, and I believe . . ."

But she would not learn what he believed, for he broke off in a fit of coughing, the exertion of the longest conversation he has had in weeks becoming too much for him. She hushes him when he attempts to complete the thought, and eases him back on his pillows, sitting by his bedside until his ragged breathing settles.

Thirty days later, Annie makes her way into the public seating area at the Old Bailey for the second time. She does not feel absolute dread; prison and ruination no longer seem a foregone conclusion, not according to her father's supporters, or to the ever-positive Mr Cluer, who has been a regular visitor to the house. She no longer wakes each day imagining the "liquidation" of her father's assets – a word which, in her imagination, has lamps, bedsteads, Mamma's vanity mirror and the Italian mantel clock being thrown into a giant pot to become pulverised into a powdery soup in a mighty crushing machine, turned by the hand of a monstrous, stone-faced judge.

The house has been abuzz with well wishers, advisors and friends helping to prepare the defence, including many writers and editors who are, in her opinion, primarily concerned for their own future publications. Mr Henry Irving and Mr John Gilbert have been frequent visitors; Mr Thomas Hardy has been in, and Mr George Gissing too.

Their "angel" Mr Harris has come often – and despite herself, Annie likes him. The illustrious editor is much younger than she had imagined, only in his thirties, with lavish jet-black moustaches and clear blue eyes – and when she remarks on his youth, he tells her with a courtly bow that he began his career early, as a boy of thirteen. "Whatever did you do at that age?" she enquired. "This and that," he replied with an engaging grin, in his American-accented voice – as he lived in that country for more than a decade – "Boot-black, labourer, cowboy . . ." She gasped, not sure if she should believe him. But he is warm and kind and does not behave in an untoward manner, although she is sure he is regaling her brothers and the other men with salacious stories when she leaves the room, judging by the bursts of uproarious laughter she hears from upstairs late into the night.

The N.V.A. have gone too far this time. Everyone thinks so, even those who privately admit that they had had misgivings about *The Soil* or *Nana* before the first trial; they all peruse the much-pruned texts of other French novels which the firm has re-issued, and declare them innocuous, objecting to them only on the grounds that they are so much diminished as works of literature. "Who can condemn something so neutered?" she hears one man whisper. "The text has been scrubbed!" said another in dismay.

Listening to this, Annie begins to form her own ideas. Perhaps it does not matter what the new books do or don't contain. It is the principle of the thing; the fact that Henry Vizetelly went on to publish any novel – any French novel – however innocuously presented, is enough to inflame the enemy. She picked up one of the books last night, unable to sleep, and turned to the title page: "*The Ladies' Paradise*, A New Edition." It no longer reads TRANSLATED AND UNABRIDGED FROM THE ORIGINAL FRENCH under the title, and it contains a prudent choice of engraved illustrations, each one pretty and inoffensive. Turning it over in her hands, Annie can see that the book must have been unbound from its green cloth-covered boards so the the printer could insert the new pages with Ernest's alterations and then re-stitch it into place. It looks virtually as new. The printers have done such fine work in a short space of time.

The original end matter, including advertisements and lists of future publications bracketing the main body of text, has been left in place; it would not have occurred to anyone to alter them; they are not part of Zola's offending work. And yet – she frowns. There at the back, below a notice for soap powder, is a listing for *Nana*. Is that as it should be? It must have been part of the original edition, but would it not have been better to cut out every mention of that title? She bites her lip, checking the front endpapers, only to find there a similar advertisement for *The Soil*.

The new company catalogue is sitting by her father's chair – it was hastily prepared and issued in January, once the expurgations were underway. In bold letters it states "Re-issue of M. Zola's Realistic Novels, in Three-and-Sixpenny Volumes, with the Original Illustrations." There is a list of the nineteen books named in the latest Bow Street summons, including *The Ladies' Paradise* and *Germinal*, as well as early Zola efforts, such as his first novel *Thérèse Raquin* and his second, *Madeleine Férat*. The firm own the rights to all Zola's work in English translation and they are exploiting this to the hilt. To her astonishment, she finds the three banned titles, *Nana*, *Piping Hot!* and *The Soil*, are listed in the catalogue too, with the words "Undergoing Revision" noted after each one; this suggests that the Old Bailey's ruling is ignored. No matter that the banned books are not "undergoing revision" at all; surely it will still appear to the casual eye, or the vindictive vigilante, that the firm are intent on defying the law. Will she question Ernest about this?

Her older brother's face is haggard from lack of sleep, and he is quick to temper. Let us get through the trial's opening day first, Annie thinks, before attempting to raise anything with him – after all, it is only the start of what promises to be quite a drawn-out affair. It might be days or weeks; the prosecution must prove their case with reference to several different volumes. At least the number has been reduced from nineteen to seven since the Bow Street hearing. Flaubert's *Madame Bovary* has been dropped from the list, due to the gracious intervention of W. T. Stead himself. At the eleventh hour, in an editorial column, he suggested that his colleagues at the N.V.A. concentrate on Zola, commenting that "judged as a whole, *Madame Bovary* is far less corrupting".

* * *

The courtroom is filling up. Mr Harris slides into the row beside Annie in the gallery and moves along, as if to make space for the friends who follow him; he sits a little too close, and his strong, muscular left leg is pressing against hers, but this is not the place or time to cause a stir. Her eyes remain fixed on the scene below, her face set. Harris turns to the woman on his other side and begins to tell her an anecdote about a judge he met once by chance, outside a certain house of ill repute. "I was only passing by, you understand . . ."

The ceremonial aspects of a Central Court trial begin: the judges file in, wearing their elaborate costumes, chains of office and wigs, and the supporting players follow in their formal attire; there are the black-robed solicitors at their shared table, set in the well of the court, and buzzing reporters crowding into their box. On the other side of the room, the wide wooden jury benches under the double windows accommodate the twelve men who will decide her father's – and her family's – future.

The audience have taken their places, some standing, some seated, many whispering amongst themselves before the proceedings begin. Some people appear to have been there all morning; Annie hears two women on her other side discussing the sentence in the previous case. Someone, perhaps a servant, had stolen a diamond ring, ". . . and two forks as well!" hisses one of the women. The thief had been given a sentence of five years' penal servitude. Would it have been less severe if they had left the forks?

Annie wishes she could see the detail of everyone's expressions in the courtroom from her vantage point – tomorrow, she must remember to tuck her opera glasses into her reticule, so as not to miss a nuance of expression below.

But there will be no tomorrow.

What happens next unfolds like a dumb show in the marionette theatres she saw as a child at the seaside. All that is missing is the jester's tune, but she can almost hear it as accompaniment to a sudden flurry of activity below, which seems conducted by an unseen hand. First, Mr Cluer beckons urgently to her father and brother and leads them to a room adjacent to the robing room, off to the right, as fast as Henry's hobbling gait will allow. This must be for the promised consultation with their Q.C. Better late than never, Annie thinks. She was most concerned when the man was not on hand to greet them on their arrival at the court. Ernest was apoplectic. Mr Alfred Cock Q.C., who had just been given a bonus payment by the generous Mr Harris "to ensure he did his utmost", could not even make himself available to have a meeting with them several days prior to the trial, as is customary, to discuss the defence. Annie thinks the man must be very confident indeed, to meet only on the day of the trial, just minutes before it opens.

Next, the three men step out from the robing room, and Annie needs no opera glass to read the faces of her loved ones; Ernest's is like thunder, and her father's, though his head is bowed as he shuffles back to his place near the table, is a picture of misery. Mr Cluer's wig is askew and he looks as if he has just seen a ghost. What is happening? Within seconds, a large, startlingly red-faced man with flyaway eyebrows, dressed in a fine black gown, scuttles out of the room at the side. This must be their famed Queen's Counsel, Mr Cock.

He waves his hand imperiously at Mr Clarke, and pushes his way around the solicitors' wide table to confer with the prosecutor and his clients. Clarke summons a junior clerk with a beckoning forefinger, and he in turn runs across to the bench, scrambling up on his chair and conveying something to the Recorder, Sir Thomas Chambers – the same judge as at the first trial. Frowning, Chambers bends his head and gives his clerk a brief instruction, and the man jumps down, scurrying back to Clarke and Cock in their impromptu conference.

Finally, Mr Cock strides back to his own side of the table with all the speed that his corpulence allows, knocking against a few fellows without any word of apology as he passes. Standing close to Henry, with Ernest and Cluer leaning in, he talks, his hands chopping the air in emphasis. All Annie can interpret, not being in earshot, is that something grave is occurring. Her father's face has lost all of its colour and he staggers a little before re-taking his seat, his bony hands clutching the edge of the table like a man holding a split mast after a shipwreck, all at sea.

Ernest appears to remonstrate with Mr Cock, who, like Punch with Judy in the puppet theatre, holds up his hand in a gesture Annie can only read as a demand for silence, if not the prelude to a blow to the ear. The man then turns, giving Ernest his back. For a moment, she fears her brother will club him over the head with one of the heavy legal tomes on the table. But instead he sits down heavily in his chair, and reaches over to their father, taking him by the hand. This is extraordinary – Ernest does not give himself to such displays of affection in public.

"What is happening, do you think?"

Mr Harris turns to her, eyebrows raised, and smiles. "I suppose they are making preparations with counsel, my dear – we are about to begin."

"Something is amiss. Do you not see? My father and brother are sorely agitated, and Mr Cock is just standing there, not even conferring with Mr Cluer." This last she whispers, close to his ear, to conceal her concern from others seated nearby. "He does not appear to be readying himself for anything."

"Now, now, Miss Vizetelly," Harris assures her, "these are weighty matters. It is not for us to guess the thoughts of our counsel. Doubtless your brother and father are experiencing a little attack of nerves, which is entirely understandable." Annie shakes her head, impatient – she knows them better. Something is very wrong.

At that moment, the court is called to order, the general hubbub subsides and the next minutes pass as in a dream. The indictment is read; the accusation of obscene libel is repeated, as well as a reminder that the defendant had been in this court just six months previously on the same count. As in the first trial, Henry is not called to sit in the dock, in deference to his age and poor health. At the appropriate moment, he rises unsteadily to his feet, facing the judge, who asks him if he will plead guilty or not guilty. After a significant pause, during which Annie finds herself reaching involuntarily for Mr Harris' arm and gripping it so tightly she must bruise it, Henry Vizetelly straightens his back and raises his chin, looking directly at the Recorder. "Guilty," he says loudly, as if expectorating the word.

A great noise breaks out, with reporters and public alike reacting to this surprise. The crowd who had assembled today came expecting a full and colourful trial, a fight between freedom of speech and its enemies – or if you were W. T. Stead and Mr William Coote, sitting smugly together just behind Mr Clarke, there was a battle promised between the purveyors of wicked, so-called "literature" and the righteous guardians of England's innocent readers. Instead, the trial is over before it begins.

The judge calls for order to be returned, and Mr Clarke stands to say that the defendant has violated the previous ruling of the court, and his recognisance of two hundred pounds should therefore be estreated. Mr Cock responds that while the previous ruling dealt with three books that have not been re-issued by the defendant, he admits that the expurgation of other titles by the same author "had not gone sufficiently far". He has read them and can attest to this himself, he adds helpfully. Whose side is he on? Annie wants to demand, but instead, she snatches her hand back from Mr Harris, who, in equal agitation to her own, has taken possession of it during the tense exchange. Her face is burning as Mr Cock adds, almost as an afterthought, that his client is nearly seventy years old and in very delicate health. Is this the extent of his legal acumen and famed rhetoric?

Ernest is then called to the witness box to testify to his father's condition. He makes his way forward and gives his oath to tell the truth. Under questioning from Clarke, he confirms that his father has suffered for some years from a complaint that has assumed a very serious character and necessitates the constant employment of medical attention. And with that, he rises to go, but the Solicitor General holds up his hand to stop him. "One further question, Mr Vizetelly. Are you a member of the firm of Vizetelly & Company?" Clarke says, in a tone of mild interest.

Technically, he is not. The firm was established when Ernest was still living in Paris, and therefore he is not named as a director, nor has he ever been contracted as an employee. In the short period he has been living back in England, translating and expurgating the Zola texts, he has been paid like any other worker they might use for the same tasks – piecemeal. And most recently, Annie knows, he has drawn no wage at all. She also knows that her father has expressly forbidden Ernest to take responsibility for the new editions, though he has offered to do so. Ernest has a wife and family to think of, and a career in translation and writing ahead of him; the implication is that he must distance himself from the firm if pressed.

Ernest looks at his father and wavers a moment – then he answers the question in the negative, saying he is a journalist and translator by profession, and if previously employed in his father's firm, he has ceased to be so. But Clarke persists, pressing him. "As the son of the defendant, Mr Vizetelly, clearly you are acquainted most intimately with the firm and the books it prints. Are you not in a position, for example, to give us an undertaking about the existing stock?"

"What of it?" Ernest cannot help but ask in return, and Annie assumes Clarke is now going to ban the sale of the remaining boxes of new editions of Zola stacked high in the warehouse. Clarke addresses the bench. "My clients, your Lordship, wish to have an undertaking from the firm, from Mr Vizetelly here, as to the destruction of all remaining books written by Mr Émile Zola." Behind the prosecutor, Mr Coote cannot suppress a thin smile. They will burn every one.

Annie offers up a silent prayer that Ernest contain himself. There is so much at stake; please, I beg you, hold your temper. But it is too late. A passionate cry rings from the witness box, electrifying the room. "You have made the defendant a pauper! What more do you want?"

Clarke is quick to reply. "Now, now, sir, we want none of

that!" But he is clearly discomfited by his quarry's resistance, and ill acquainted with being thwarted.

"I have nothing else to say," Ernest adds. "I do not belong to the firm of Vizetelly & Company, and I know nothing about it."

"You may step down," Clarke says.

The Recorder announces he will now pass sentence. It is useless, he says tersely, consulting some documentation laid before him, to fine the defendant anew, as he appears to have no means to pay a further penalty. His recognisances of two hundred pounds must be estreated, as requested by the prosecuting council, and he will go to prison for three months, sentence to commence at once.

The officers of the court move forward, gently helping Henry to his feet, and start to lead him from the room. It is so unexpected and so final that Annie rises, gripping the balcony rail in front of her seat, meaning to call out to him. Let everyone stare at her, and the Sheriff's men throw her out in the street; she will not flinch. But as it is, no sound emerges from her open mouth. She has no voice.

Ernest and Cluer are in close conference below; Frank and Arthur have joined them, their faces grave and urgent. Cock is standing to one side, glancing at some papers and looking not at all ruffled by his abject failure to defend the case. The courtroom has erupted in excited chatter, and now Cluer must shout to make himself heard at the bench.

"Your Lordship, we have a request, if it please you." The judge, in the act of rising, his papers neatly stacked, looks up. "My client's sons request permission to speak to their father." It is too late – Henry has just disappeared through the small door in the far wall, which leads down to Birdcage Walk and on to the holding cells next door. "You may apply at Newgate to see him now," Judge Chambers says with a dismissive wave. A moment later, he is gone and the trial is over.

It is only when Mr Harris tucks a voluminous silk handkerchief into her hand that Annie realises that her face is wet with tears.

11. *July 1889, Holloway Prison*

"Gissing won't sign." Henry crushes the message, contained within the pages of a Walter Scott novel he has requested from home, and lets it fall to the floor next to his bed. Despite this news, today is a better day than most, for after a fortnight of agony and little sleep, he has been moved to the other end of the hospital ward, making it much easier to reach the bathing rooms, where he can find some respite from the constant, stabbing pain of his stricture.

He cannot escape, however, from the incessant noise of the crowded sleeping area, which is filled with the cries and complaints of fellow inmates, many of them in worse health than him. Last night the man on his right was vomiting blood, spraying it over his bedcovers and spattering the tiled floor between them; this morning he was gone when Henry woke, and a younger man lies there now, head wrapped in cotton bandages like a mummy, with only his lips and mouth visible. It is unclear whether he is conscious, but his narrow chest rises and falls under the sheet. Henry hopes they replaced the bed linens for him, but he doubts it; cleanliness is not next to godliness in Holloway Prison.

At least he is not in Pentonville. After the trial, his sons had hastened round to the door at Newgate, as they told him later, only to find that he had already been dispatched to that notorious prison for serious criminals, where evidently he had collapsed in a faint. Henry remembers nothing of this. They pleaded with the authorities and he was soon transported to Holloway Prison, or "Holloway Castle" as it is commonly known, due to the grand turreted gateway and crenelated Gothic façade. It is not much superior to Pentonville in terms of the draconian conditions within; there is a total infestation of lice, a high occurrence of lunatics and limited sanitation. But there was a bed with a mattress available for Henry in the newly built hospital wing, which is greatly preferable to the hammocks with horsehair mattresses used in the crowded cells.

Oddly, he is not in low spirits. The pressures of the two trials had squeezed him so tightly over the last year that the release, even to begin a prison sentence, has been an improvement, like removing a pair of ill-fitting boots. Dread is always worse than the actual event, as he would often tell his children when they were facing some particular challenge at school; this is one more example. He can count his blessings, for he is not in the workhouse, nor is he charged with the cruel and fruitless tasks of those men sentenced to years of hard labour, who are required, for example, to rise at dawn each day and turn an iron wheel set in the stone wall of the prison yard, positioned as if it might produce some practical result, such as milling grain or causing water to flow. In fact, the contraption does nothing at all but break the backs of the men, some of them older than he is, who are forced to stand there for up to twelve hours a day, cranking the heavy wheel round and round, only to return to this position the following morning to take up the charade again.

It is not the first time Henry has seen the inside of such an institution. As a boy, running deliveries for his father's printing firm, he was required on several occasions to visit writers and journalists who had been convicted of this or that offence but were still submitting copy from within prison walls. He can see himself as he was then, a skinny lad wearing his older brother's long coat, hopping from one foot to the other, stalk-eyed as he waited, taking it all in: the terrible smells, the cacophony of voices, the filth and the damp, and that old man with one eye who frightened him so, tugging at his sleeve and miming the act of eating to beg for a crust. Prison conditions were far worse then, before the reforms of the last few decades. But to a young lad, "it was as good as any play, the kaleidoscope inside these places," as he had written yesterday. He is making notes for a memoir, a task that keeps him entertained, and transports him, albeit fitfully, to better times and places.

Nobody tells you how dull prison is, how monotonous the daily routine, how relentlessly blank the grey walls and the eyes of your fellow inmates, most of whom marvel at Henry's penchant for reading and writing each day. In the face of boredom, Henry has time to think, to reconstruct past events and imagine future remedies; he can engage in deep reflection, something that his hectic, creative life has never afforded him before.

Despite the initial shock of his sentence, and the consequent loss of his business and other assets, he is determined to fashion a productive regime for himself and plan for the future. Henry is privileged enough by his status to be allowed some supplies from without, delivered by his family and friends: a few books, some decent food, and even one or two pieces of furniture. He has asked for writing materials and his small table and a soft chair, which have also been allowed, and he aims to make notes each morning for the memoir, if he has the energy. This should allow him to have something to publish when he is able to return to work, he tells himself.

He still suffers from the persistent urethral stricture that has plagued him for years. He eagerly awaits the youthful, harassed medical officer who visits the ward in a rush most days and offers him some relief, using the prevailing dilation techniques to help ease the passage of urine from his distended bladder. Otherwise, he is reliant on a warm salt bath, but this is a luxury that is hard to come by in prison, where the others are jostling and shouting for their turn, and you must re-use the previous man's dirty water – none too warm unless you are first to the bathing area. His new location makes this more likely, and this in turn fuels his natural optimism.

So Gissing won't sign the petition, he muses, as he lays out a sheet of paper to write to Ernest and thank him for the book and the message, as well as his wife Marie for the neat parcel of cheese and portion of meat pie she has sent. Ernest and George Moore are preparing an urgent appeal to the Home Secretary, calling for his early release. Henry's help has been enlisted in suggesting signatories. So far, all of his proposed friends and associates have complied, including du Maurier, Gosse, Rider Haggard, Havelock Ellis, Symons, Irving and many more. Even Hardy has signed, though he loathes G.M. almost as much as the Irishman hates him. "Where was he during the trial, I ask you?" Moore wrote in aletter to Henry last week, underscoring the question twice.

Henry has compassion for Hardy and all authors – he knows the man distanced himself from the trial due to potential difficulties he anticipates with his new novel, *Tess of the d'Urbervilles*, which he is hoping to publish soon. There is a difficult section

216

involving the ravishing of the heroine, and Hardy is now considering its excision in the light of Henry's sentence. Not simply
"softening it" somehow, but replacing it – and some other details
– for mass-market serialisation and in volume form. He has indicated that he hopes to publish the full version in the *National
Observer*, an intellectual's journal with a circulation in the low
hundreds. This seems the only way to avoid censure: write for a
very small and elite audience.

Some writers, including the ever-rebellious Robert Buchanan,
have refused to sign the petition for Henry, but in his case, it is
due to the fact that he has written his own letter to the Home
Secretary about the matter, titled "Concerning the Proposed Suppression of Literature", in which he makes plain once more his
long held belief in free speech as the measure of a civilised nation.
Buchanan did tell me, Ernest reported to Henry on his last
visit, that he could not subscribe to the appeal's wording since
it describes Zola's novels as "masterpieces", a verdict they do not
merit. That snide note made Henry chuckle; writers were ever
thus – such admixtures of idealism and envy.

As for George Gissing, he is a cautious and a bruised man.
Early in his career, he wrote a novel titled *Mrs Grundy's Enemies*
and struggled to find a publisher; he was so disheartened that
eventually he burnt the manuscript. A month before the latest
trial, his realistic novel *The Nether World* had been decried as a
piece of "Zolaism", although one critic did acknowledge that "at
least it was English". He is on dangerous ground if he speaks out
now. Quite apart from this cause for reticence, Gissing had always

maintained that Zola should be read in the original French: "If people are so desperate to read it they can put themselves to the trouble of learning the language!" Ever the schoolteacher, Henry thinks.

Seeking other high profile supporters, G.M. had said he would not even bother to ask his friend Oscar Wilde; he's about to publish his new novel, *The Picture of Dorian Gray*, in serial form in *Lippincott's Magazine*, which may provoke more scandal than Zola, or so gossip has it; his signature might do more damage than good. In any event, the plea will be sent to the Home Secretary next week, with plenty of notable names attached. It is gratifying, but Henry knows this is about more than his personal wellbeing. Aside from the threat of future prosecutions, the verdict at the Old Bailey casts a long shadow of self-censorship over many writers' current endeavours, as Hardy and Gissing have already shown. And how many great novels will perish unborn in future?

Henry is still furious with the arrogant Mr Cock, who had had no appetite for this fight, despite his pugnacious reputation – the man has even pocketed his pre-trial "bonus" from Frank Harris, though he did nothing whatsoever to earn it. When they had finally met him that dreadful morning, in the little room off the well of the court, just minutes before the trial was scheduled to begin, Cock had begun the briefing in a tone so dour it seemed to Henry he was more prosecutor than defender. "Well, gentlemen?" he had said. "Here is our defence, sir," Ernest had said, offering him the neat summary of salient points they had drawn up with

Cluer. The Q.C. took the page and looked at it askance. After a moment he thrust it back at Ernest.

"This is impossible. There is no defence. You must throw yourself on the mercy of the court," he said, and with that he turned on his heel and left the room. Astonishing though it still seems in hindsight, that was the end of the consultation. It was impossible to request new counsel, which was Ernest's immediate thought – if they did so at this late hour, they would be fined, which they could not afford. With the clock ticking, they had begged Mr Cock at least to consult with the prosecutor and the judge, to ascertain if there was a chance of Henry avoiding a prison term, and whether there might be some reduction of the bond, given their straitened circumstances. But they were unrelenting. Henry's blood boils to think on it again – for inside the fragile cage of his old and battered body beats the heart of a man who once believed in justice.

His greatest regret is that he might have made the public case for freedom of speech in literature. It had been his intention to speak out at the Old Bailey, for the judge and all the world to hear, and argue for that essential liberty that allows creativity, invention and sometimes genius to flourish. His defence was to call on witnesses from within the cultural realm who would speak eloquently to this theme; it was all planned to the last detail. He does not see himself as a martyr, though some have used the term – quite the opposite; he is a disappointed man who was unable to speak out against tyranny.

Now the industry he knows and loves so well has not only lost a series of French novels and an enterprising publisher and his small firm – they have lost the right to protest; like Philomela, their tongues are cut out. Only the brave or foolish few dare to try. There is Robert Buchanan again, who added to his private appeal for Henry's release with a series of long letters to the press about the larger significance of the trial and sentence. Even in the letters pages of W. T. Stead's *Pall Mall Gazette*, he argues that "literature should not be pronounced on by criminal tribunals . . . the moment we summon the policeman, we attack the privileges of private judgment and imperil the freedom of all literature."

In the same edition, Henry's youngest son Frank makes his own eloquent outcry. Henry is proud of the boy, who has just announced his intention to quit England in disgust and make for New York to pursue a writing career. His father is delighted to read the letter, even if it will fall on deaf ears. It concludes nicely with a quote from an essay on Lord Byron:

> We know no spectacle so ridiculous as the British public in one its periodic fits of morality . . . Once in six or seven years our virtue becomes outrageous. Some unfortunate man is singled out as an expiatory sacrifice . . . and if he has a profession, he is driven from it. At length our anger is satiated. Our victim is ruined and heart-broken. And our virtue goes quietly to sleep for seven years more.

The N.V.A are going from strength to strength, their influence spreading. In the aftermath of Henry's trial both the *Decameron* and the *Heptameron*, titles they have long sought to ban, are ordered to be withdrawn from booksellers and libraries; ironically, the novel that Lord Campbell, the author of the 1857 obscenity Act, had specifically excluded from its reach, *La Dame aux camélias*, has also been suppressed.

The *Pall Mall Gazette* has run a congratulatory interview with N.V.A. secretary William Coote, in which he claims that even the publishers of Holywell Street are now asking him to vet their wares before issuing them, warning anew that "we will not allow England to be flooded with filth". The interviewer asks him at one point if he gives any credence to the argument Henry's pamphlet set out to make, that Shakespeare is as obscene or more so than Zola. "But Shakespeare is a good writer!" Coote dismisses him, aghast at the comparison. The fact that the Bard of Avon is also English is implicit, when he adds that "our youth cannot be polluted any longer by having the most revolting and hideous descriptions of French vice thrust on their attention".

Henry hears from Moore that due to the work of associates of Coote, a large shipment of Guy de Maupassant's novels has been stopped at the port in Dublin and destroyed. Henry shuts his eyes, imagining the books in their etched leather covers being tipped overboard, tumbling down through the brine to rest on the floor of the silted harbour like the corpses of so many drunken sailors. This is real tragedy, not just an old man huddled in a lukewarm bath in a malodorous room in an ugly castle of a prison to the north of the city of London. After all, he is required to serve only three months – less, if the petition succeeds – whereas the precedent that has now been set for censorship and punishment of "obscene libel" without any consideration of literary merit is likely to endure for many years to come.

"Only" three months: Henry does not mean that the sentence sits lightly on him. His health cannot improve in these conditions; he fears infection and contamination with disease in his weakened state. He misses his children and the feeling of sunshine on his balding head; he longs for a glass of Madeira each evening, and above all, he is haunted by thoughts of the Vizetelly family future. Where will they go? What will they do? He might as well be with the felons outside, turning one of those benighted wheels in the yard each day, for the weight of these worries is just as great.

* * *

Now it is August, and the noonday sun strikes Henry with full force as he steps forward from the queue of men at the prison gates when his name is called. He can see his sons, and Annie too, straining to locate him amidst the crowd gathered outside. He is a free man, but he is broken. The many weeks of poor hygiene and haphazard medical attention in insalubrious quarters have ruined him physically as surely as the court's verdict ruined him financially.

The petition "Voices for Vizetelly's Release", ultimately signed by one hundred and fifty prominent writers, artists and publishers, had failed; the Home Secretary did not relent. "I cannot advise her Majesty to intervene in this case," came the terse reply. Examples must be set, and if one publisher were to walk free, what would happen to the next offender, and the one after that?

In any event, Matthews has other, weightier concerns at this time. Jack the Ripper is still evading capture, and another woman has been found in a Whitechapel alley this month, her throat and stomach slit wide. In the midst of dealing with this ongoing nightmare, it is easy to dismiss an appeal from a pack of bohemians. It is also possible that Ernest had gone too far in his accompanying letter, in which he derided the jury and the officials of the court for being unfamiliar with French literature; a general does not like to see his foot soldiers belittled.

Henry is outside the gates now. In his right hand, he carries a cane the medical officer has given him; he can no longer walk without it. In his left, he clutches a few treasured possessions, including his bundle of notes for the memoirs he will write once he is settled in new lodgings the children have found for him in Putney. Gus Sala lives there, by the river, so he knows the suburb, and while it is not as fashionable or practical as Covent Garden, it is inexpensive and leafy – a place to lick one's wounds. Annie will be on hand to take care of him, as ever.

There she is now, a picture in her best blue hat, which matches her eyes – her mother's eyes. Thank heavens Elizabeth did not live to see him emerge from the high iron gates of Holloway Prison. Annie steps forward to embrace him and he nearly falls, steadying himself with the cane. "Lightly does it, my girl," he smiles. His sons stand in a serious little cluster; each one of them dismayed at the sight of him, though they pat his shoulder carefully and tell him he looks well. He is so thin now he might break, Arthur thinks, trying not to stare at the cane, the mottled hand

and child-size wrist. I am taller than he is now, marvels young Frank: Papa has shrunk in prison somehow, his upper back developing a slight curve, which has cost him a few inches.

Ernest carefully guides his father to the waiting carriage they have borrowed from Frank Harris to collect him. Now for Putney, and a bottle of Henry's favourite champagne, rescued from the bailiffs when they came to take most of their furniture and stock for auction on the sorry day the Vizetellys vacated Henrietta Street.

Now for the future, Henry thinks, sinking back onto the plush cushions – whatever it may hold.

12. *November 1891, rue de Bruxelles, Paris*

Alexandrine Zola.

Alexandrine Zola reaches up and twists the socket key that switches on the electric light bulb in its wall sconce. She switches it off again, then on once more. The lamp dazzles, even in daytime, being so much brighter than candles or gaslight. It is her private pleasure to do this when the servants and her husband are out – it would be mortifying to be caught at such child's play, but it delights her, and the fact that they are the only people in their street to have installed electricity adds to her contentment.

Some friends of Zola's, the painters, hint that for their taste it is over-bright, and lacks the romantic quality of candle and gaslight. Well, let them have their acrid lamps, their *chiaroscuro*; she is a pioneer of the modern – and on grey, cold days like this one, when the city never really shakes off the semi-darkness of morning, she does not wish to live in the shadows. This apartment, which ranges over two floors and can feel cavernous, is difficult to heat no matter how much the housemaid feeds the fireplaces. There is something about this white electric light that gives an illusion of warmth, mimicking a blast of country sunshine.

She settles herself in her favourite chair, covered in a rich brocaded velvet, and pulls a soft rug over her lap against the chill, smiling to find that her favourite pet, little "Monsieur Fan", is quick to follow, tail wagging as he snuffles and wiggles into his customary place, tucking himself under her ample bosom. "Hello, dearest, how are you today?" She leans down and plants a kiss on the crown of his wiry head, then rubs the space behind his ears, which he adores. "*Maman* must cut your little nails, *chérie* – you make a horrid clicking noise on the parquet when you run, and that won't do, will it, my angel?" Monsieur Fan closes his eyes in ecstasy and his mistress continues the ear rub, murmuring little admonishments and endearments all the while.

A tap at the door interrupts her. "Madame? Shall I l-l-leave your letters here?" The new maid, Sylvie, is too timid. It will not do; Alexandrine expects her servants to have spirit, to get on with their duties without troubling her with every little detail. It is so difficult to find that in Paris these days; she will have to bring one of the girls up from Médan to live here. Country-grown servants are made of sturdier stuff. Sylvie, hovering at the threshold, big eyes fixed on the electric candle as if mesmerised, is a little wraith whose voice trembles if she is asked her own name.

"Give them to me, please." Alexandrine holds out her hand for the packet of letters and begins to sort them automatically, separating those meant for Zola, ready for his return from his daily walk. "One moment. You may take his upstairs." As ever there are also a few fat parcels, people sending him manuscripts he will somehow find time to read, and letters from people begging him for money – she will deal with those. She makes a tidy pile, with the most pressing items for Zola at the top. First is a letter from Ernest Vizetelly, which is likely to contain a banker's cheque. She has come to recognise his spidery hand, for, as her husband's agent, he has reason to write often,

It was odd, Zola had remarked, when Ernest first wrote to enquire if he might look after English rights in his work, only a year after his father's trial. Had not Zola's work landed the man's father in prison, and caused the collapse of the family firm? Who could understand these people? Alexandrine was more outraged than her husband by the whole affair. Not only did she feel sorry for the old man, she also calculated the drop in rights income that would result. Zola shrugged it off at the time, as he seemed to do with so many practical matters. "They underpaid me in any event; I am sure we will find other publishers in England when the dust settles, who will offer better terms."

Ernest's initial idea, two years ago, was to do just that. He proposed to translate Zola's penultimate novel in the Rougon-Macquart series, his "war novel". *The Downfall* describes the humiliation of the French by the Prussians in their brief and brutal conflict of 1870–1, which marked the end of Napoleon III's Second Empire. The subject matter was ideal – what could please the English more than a story showing that the French have no idea how to conduct a successful war? Zola had to smile. Ernest said he thought he could arrange for the English rights to be acquired in London at an excellent price, at least four thousand francs, twice the amount his father had paid in bygone days. The London firm of Chatto & Windus had expressed interest in the entire Zola catalogue. He realised this might surprise M. Zola, but assured him that he still had a loyal audience in England and this book did not suffer from the problems that had caused difficulties in the past. Quite the contrary, Ernest said, it will be sought after for its theme, and is most unlikely to cause offence, even to those who prosecuted his father.

Ernest had explained that he would present a "reformed" Zola to the English publishers, as a writer whose subjects had become more suitable. As for himself, he was a former war correspondent (England's youngest ever), and therefore uniquely qualified to translate *The Downfall*, with his intimate knowledge of matters military. In addition, he offered to find a home for *Money*, the

228

eighteenth Rougon-Macquart novel – this salutary tale of speculation and greed, set in the Parisian banking world, would, he felt sure, return Zola to his *L'Assommoir* status as a moralist, writing about vice and greed as a warning to readers not to follow in his characters' paths.

"I notice he does not offer to translate *The Human Beast*," Alexandrine said, when Zola shared Ernest's proposition with her. She was referring to "the railway story", the seventeenth Rougon-Macquart novel, a visceral, documentary tale of obsession and murder which paints a world and a clutch of characters that might spring from Dante's vision of hell. In Zola's initial sketch of this book, he wrote: "I would like, as a subject, a violent drama capable of giving nightmares to everyone in Paris."

It had garnered some remarkable reviews in France when it appeared in serial form at the end of 1889. *Le Figaro*, the same organ that published the Manifesto of The Five against Zola just a few years earlier, now called him "the poet of man's darker side". Anatole France, who had loathed *The Soil*, proclaiming it "a heap of filth" and going so far as to say he wished Zola "had never been born" when it was published, now compared her husband to Homer, hailing him as "the great lyric writer of our time".

"I think it will be some time before the English are ready for that one," Zola said. Alexandrine made the assumption, having little knowledge of the English, that they preferred their violence in fiction to be dressed in uniform and accompanied by cannon fire, rather than directed against defenceless women by a sexual maniac. Perhaps they get enough of the latter in their daily newspapers, she mused; a killer of female prostitutes, following in the footsteps of Jack the Ripper, has just been executed in London. He was a doctor whose favoured weapon was strychnine, administered in glasses of water he gave to his unsuspecting victims.

Ernest's original business proposal also stated that he would take a modest percentage for making translations as well as seeing to all the arrangements with publishers. He asked less than the average rate – not quite a third of the sale price – in the hope that M. Zola would do him the great honour of allowing him to represent his interests. Alexandrine has encouraged the relationship from the outset. Ernest is a good agent; his efforts had brought financial rewards from a source she had thought lost.

She is more worldly than her husband, and more capable at managing their finances. She never forgets the first decade of their marriage, when they were hard pressed for money and struggled to take care of his ailing mother. They often went without a hot meal for days, moving from lodging to lodging around Paris. At the end of the war in 1871, they were reduced to begging a bed from friends, after she had to sell their mattress for food. Even when he got his contract with Charpentier, allowing him to continue writing the Rougon-Macquart saga, he did not earn much; the early books did not enjoy great success and they only started to see significant returns after he wrote the seventh book, *L'Assommoir.*

Look at them now, owners of this grand, elegant apartment in the ninth arrondissement, spread over nearly two hundred square metres, with its tall windows and pretty interior courtyard. In this fine street they are surrounded on all sides by neighbours who bow to them when they pass by. These are the Parisians who would not have deigned to give the young poet and the artist's model a second glance when they were first married.

Those old days were hard days, she thinks, idly rubbing Monsieur Fan's ears. But there was joy, then. She can remember how Zola would tease her, calling her his "thrifty little wife" when she managed to set out a meal for him and their crowd of bohemian friends, including Cézanne, Manet and Renoir. She could conjure something from almost nothing, perhaps a few vegetables or cheap ends of a joint of beef or lamb, wrapped in her light, perfect, flaky pastry. "Exquisite!" he would cry, pulling her close and planting a kiss on her cheek. In their room at night, he would tease her, calling her "Lou-lou", pulling at her ribbons and making her laugh. What must their hosts or landlords have thought of them when such sounds seeped out from their bedchamber? Ah, she thinks with a pang, whatever happened to that laughter behind closed doors?

She shakes herself out of this low mood, as she must, and turns to her letters. Invitations to this and that – parties, exhibitions, salons. Monsieur and Madame Zola do not go out together often on winter evenings in Paris; the cold seems to find its way into her bones, and she prefers an early night. Of course, if the occasion is sufficiently important, perhaps an invitation to the opera or a political event, she will go, arrayed in her finest jewels and furs.

This summer Paris hosted the *Exposition Universelle*, which had been a lovely diversion. The Zolas were treated like visiting dignitaries, going up in the new three-hundred-metre-high tower by Gustave Eiffel, and visiting all the colourful exhibits, set out like souks with their foreign wares. She enjoys being "Madame Zola", with all the prestige that entails, and if her famous husband is gruff or rude, as he so often is lately, she expertly smooths things over, apologising for his distemper; he is so oppressed with work at the moment, you see, he is completing his *magnum opus*.

They see less of each other altogether these days; when she is in Médan, it seems he must go to Paris often for his research. When they are both in Paris, he is out for hours each day, walking the city – some of the weight he lost a few years ago has crept back on, and he therefore needs regular exercise, in all weathers. She would not join him even if she were invited to, for she is fatigued much of the time and prefers to sit in the vast salon and receive her favourites, such as her cousin Amélie and the children. Sometimes she and Zola will talk of travel; she has always wanted to go with him to Italy. He says that when he finishes the Rougon-Macquart series, perhaps they will do that at last.

The end is in sight for the work that has dominated their entire lives together. He is engrossed in the twentieth book, *Doctor Pascal*, a kind of summary of the series, he tells her, and a scientific exploration of his ideas about heredity and environment. She has seen a few pages on his desk, and they suggest that a love story also plays a part in the piece – but he will show her when he is ready, as he always does.

A letter in an unfamiliar hand is next in her pile. She opens it. It is short and devastating. "Your husband has had a mistress these last three years, and fathered two children with her, an infant and a two-year-old. Her name is Jeanne Rozerot." It gives details including a Paris address where she might find the woman, and it closes without a signature. She turns it over. There is no identifying mark.

Jeanne ... the maid. That girl at Médan, who came with them on holiday some summers past, the tall one who cycled with Zola down country lanes? The one who abruptly left her employ. Alexandrine reads the letter again, her face growing hot. Her breath quickens; she feels as if she is suffocating, as if the air was sucked from the room when she slit open the envelope. There is a sharp pain in her breast. She reaches up and presses on her heart with both hands as if she might stop it from shattering, or leaping from her chest. The little dog in her lap whimpers, sensing her distress, then jumps to the floor in terror when she throws back her head and roars. She cares nothing for the servants or the neighbours now. As she wails her heartbreak, the thought comes: if this is true, she will kill him. And herself. And in that moment, she knows it is true. This is no prank; it makes absolute sense of everything. A violence surges through her like a current that cannot be extinguished. She will never recover, never forgive, nor ever be happy again.

Sylvie comes running. "Madame, what is it?" She fears her lady is dying, or perhaps having a brain seizure, like her old auntie. A sudden, vicious gesture assures her that Madame lives – as she watches, her mistress gives a vicious kick to her adored little dog, who is barking and grizzling on the floor in front of her, then bends double, her body convulsing. Sylvie backs out of the room and runs for help. The cook is at the market, there is nobody about. Then she sees Zola's hat on the table by the door; thank God, he's home. He slips in and out of the house so quietly, she has noticed, it is hard at any given time to be sure of his whereabouts.

She takes the stairs, two at a time, and bursts into his office above. He is already on his feet, standing by his enormous desk. "Good Lord, what is that noise?" he demands. She cannot speak but opens and closes her mouth like a beached fish gulping air – then she points towards the door, hand quivering. From the room below issues such a cry that it seems to break through the floorboards: "ZOLA!" In that one word is compacted such a universe of fury and hurt that instantly, he knows. He grabs for paper and pen, and whispers to the terrified girl, "You must take a message." He scribbles something and gives her a nearby address for his trusted friend, Henri Céard. "Run," he urges. He has written, "I fear the worst – please, take her and the children to safety, immediately."

Sylvie hesitates, and Zola grabs his coat from a hook on the wall, draping it round her, drowning her slim frame in its black woollen folds. "Run girl, now! It is urgent! Go!" The girl stumbles from the room and clatters down the stairs.

He must collect himself. He covers his face with his hands for a moment, rubbing his cheeks as if washing his face. The moment had to come. It is surprising, he muses, that it has taken so long – he must be a better actor than he imagines. Guilt and apprehension overwhelm him. She may calm down if he leaves her to recover for a while. He listens – there is no more sound from below. Anxiety causes him, as ever, to gasp for air. He sits down and tries to count to ten, to take those deep slow breaths that bring him ease, but he can only manage three exhalations, while he struggles to think what he can possibly say to his wife of nearly thirty years upon her discovery of his love affair with Jeanne. He hears a rapid clicking sound, and looks up – there is her little dog, standing at the door, ears and stubby little tail up, whining like a baby. Like his little Jacques when he wants more milk. He must face his wife. It is time.

But Alexandrine is gone. She has thrown a fur around her shoulders and is striding down the street in the direction of rue Saint-Lazare. People step out of her way as she passes, her swollen face and blazing eyes a warning to all. In her mind's eye she imagines bursting in and finding the lovers together, framed in the doorway, a diabolical version of the Holy Family in a Renaissance painting, with a baby at that slut's naked breast, and a toddler standing alongside holding a wooden staff, chubby hand resting on his father's arm. His father. Her husband. Zola.

Her step quickens – despite her bulk and the crowds and the cold, she is nearly running now, turning left at the corner, and now she is picturing Zola running down this road too, consumed with lust, scurrying along to his pretty young mistress each day when all the while he pretended to be walking for his health . . . The thought chokes her.

The enormous, stunning pretence. Three years, says the letter crushed in her gloved hand. He has made a fool of her for three long years. No doubt all of Paris knows. It is considered usual, even run-of-the-mill, for a middle-aged man to have a young mistress here, and to parade her around the city quite openly while your matronly, dried-up, greying, misshapen, unlovely and unloved wife is left at home, carefully reading your manuscripts for errors, tending to your household, feeding your friends and placing fresh flowers on your desk each morning.

She utters a sound so guttural and strange that a child clinging to his mother's hand as she pushes roughly past them cries out in fear. The mother stares and pulls the boy close to her skirts, clucking disapproval. What does Madame Zola care? She is nearly there. There is the tall bell tower of the church of Saint-Trinité, and there, to the left is the street. She knows it well – she was born barely a few hundred metres away. Somehow this compounds the insult. How dare he? How dare they?

Number 66 is just past the corner; she looks up at the windows of the tall, flat-fronted building where the letter has directed her. There are lace curtains; it is clean, well kept. Not grand like her own home, of course, but it is a good address. Renting an apartment here must cost a pretty penny, she thinks in passing, though that hardly matters now. She pushes at the outer door, which swings open into a communal hall. On the tiled floor before her is a child's toy. She crushes it with her heeled boot. I want to be covered in her blood, she thinks wildly, my hands, my dress, my face; I want to be steeped in the blood of Jeanne Rozerot and her bastard children. Where are they? The building is divided into

Zola with his mistress Jeanne and their children,
Denise and Jacques, circa 1890s.

many apartments off a central staircase. She unfolds the letter, a damp ball in her hand, a blur of ink – and tries to decipher whether it tells her which floor the flat is on. She is overcome, sinking to a crouch, chest heaving, desperately calling on her last reserves of strength to climb five sets of stairs.

When Zola arrives the door to Jeanne's apartment is still ajar as Alexandrine had found it. Céard must have bundled them out so fast he didn't bother to close it. Good man – he lives nearby, but he must have made tremendous haste, acting immediately upon receiving the note. Zola enters cautiously, expecting to find the place vandalised, furniture upturned, linens slashed – in other words, the scene he would create in a novel of this sorry story. He knows his wife's character well; she is capable of anything in a temper.

But there are few signs of disruption, some of which could easily have been created by Jeanne as she made a rapid retreat. She would not have questioned Céard, he is sure of that; she is an obedient woman with a kind heart, and they have talked about the day when their secret might come out. How exactly it happened, Zola does not yet know, but he is sure someone gossiped, for Paris is a world of gossip. His guilt increases; he has been careless lately, taking the young family for walks in the Tuileries Gardens when the weather is fine, and to a popular café nearby for lunch.

At first, the place appears to be deserted. He is not certain Alexandrine is there until he makes a circuit of the other rooms and comes into the parlour. He jumps, exclaiming aloud when he finds her sitting like a statue at the piano. He has recently employed a teacher for Jeanne, and she loves to play to the children. Her sheets of music are still there, lying open as if she had been interrupted in mid-song.

"Sandrine . . . Lou-lou . . ."

"Don't!" She slams her heavy hands on the piano keys, making an ugly chord, and closes the lid with a bang. Despite his desire to placate her, Zola feels briefly irritated by this. His wife has always been volatile and prone to drama, and it does her a disservice; it is melodramatic, undignified.

Behind her is a reproduction of the Greuze painting, "The Girl with the Broken Jug", with the model's face so like Jeanne's. Below the painting, the pretty *escritoire* he bought last year, decorated with trailing painted flowers, has been destroyed, the baize-inlaid writing surface ripped off its wooden hinges, entrails of letters and writing materials scattered to the floor. A bottle of ink has tipped on its side, pooling black on the woven rug. He goes to reach for the precious letters, all in his own expansive hand; they were sent from Médan, and even from the flat nearby, penned when he could not escape for an afternoon, messages full of love and silly drawings for his children, with gratitude and endearments for their beloved mother. From where he stands he can see the tail end of a sentence: ". . . have transformed my life." He moves forward.

"Stop!" Alexandrine barks.

There is nothing he can do. Briskly, silently, her lips pressed together, she gathers up the papers as he watches and takes them over to the still-smouldering fire, which she prods with an iron poker before tossing the pages in to burn, stabbing at them as if they were enemy soldiers.

"You cannot destroy history this way," he says, reasonably enough, at least to his ear. A mistake. She turns on him, the hot poker in her hand, and he takes a few hasty steps back, beyond reach. Her familiar face is distorted with hatred. "Do not think you can lecture me about history today. I who am your history, I who have been with you every step of your journey, I who have sacrificed my life to you, and given up everything for you! I who am inseparable from your life's work, Émile Zola! I married you when you began with your wretched Rougons and now you wish to toss me aside at the finish – and for what? Some stupid young whore, some nothing girl with nothing in her head and nothing in her name whose only asset is her womb . . . how could you?"

Her normally pleasing voice has lowered an octave, thick with anger and pain. He shakes his head. What is she saying? He has no intention of throwing her aside. How can he reassure her? She has begun to shake, finally overcome by the shock, tears flowing down her weathered cheeks. Somehow, he loosens the poker from her grasp, lays it gently on the hearth, and coaxes her out of that room, easing her down the stairs. He takes her home and convinces her to lie down awhile. "Rest," he says gently, closing her door, certain that the prudent way forward is to stay calm. He will send immediately for her cousin Amélie, and leave them to talk and cry, for he knows it is better when women are healed by women in matters of high emotion.

The depth of Alexandrine's feelings does not surprise him, but he has an idea that her reaction goes beyond the legitimate and natural response to such a discovery. It is as if she is once again the young woman of twenty whose newborn child has been taken from her breast to a foundling hospital, or the orphan girl who cries each night for her mother, lost to cholera when Alexandrine was eight years old. She is caught up in an agony of history, and that is why her first response was to try and destroy it, to burn his letters to Jeanne. He can intuitively understand this. Alexandrine has thrown herself into his life, developing an identity that is entirely based on being "Madame Zola", the great writer's loved and loving wife. As false as that has become in recent years, it is a façade of her own making and she is not prepared to see it fall.

* * *

She has ranted and screamed and he has let her, for several days – he can tolerate most of it, but she frightens him with the violence of her anger at Jeanne and the children. Her imagination is operatic – she repeatedly tells him of her fantasy that she is covered in their blood, that she has slit their throats, or that she is kicking a dying Jeanne, who is writhing on the floor in agony after drinking a glass of poisoned water. He writes to Céard, "My wife is behaving like a lunatic – can you come?"

He prays she will tire of her macabre fantasies soon, and until then he will listen patiently. It is the least he can do. He tends to her, bringing her favourite food and drink on a tray, and does not flinch when she upends it on the floor. He or one of the servants is now on duty in her room at all times, for as the days pass he has become convinced she is as capable of suicide as she professes to be of murder.

If he can somehow navigate their broken vessel back to dry land, then they will have a civil conversation in which he will assure her that he cannot imagine leaving her. She speaks of divorce in the midst of her shouting and sobbing, though it is only recently legal in France, and very rare – and he refuses to entertain the idea. "You are my wife. You always will be." This does not assuage her. She weeps all the more, pitching any small object near to hand at his head, aiming to wound him. It is as if he has told her that he rejects her totally and is leaving her forever. She cries out that she does not want more lies, she wants the complete truth. "You, you who write and speak of truth with such almighty grandeur, the great Zola, the self-appointed scourge of hypocrites – you are the worst of them all!" She spits at him, like some harridan of the gutter, a creature of Gervaise's slum, not the lady of a fine house. He nods sadly, spreading his hands, palms upward, and admits it is true. He is the worst. What else can he say?

Henri Céard arrives, and Amélie La Borde. They are sworn to secrecy, the only visitors admitted. Amélie has never warmed to Zola, and does not mask her disdain now, but she is practical and unsurprised; the French woman is familiar with this terrain. She is good to Alexandrine, and her visits have a pacifying affect, so again he steels himself to practise tolerance. He is the guilty party, he must bear his penance. Céard brings him news of Jeanne when he calls, and carries messages back to her and the children. "Tell my little Denise," Zola writes, "I think of her and of you every morning and every evening, and if she does not see her father for a time it is only because he is very busy elsewhere."

Céard is also a good listener for Alexandrine – she has always liked the man, who is an artist, a critic and a novelist like her husband, though much less successful. Of course, she is unaware of the co-conspiratorial role he has played in Zola's affair. He is a natural appeaser. After one visit, he writes to Amélie, who takes turns with him to visit, "You will find her calmer . . . I do not pretend there will be a permanent solution. But I have told her not to make any rash moves. She speaks of leaving, of finding work, *et cetera*, but I have told her not to decide quickly." Healing hearts is hard labour, Céard thinks, and he writes to Zola to ask if he is actually considering leaving his wife now that the truth is out.

"To leave the person who has shared everything with me, who has given me unconditional love, even though this is now transformed into unconditional hatred, would be throwing myself into the unknown," Zola replies. As much as he adores his mistress and the children, to abandon Alexandrine would be to abandon himself. She is – or has been – his ally, the sister he never had, the companion of his fears, a mother and a wife in one, and he still needs her. If he is caught in the proverbial "love triangle" which he has so often detailed in fiction, then Alexandrine is the base of it. Without her in his life, he is sure he would have been a writer, but he doubts he would have constructed such a phenomenal literary edifice. She has been the engine of the Zola machine.

When Alexandrine comprehends this, she will allow her sense of self to be rebuilt. She is still Madame Zola. They will not alter their living arrangements or their plans. She will go forward with him publicly, to all outward appearances unaltered by this scandal, and Jeanne will stay in the shadows, willingly. Zola will not renounce his mistress – she has borne him children, and he could no more do so than cut off his arm. They will have to find some middle ground, a compromise arrangement.

At first, there is a taste of triumph – Alexandrine has won, she has maintained the *status quo*. But soon enough, the jealousy roars back, as she relives the events of the last three years, and runs through dates in her mind like rosary beads, each time halting at some new hurt. One night, while plaiting her hair before bed she blurts out, "So when we were having these curtains hung, as I was standing here directing the men to hang these very curtains, you were becoming a father. Is that it? Have I got that right?" And Zola would nod, sadly, and try not to hurt her further, but for a moment, he loses himself in thinking of the excitement of that time, of the tremendous days before the birth of Denise.

He would send coded messages to Jeanne's doctor and receive news in return from Céard via adverts in the daily paper, ensuring he was always fully informed of progress. His face softens as he recalls the great day when the news came. At last, he was a father. That day, he wrote to his publisher Charpentier, with a mysterious postscript: "I feel once more as I did when I was twenty, ready to devour mountains." His reverie is broken by Alexandrine hurling her silver hairbrush at him, missing her mark and shattering the window behind him. And the screaming begins again.

Sylvie hands in her notice early on. Her n-n-nerves, she stutters. Other servants come and go. Eventually, Zola soundproofs the large bedroom, padding the walls with fabric and mattress stuffing to contain the horrendous sound of his wife's grief and anger. This room becomes the only place in which she chooses to vent her rage. In public, she takes his arm. At table, she passes wine and offers him salt. He longs to suggest that he has his own bedroom, but this would be an act of war and so he stays on in their vast cold chamber, in their great carved bed, each of them clinging to their respective side all night, like shipwrecked mariners on the rocks, despairing of rescue.

After considerable interruption he returns to his writing of *Doctor Pascal*. The protagonist is Pascal Rougon, who has lived and practised medicine for thirty years in Plassans, the southern town modelled on Zola's childhood home of Aix. Pascal is occupied now with classifying his family line, using a series of case studies within the family history to examine the troubling effects of heredity. Pascal is his author's alter ego; he is expressing Zola's scientific beliefs, as well as summarising the events of the series.

Into the doctor's life comes a charge, a beautiful young niece called Clotilde. Initially she challenges him about his project, on religious grounds. Gradually they begin a romance, despite the thirty-year difference in their ages, and he teaches her the rational grounds for his theories about the chequered history of the Rougon-Macquart family and their tendencies to sexual violence, alcoholism and criminal insanity. Pascal's overbearing mother,

Felicité, discovers his intentions and is outraged (far more so than by his affair with the girl); she will not have their dirty linen washed in public. She sends an anonymous letter to Pascal, decrying his actions.

Zola also plans a climatic sequence in which Pascal is taken ill and, as he dies, Felicité arrives and burns all of her son's papers in an attempt to obliterate the family's true history. The image of Alexandrine, red-eyed and furious, incinerating his letters in Jeanne's grate, hovers before him as he creates the scene. Is this fair? Of course. Plundering his own and his loved ones' lives, even the most private and agonising moments, gives him no pause. What could be more authentic for any artist, than to ransack one's own emotional storehouse, or one's wife's? His poor friend Guy de Maupassant, now incarcerated in an asylum after a suicide attempt, once wrote that "the gaze of the man of letters is like the hand of a thief, forever stealing . . . he plucks and plunders, without respite."

The book's lyrical celebration of an illicit love affair with a younger woman will enrage Alexandrine afresh when the book is done, but he hopes to temper her response. He had intended to pay homage in this final book to the memory of his mother – but he will now add "and to my dear wife, I dedicate this novel which sums up and concludes my whole work." She will be pleased – and he will take her to Italy soon. She will like that.

It is as well that Alexandrine will never read the inscription in the edition of *Doctor Pascal* that he gifts to Jeanne: "To my Clotilde, who gave me back the gift of my thirties, and to my Denise and Jacques, the two dear children for whom I wrote this, so they know how I adored their mother."

He writes to Vizetelly to tell him the last of the Rougon-Macquart series will be ready before long, assuring him that like *The Downfall*, "It contains nothing to offend the prudery of your compatriots." On reflection, he adds, "I give you full authority to modify any passages that may seem to you to be *inquietants*."

When spring comes and they return to Médan, he will settle Jeanne and the children in a charming cottage he has found across the river, a few kilometres from the villa. As he sits at his desk of a morning, facing those tall windows, he will slip his opera glasses from their leather case and remove the black velvet cloth. Holding them up to his eyes, he will be able to watch Denise tottering on chubby legs in the grass, her joy palpable even from such a distance. He will find her lovely mother, head bent, unaware of his observation, sitting on a rug nearby under the shade of a spreading chestnut tree. Jacques' dark head will be buried in her bosom as he suckles, his left arm raised straight in the air, like a flag in happy victory. Thank you, my son, he will whisper, for giving me the final image in the final chapter of my life's work.

13. *September 1893, London and Surrey*

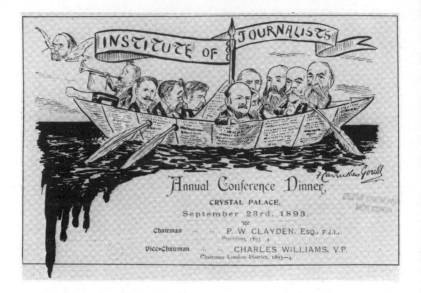

INSTITUTE OF JOURNALISTS

Annual Conference Dinner,

CRYSTAL PALACE,
September 23rd, 1893.

Chairman ... ... P. W. CLAYDEN, Esq., F.J.I.
President, 1893–4

Vice-Chairman ... ... CHARLES WILLIAMS, V.P.
Chairman London District, 1893–4

"Well? What am I to say to Papa about this?" Ernest asks his wife, holding up the invitation. Marie makes no answer other than a typical and irritating little lift of shoulders and eyebrows. She is preoccupied, two pins held in her mouth and another pushing through the thin fabric of the hem she is sewing, so that their three-year-old daughter Dora can wear her older sister Violette's cast-offs. She has adapted well to their reduced circumstances, Ernest concedes, though she still infuriates him with her insistence on ritual and appearances, her French sense of what is

248

"done" at table or in public. "Why eat mutton on fine china?" he grumbles, and she replies tartly, "As long as they do not wrest my mother's china from our hands, I shall use it as I please."

Nothing has gone right these last three years. Ernest's earnings have been so meagre that they are now living in what he calls "the slum" near Hurlingham, in Southwest London. The family of six (three girls now, aged two, three and eleven, and his nine-year-old son Victor) are living in a few dark rooms. When he comes home of an evening, after spending another day in town endeavouring to find a little journalistic work, Ernest must push past the street urchins sitting outside the public house on the corner, quaffing their beer from pewter mugs and shouting obscenities. Once indoors, the smell of damp and the noxious coal fire greet him, and the clamour of young children at play. He can never seem to find any peace.

Brocade curtains hang incongruously at the front windows, a legacy of Marie's privileged past, and the décor consists mainly of piles and piles of books, many of them rescued from the bailiffs who descended upon Vizetelly & Company. Dozens of cloth and leather-bound volumes are stacked in corners, on chairs, even cluttering the staircase – or piled high next to a wooden table in the little room on the first floor where Ernest works. When he cannot generate enough money to pay the rent, he goes to the pawnshop with some last little trinket, or a handsome illustrated volume from his father's library, if he must.

His income is largely dependent on the man whose books ruined his father. Two years ago, when he arranged to act as Zola's

English translator and agent, he had his qualms, but his father had given him his blessing. He knew Ernest had to earn a living, and Zola was never their enemy.

His next translation will be Zola's new project, modest in scale compared to *Les Rougon-Macquart*. Titled *The Three Cities*, it is a trilogy of novels about faith from an avowed atheist. He will begin at Lourdes, and include stories set in Rome and Paris. Chatto & Windus have pledged to buy the rights for a significant sum. Andrew Chatto has been very good about Zola. He is a true entrepreneur, and detects that the wind is changing with the dawn of the new decade; although several other English publishers declined any association with Zola when Ernest first approached them, Chatto is willing to take the risk that the right French novels, carefully chosen and translated, will not invite prosecution. He believes that the influence of circulating libraries and the N.V.A. is waning, the public growing tired of these moral arbiters. The success of Zola's war novel *The Downfall* has encouraged him.

This year he will publish *Doctor Pascal*. Zola had been certain this "scientific investigation" could not offend the English reader, but Ernest was asked to make a circumspect translation. A Victorian "fear of the bed" still stands, whatever else might be changing in society, and the lovers' richly described first sexual encounter is conveyed in the Chatto version in a few abstract lines, before dissolving into a new chapter in which they are happily breakfasting on the following day. Ernest's translator's preface apologises for "the omission of certain passages" but hopes it does not prevent the reader "from understanding the drift of M. Zola's narrative". There will be many who will not agree, but Ernest loves this final novel best of all the series, and is convinced of its "perfect style".

Zola's name is still a great draw to the book-buying public, as is so often the case when an author's work is censored; his friend Flaubert had proven this tenfold in France before him with *Madame Bovary*, another book that Chatto will soon re-publish. Be that as it may, Ernest is fearful that the wind might turn again, and he grows increasingly impatient for delivery of the *Lourdes* manuscript.

But Zola, having finished his "life's work", is in no hurry to deliver *Lourdes*. His personal situation is much changed, and well Ernest knows that fatherhood is a great distraction. He is guessing about this to some degree, based on rumour and on the content of *Doctor Pascal*; Zola is certainly not prone to discussing his private life when he writes to his agent. Ernest responds to him with alacrity when the author does make contact on business matters, dealing with the query and then, if the mood strikes him, unburdening himself as if to a lifelong confidant, touching upon such intimate matters as his wife Marie's ailments and his children's schooling. It is a kind of role-reversal, some would say: the reserved Englishman opening himself up over several pages to the intemperate Frenchman, whose replies usually consist of two or three lines.

Perhaps Ernest shares his woes with Zola because he cannot do so with his father. Henry is living still, which is a minor miracle, considering his ill health and the woes he has suffered – but under no circumstances would Ernest add to the old man's burdens by describing his own. Henry is occupied with completing his memoirs, which he has decided to call *Glances Back Through Seventy Years*. He has shown chapters to his children and they have complimented him on his ever-fluent style, his lightness of tone and his gift for the telling anecdote. There is an appealing humility in the way he has captured the remarkable view from his front-of-stalls seats in London, Paris and Berlin for some of the most turbulent moments of the last century. Henry's old friend, Charles Kegan Paul, who is celebrated for his attention to aesthetic design in his books as much as for their radical content, has already committed to publish the work on completion.

But "glances" is the apposite word – it is not a searching and fearless inventory; it is a series of vignettes, and a reasonable assemblage of dates and incidents (though Ernest has had to correct a number of these), presented in Henry's charming and digressive style, with vigour and wit. The problem with the work is that it is stunted: he has decided to finish around 1878, on his return to London from Paris, thus avoiding an account of his final business ventures and the hardships he endured for publishing the works of Zola. "The book is too long as it is, dear boy; it will run to two volumes!" Henry tells Ernest.

* * *

Ernest makes the weekly journey to Tilford in Surrey, where Henry lives at Heatherlands, a small, plain cottage that Annie found when London was no longer affordable. Henry had finally admitted defeat after trying and failing to re-establish himself in

252

the publishing world with one project after another. One day he confessed to Annie that he no longer had the stomach for it, saying, "Everything goes wrong, though I strive and strive and work like a slave," and adding, "I am tired of existence." Alarmed, she sought to cheer him by returning him to the country views of his boyhood, when he was at school in leafy Chislehurst. On fine days, if he is well enough, she takes him to the village green to see the local teams play cricket, and he delights in this, muttering commentary and advice about their poor technique that the players mercifully cannot hear.

Annie is assistant, housekeeper and nurse in one; there is no money for outside help, and little enough for their daily comfort. Their circumstances are so reduced that Henry has been compelled to apply twice for a grant of assistance from the Royal Literary Fund. Annie is about to tell him they must do so again, or risk being without a roof over their heads by Christmas. It hurts his pride to ask for charity, but they have had no choice.

"Resentment," Henry says to his son, who has decided to raise the matter of the Zola trial and the memoir one last time. The old man is propped up against a pillow in his bed, where he spends most of his days. "As we know, the word derives from the Latin: intensive prefix 're' and the verb 'sentir', to feel. If I re-feel, that is, if I re-live in the telling those scenes at the Old Bailey, or if I paw through boxes of vitriolic cuttings from the popular press, or go so far as to pick up the N.V.A.'s rabid pamphlet *Pernicious Literature*, and review Samuel Smith's diatribe against me in Parliament, then I shall drown in a sea of resentment, I know it. And this will not hurt my enemies; it will only re-open my wounds. Therefore, I choose not to look back at this sorry experience.

"But you can set the record right, Papa. You can tell people what happened, and how we were badly misrepresented by our counsel, and in what way you intended to fight the case, for the sake of literary freedom—"

"Intended. But I did not."

"You were ill!"

"Yes, and I was afraid, which is implicit in my guilty plea. I did nothing for the cause, as you call it, except set it back. Look at the landscape now." He waves at the window, as if the corpses of transgressive literary lions were lying belly-up in the fields outside. "Wilde is denounced, Shaw is censored off the stage, our own G.M. has written just one novel these last four years, and Hardy is bowdlerising himself. The bravest act any author can contemplate is to publish new fiction in obscure and costly journals or elaborate private editions which hold no interest to the justice system."

Annie intervenes, the evening paper lying open in her lap, half read. Like her brother, she is disappointed by her father avoiding the issue. She wants nothing more than vindication of his name. "Papa, you forget: Mr Moore was here only days ago, showing us the serialisation of his new book in the *Gazette*; he says this could never have been published when Mr Stead was editor, but he is gone. And Mr Chatto is doing well with Ernest's translations . . ."

This would be the ideal moment to tell Henry about the invitation from the Institute of Journalists. It is printed on heavy card, edged in gilt, announcing a gala evening in London, at which Émile Zola is to be one of the guests of honour. It seems as bold a declaration of the redemption of the author in England as you could wish for – at least within the press corps. Henry might be delighted that time is bringing the change he once predicted – and rather swiftly, at that. On the other hand, the fourth estate's evident *volte face* could make him angry, since it has come too late to benefit him. Or more likely, his response will fall between the two, given his balanced view of most things – as a long-standing member of the Institute, he will know that it is entirely in keeping with tradition to invite foreign dignitaries to their annual confer-ence in London, and Zola is the chairman of their sister union in France. This is not so much a miraculous moment of salvation as a prudent gambit by the organisers; Zola's fame (and infamy) will help to ensure wide interest in their event.

The moment passes, and Ernest does not speak up. Annie brings tea, and offers some soft, sugar-dusted sweets arranged on a plate. "What are they?" Ernest asks. "Turkish delight!" she replies with a smile, "Absolutely delicious. Try one. Edward brought them last weekend. He is so thoughtful."

As if to compound Ernest's misery, his elder brother Edward has just settled in London after many years abroad as a war reporter, acting as if he has never been away. He visits Henry, who is delighted to see him; he teases Annie and gives her pretty little gifts; he regales the younger boys with stories of his adventures in the Mid-East wars and in Africa, where he organised the troop of men who found the lost explorer Stanley in the jungle. Dapper and confident, he needles his well-named younger brother, who bridles with every comment. To cap it all, he has brought home with him a young French wife called Marie, like Ernest's wife, and she has recently borne a delightful baby daughter on whom Henry dotes. Edward's assumption that he can just walk back into a life he has abandoned for years and pick up where he left off is infuriating – and now it seems he is setting aside journalistic pursuits to translate French literature into English, something he had dabbled in as a young man in Paris.

This is Ernest's business now, his livelihood! Yet there is Edward, casually letting it drop in conversation that he should like to undertake an English version of Zola's earliest works of fiction, his *Stories of Ninon*, and wondering aloud if now is also the right time to consider a new translation of Zola's first novel *Thérèse Raquin*, as if it were his familial right to mine this seam. An observer who was familiar with that novel might say that Ernest, ever the awkward, less adept brother feels much like Camille beside Edward's handsome, self-assured Laurent, with the shared object of their affections being Zola.

Can things get any worse? The invitation burns a hole in Ernest's jacket pocket, as he grudgingly takes another sweet from the plate. These spongy little squares are indeed delicious, though he fears most of the sugar has missed his mouth and landed on his black trousers; the grey shawl wrapped round Henry's bony shoulders is dusted with the stuff. How typical of Edward to be so inconsiderate.

Zola had written to Ernest about the invitation a few weeks

earlier, soliciting a view as to whether it would be wise for him to accept. He is now Chairman of the *Société des Gens de Lettres*, and it is in this capacity that the Institute wishes him, together with several esteemed colleagues, to attend. They have asked him to speak on the topic of anonymity in journalism; it is widely known that the themes of taking responsibility and pride in one's work are dear to Zola, and he is vocal about this in France, where, as not in Britain, the signed newspaper article is an established practice.

Ernest responded to Zola's concerns immediately and encouraged him to say yes; it would only do him good and, though he does not say so, by association, his translator and agent will benefit too. He tells him that the English press corps, four years on from his father's trial, "like to think you have undergone some great change since *The Soil*," and adds, "Your presence in London might help clear up past misunderstandings."

Zola is by his own admission not a good traveller, and despite the assurances of his agent and other English friends, he is concerned about the reception he will receive. Ernest offers to meet Zola at Calais and conduct him to London with his group – and Madame Zola, of course. He will organise a series of interviews; he will even give Zola a tour of London, for this will be his first ever visit. Ernest draws up a detailed schedule, with a few hours set aside each morning for press interviews at the Savoy, where Zola will stay as the Institute's guest. Henry James wishes to dine with his friend; George Moore has proposed a riverboat trip down to Greenwich, and there must be a luncheon with Andrew Chatto. Ernest will also take Zola to see the Turner watercolours at the

National Gallery, and give him a tour of the East End of London, which he knows only through reading translations of Dickens' work. The Authors' Club would like to arrange a dinner, and, alongside all of these entertainments, Zola, as one of the French delegation of journalists, will give his paper at the Imperial Institute, attend a reception at the Guildhall in the presence of the Lord Mayor, and enjoy a final gala event at the Crystal Palace. It is going to be a busy week.

"Are you to be paid for running around London after Monsieur, lifting the hem of his coat out of the mud?" Marie asks, when he describes the busy itinerary to her. "Certainly not, it is an honour to be asked," Ernest snaps back at her, ruffled by the image. Marie has said before that she feels Ernest has undersold himself to his famous client; he is no businessman. Her husband does not know that last year, desperate to take her children out of London to the seaside for a brief holiday, she wrote to Zola herself, begging him to forgo five hundred francs that rightfully belonged to his translator, but which Ernest had foolishly waived in an effort to ingratiate himself. The author, or rather, his wife, who had kindly replied on his behalf, had agreed to her request.

Henry Vizetelly has not been invited to the conference or any of the other events. It might have been possible; the Authors' Club had particularly asked for him. "No, no – his health is poor," Ernest had replied. What he really meant, though it also true that Henry is largely bed-bound and would struggle to sit through any public event, is that it would create too much of a scrum; he cannot put his poor father through the frenzy that would result from him coming face to face with Zola in a room packed with eager reporters. Better to bring Marie, who will be delighted at such a splendid outing. But the problem is not resolved. Zola's presence in London will be widely reported, and Henry will certainly come to hear of it. What to do?

As it turns out, when the day draws near, the papers are filled with reports of striking coal miners, eclipsing all other topics. The falling price of coal has lately caused pit owners to reduce workers' wages. Across the country, more than two hundred thousand men, led by the recently formed Miners' Federation, are demanding improved safety measures and conditions, and what they have termed "a living wage".

On September 5, riots begin in pit villages in Yorkshire and Derbyshire, and the protest spreads to Scotland. In Featherstone, near Bradford, a local magistrate "reads the Riot Act", indicating that anyone who does not disperse within an hour will be arrested. A group of soldiers are summoned to enforce this, with the approval of the Home Secretary. As the hour elapses, with no sign of surrender, the magistrate asks for warning shots to be fired. The crowd of protesters assume they are blanks and stand their ground until the troops open fire again. In the ensuing melee, eight men are shot, two of them killed. There follows a huge outcry in the press, and a sense of unity amongst other workers is building in factories and fields across the country. The atmosphere is tense, unsettled – and the government refuses, at least for the time being, to intervene.

The coincidence of this occurring just as the author of

Germinal is about to set foot on England's shore does not escape Ernest, nor will it go unremarked by some newspapers. Zola's thirteenth novel in the Rougon-Macquart saga had been a sensation to rival *L'Assommoir* or *Nana* when it was first published in 1885; to date it has sold more than eighty thousand copies in France alone, and it had also enjoyed great success in England.

The hero, Étienne Lantier (a son of Gervaise Macquart, tragic heroine of *L'Assommoir*), loses his job as a mechanic in Lille, takes to the road and finds work in a mining community in Northern France. He is horrified by the working environment and the abject poverty, and ultimately leads the men in a strike. A vast, layered and distressing story, particularly for the anxious middle classes, it is yet considered by many to be Zola's masterwork, and a defining story for a generation of working men. "Germinal!" will be the rallying call of striking French miners for decades after its publication, despite the reality of its bleak ending. As the title suggests, a seed has been planted – if not for revolution then certainly for evolution.

Should Ernest counsel Zola to make mention of the striking miners in his speech, or even to appeal for intervention? This would be in keeping with Zola's principles, and, if carefully phrased, might not provoke his detractors, for everyone wants some end to the escalating crisis. Even if his visit is too brief to allow for him actually to visit the English miners to give them some words of encouragement, might Zola raise a glass to the fallen of Featherstone at the end of his speech?

Ernest does not, in the end, suggest anything of the sort, nor does Zola speak of it when he arrives, though he cannot be oblivious to the miners' situation. Perhaps it is just as well; despite the uncomfortable irony of Lantier's creator feasting with the Lord Mayor while, just a few hundred miles away, coal miners and their families are dying of want, Zola has engendered enough controversy in England to date. Ernest considers it his job to smooth – not to ruffle – feathers. He must help himself, and his own career, as Marie always tells him.

* * *

Ernest had not expected such fanfare. There is a state procession underway at the Guildhall that would befit visiting royalty; music plays; a red carpet has been set out, bejewelled ladies and gentlemen are arriving in finest evening dress, and here is the guest of honour, elegant in his black frock coat, his hair swept back from his forehead, with his wife behind him, draped in furs, being greeted warmly by the Lord Mayor.

The status accorded to Zola on this visit was made apparent when they arrived by train in London a few days earlier: they were met with speeches from the stationmaster and the editor of the *Daily Telegraph* on the platform; throngs of people called out Zola's name. Alexandrine was amazed, and looked to Ernest for an explanation. "They behave as if he were a stage actor, not an author whose works your courts have banned!" No-one is more aware of this than he, and in truth, it is hard for him to account for this enthusiastic welcome. He can only surmise to Madame Zola that the trial has made her husband a household name here. "So, he is infamous, rather than beloved," Madame replied drily.

Zola greeted by the Lord Mayor of London at the Guildhall.

"Like a criminal." At that, Zola laughed. "Ah, the English – I no more understand their attitudes than I do their language." He is dependent on Ernest and a few other friends for translation, and alighting from the train, he and his wife apologised in French for their lack of English as they graciously met the noisy crowd.

All the way from Calais, Ernest had studied Alexandrine with some curiosity – whenever he could do so unobserved. He is fascinated by her dignity and composure, considering her husband has recently fathered two children by a woman half her age. Perhaps she is unaware? Though his friends in the literary world in Paris speak casually of Zola's mistress, Madame Zola would not be the first wife to be oblivious. She smiles and nods with queenly aplomb, and holds Zola's arm as if they are one of those couples whose marriage of three decades has only improved with age, like the finest wine.

There is one telling moment, when two little children playing on the platform tumble into Zola's path as they make their way through the crowd. He bends down to tousle their hair, smiling at their pink faces and chucking the little boy under the chin. In that instant Ernest sees Alexandrine lose her guard. A look passes over her face that he can only perceive as violent, but she recovers herself so swiftly, turning to share a smile with the stationmaster by her side, that he thinks he might have imagined it.

Robert Sherard, one of Zola's retinue from Paris, is an expatriate English writer who has recently published an admiring biography of Zola. He is seated next to Ernest and Marie at the dinner at the Guildhall, hosted by the Corporation of the City of

London for the assembled journalists. Ernest is not impressed with Sherard's book, which is really a stitched-together series of interviews. One day, he thinks, I may undertake a better biography, when time permits; who knows Zola's life and work as well as his translator and agent? I have lived inside his words, not merely taken wine with him at his table.

A handsome blond Englishman in his early thirties with impeccable French, Sherard has the confidence of an aristocrat. Ernest can imagine why, as is rumoured, Oscar Wilde is mad about him. But he has an eye for the ladies – that much is evident in his conversation and his manner with Marie, who is clearly charmed. He is the sort of man who, like his dashing brother Edward, instantly makes Ernest feel inadequate.

In an effort to divert Sherard from paying such attention to his wife, Ernest asks him what he knows of Wilde's latest novel. The censors in London banned a production of his play, "Salomé", which was to have starred Sarah Bernhardt, last year. "Not a novel at all, nor another tragic subject," Sherard replies, waving his glass and slurring his words. "He is completing another society comedy for the stage, I believe, to follow the success of 'Lady Windermere's Fan'. I know only the title: 'The Importance of Being Earnest'." He winks at Marie and drains his glass.

Safer ground, Ernest thinks. Wilde will have to watch his step; times were not changing fast enough to allow for his more extreme ideas and lifestyle, despite his popular successes in the theatre, or the celebration of the previously "monstrous" Zola here tonight.

Marie whispers in his ear now, pointing out a few friends and commenting on Madame Zola's superb diamond earrings. "What kind of fur do you suppose she's wearing?" Ernest half listens, surveying the room, wondering if his nemesis, W. T. Stead, is present, if he would dare to show his face after all his editorial columns against Zola. He is no longer the editor of the *Pall Mall Gazette*, having resigned three years earlier to found his own journal, the *Review of Reviews*, which synthesises "the best journalism from around the Empire". Though less involved with the N.V.A., he continues to be a campaigner for various causes, recently advocating the new international language Esperanto in his monthly column. To his relief, Ernest cannot find Stead; the Institute has nearly three thousand members and at least half of them must be in attendance tonight. There are too many tall, bearded journalists to distinguish one from another in the hazy lamplight. If he does pass Stead in the throng later, he will spit in his eye. He moves the wine decanter out of Sherard's reach and pours himself a large glass before the man drains it all.

At the conference at the Imperial Institute the following day, the chairman of the British Institute gives Zola a warm welcome "from his fellow journalists". Zola smiles shyly as he gets to his feet, his papers in hand, and sets his top hat aside. He begins immediately, rather than allowing the enthusiastic applause to develop and end. His head is not turned by this reception, Ernest knows. The tributes made to him today mention his long career in journalism rather than his novels, as if they can uncouple him from the works of fiction that caused many in the room to criticise him in the recent past. Ernest shakes his head. Hypocrisy is alive and well.

"I have noticed," Zola had observed to one interviewer at the Savoy that morning, "that the Frenchman is more liked in England than the Englishman is in France." "Why do you think that is?" the man had asked eagerly, pen poised to record Zola's wisdom. "We have been isolated for so long, we have a grievance against the rest of our neighbours," Zola answered slowly. "For all that, this dislike of the English is as unfortunate as it is silly . . . I am quite positive that you like us, and I shall give the widest publicity to the fact; may it be productive of some good in our future mutual relations!"

He is also asked repeatedly by the press about his failure as yet to be chosen to join the French Academy, despite being nominated many times. One reporter wondered if he thought this visit would influence the members in his favour. His reply, though misreported as a sign of his desperate ambition to be chosen as an "Immortal", was terse: "This sort of thing would not guide the decision of the Academy." Ernest had hurried that fellow out of the room, and ushered in the next, a sycophantic gentleman who asked if Zola would consider writing something set in London in the future. He was charming in his response. "I am sorry I saw London so late in life and that having come, I cannot stay longer. My dear wife was only saying to me this morning, 'This is a city for you!' What might I have written on this colossus had I been here sooner?"

One morning, when there is a blessed pause in the parade of visitors at hotel, Ernest pulls some old newspaper cuttings from his pocket and lays them out in front of Zola. "What is all this?"

Zola is unable to read the various articles from English papers, though he can see immediately that they all feature his name. "I – it concerns my father," Ernest says. "These are a few reports of his trial, four years ago."

"What an injustice," Zola says, shaking his head. "My wife and I were very sorry to hear of it." He adds that he was surprised, too, as he had faced similar difficulties at home, but had never been prosecuted. "You do not have to contend with the ignorance of narrow-minded, power-mad vigilantes we have here, Monsieur," Ernest says, "nor with their cronies in government who step to their bidding." "We have our own versions in France, I assure you," says Zola.

Ernest is blaming the wrong people, he suggests. At first, he too had thought the Establishment and the legal system were at fault, but it occurs to him now that the real problem lies with England's contemporary writers, many of whom he has read in translation. The English reader was so used to reading novels full of "artful reticence" (books which in his opinion are far more capable of corruption than his own work) that they could not stomach his "rough frankness" – this is, he believes, the root cause of the unjust trial of Henry Vizetelly.

Ernest cannot meet his eye. He clears his throat, hesitating. But he must go on; when will he have the opportunity again?

"I do not wish to offend, Monsieur Zola, but . . . you were reported in the English press as saying that you were in favour of his sentence."

The silence that follows is agonising. Ernest wonders if he has just done himself out his job. Zola removes his pince-nez and rests his head on his hand a moment. He slept badly last night, in the unfamiliar bed, and it has been a long morning. He wishes he could read English – but there is no need. It is obvious that he was misrepresented, his words twisted; it is ever thus, he explains to Ernest. "The more famous the subject, the more grossly they distort his words. Truth is lost for editorial ends. Look here – the *Pall Mall Gazette*." He taps his finger on one of the articles. "You would not believe it. They sent a boy to talk to me, barely out of school. He took down every word I said, but I expect he altered them to meet the needs of his editor, like an eager pupil before his master. This is not journalism as I understand it – and until these cowards are required to sign their work, they will go unpunished." At this, he pushes the collection of articles away from him in disdain.

Ernest gathers them all up in haste, and thrusts them out of sight. "Please, dear sir, no more. I fully understand." Zola gazes at him, and reaches out to touch his shoulder. "I am sorry for your troubles. I too had a father I loved."

* * *

The reception at the Guildhall, and Zola's beautifully executed speech on journalistic responsibility the day after, are followed the next night by a special concert at the Royal Opera House in Covent Garden; famous writers, actors and artists gather around him, and the papers are full of excitement about the forthcoming gala fireworks night at Crystal Palace – every detail of this lavish, week-long conference is reported, perhaps as an antidote to so much

268

bad news breaking at the same time. The trouble with the coal miners continues, and the deepening American economic depression is making its impact felt in Britain and beyond.

At the cottage, Annie sees the articles about Zola and hides the papers from her father for a few days. She is outraged that the press are, for the most part, singing the praises of a man so recently vilified. What has changed, in three short years, that allows a man once blasted for writing "pornography", creating novels that are only "fit for swine", to be fêted by English journalists and *litterateurs*? It feels like a slap in her father's face – and she knows, from Marie, that Ernest is right in the middle of it all. She cannot blame him – she knows that his finances are such that he must keep Zola happy, but it is nonetheless galling.

Henry is calling out again. "Annie! Have they brought the papers?" He has a daily habit of reading them, even now, when he is out of bed only a few hours a day, spending the rest of the time drifting in and out of sleep. He has been distressed to hear that the papers have mysteriously not arrived this week. "I don't know what is happening, Papa," Annie says, as she bustles in to prop him on his pillows and give him his morning tea. She pauses in mid-step. He is already sitting up in bed, his face serious, with his hand resting on a pile of folded newspapers. "Not your best hiding place, my dear. I found them when I was looking for one of my old wine books last night."

Annie blushes. "I wanted to save you—" but Henry holds up his hand to stop her and smiles. "Annie Elizabeth. Don't fret. I am an old man and a robust one, at least in my mind; I can absorb any news at all at this point in my life. Besides, Edward mentioned Zola was coming to London, when he visited."

She sits in the chair next to the bed and takes his hand. "Did you wish to meet him? After all that's happened?"

"It isn't necessary. Of course, I am curious . . . But I have been privileged to read most of what he's written, and I feel sure I know him well as a result. It would have been too trying, and too controversial, to bring us together." He sighs, and pats her hand. "It is an irony, of course, that while I am completing my book, I read of this enthusiastic reception . . . But it is a good thing. A sign of the times."

"Papa! Nearly every journalist who called you evil and depraved and – and a pornographer . . . they were all there, applauding him! And I'll warrant that Mr Gissing, who refused to sign the petition for your release from prison, was toasting Monsieur Zola at the Authors' Club reception too! It seems so—"

"Unjust? When did we live in a just world, dear child? And we are not the only ones to notice the paradox, I daresay." He sets his spectacles on his nose and opens the *Westminster Gazette*, reading aloud in his quavering voice. "No man ever received a more courteous and respectful greeting than he, yet it is only a few years ago since his English publisher, a man with a name respected in English journalism, was hauled to prison for publishing what at most was but a bowdlerised edition of one of the Sage of Médan's most harrowing dissections of moral cancer. How changed today!"

"Yes, indeed." Annie is indignant.

"Change – that is what we wanted! This is a vindication I thought would take decades to come! And though it does not help our situation now, it is more than I thought I would live to see. Or read of," he adds wryly. "And now, Annie, do you have my daily paper?"

She runs from the room and returns in a moment, handing it over with a little bow, and waiting for him to open it and read the society pages. "This is the last night of the conference," Henry says. "Eight hundred people at Crystal Palace for the closing gala and fireworks, apparently."

Annie has never seen any fireworks herself, though she has heard their thunder outside, generally on Guy Fawkes night, when it is too dangerous to go out of doors. In London and around the country, many are scalded and even killed by the displays, with their powerful crackers, squibs and rockets filled with gunpowder. She has read about them often, however, because the English, particularly the royal family, adore them at their festivals and fêtes. She can only imagine the giant flowers and pinwheels of coloured light unfolding in the night sky, rockets like shooting stars careening across the heavens.

That night she settles her father to sleep, his face peaceful and his breathing even, for once. "Sleep well."

She moves to the desk and sees that he has arranged his manuscript pages in a pile, inside a cardboard cover. On the first page there is a verse, newly added after the memoir's title, an extract from Christina Rossetti's "The Thread of Life".

And sometimes I remember days of old
When fellowship was not so far to seek
And all the world and I seemed much less cold
And at the rainbow's foot lay surely gold
And hope felt strong and life itself not weak.

Annie replaces the page, tears in her eyes, and covers the book again. She moves to the window and draws the curtains closed, overlapping them at the centre so that no early light will wake him.

* * *

At Crystal Palace, Zola and Alexandrine stand and bow to the assembled crowds, to the Lord Mayor and Lady Mayoress, the visiting dignitaries, and to Charles Russell, President of the Institute of Journalists. Russell proposes a toast and the assembled members of the journalistic fraternity and their families and friends join him in a ragged chorus of "To the Foreign and Colonial Visitors". This done, he gives way to their most distinguished guest, Monsieur Zola, to respond. Zola stands, clearing his throat, and begins. He has been assured that most of his audience will comprehend French, being educated men.

"Gentlemen, above the secular hatreds of races, beyond the accidental misunderstandings of nations, beyond the personal interests, jealousies and outrages which overturn Empires and Republics, there is a tranquil kingdom, vaster than the vastest, the kingdom of human intelligence, of letters, of arts, and universal humanity. It is in this unbounded kingdom of sovereign peace that our Molière and Corneille grasp the hands of your Shakespeare, and it is there that they can also offer their hands to Goethe and Dante. In that realm, there is only one country, that of genius, and it is to this common country that I desire to drink." The guests raise their glasses, crying out, "To our common country!"

The band strikes up "God Save the Queen", everyone rises to their feet to sing, and soon the fireworks begin: hundreds of skyrockets sprawling about the sky like young stars in the making. The noise is tremendous – people cover their ears and some flinch in terror. There are admiring oohs and aahs at the initial figures, including a perfect palm tree etched in green light, surrounded by rays of golden sparks. One bright flash reveals that the guest of honour is stifling a yawn; he is not so amazed by fireworks, and it has been such a long and busy week. The Lord Mayor notices this, but he is unoffended; he knows what it is to stand for endless ceremonies at this age. His wife nudges him – she saw it too, and is ready to remonstrate, when the Lord Mayor whispers to her, "Wait until he sees the finale."

With a roll of drums, the band changes their tune to *La Marseillaise*. Zola and Alexandrine exchange looks of surprise; he bows his head to his hosts for doing him this honour; Charles Russell simply points upwards. The next round of rockets sing into the sky, and as they break, they create a new pattern, a grand setpiece – not a starburst nor another spinning wheel, but a clearly identifiable fire portrait of a man with a high forehead, pince-nez and a pointed goatee beard. Cheers and wild applause break out. Zola is astounded, and what's more, Alexandrine is laughing with delight and clapping her hands, for the first time since he can remember. As they all gaze up at the image, it lingers in the air, ghostly, wreathed in hazy smoke, for several long seconds before it disintegrates. One after another the lights fade and are gone.

* * *

Everything is still. The village green in Tilford is covered in feathery hoar frost, the church bells are silent, and the raggle-taggle mummers, their leader made up as a mangy horse with dirty ribbons flying from his mane, have finished carousing and gone home to sleep off their excesses. It is a new beginning, and Ernest Vizetelly has hope today. The first of January has always been his favourite day of the year – a short window of time when everything seems possible, before his natural pessimism slams it shut again.

1894. This year, our fortunes will change. This year, Marie will have another child. This year, I will write a book – not translate someone else's, but write my own. As his father's house comes into view, he takes a deep breath, and the air burns his throat and lungs. He carries an awkward bundle – he is the "First Footer" this morning. This seasonal tradition of making a pilgrimage to loved ones, bearing good wishes and gifts that augur abundance, is a family favourite, and he comes armed with coal and bread.

In his pocket, he carries a special present for Annie – a perfect orange, studded with cloves by his wife. For his father, he has a small flask of good Scotch whisky – another traditional gift, something to keep the chill off the old man during the long winter nights. He crunches up the path to the cottage and knocks. It is not even nine o'clock, but it was important to him, though he had to rise before dawn and endure the long uncomfortable carriage ride in icy darkness, that he arrived before Edward or Arthur.

There is no response, so he sets down his gifts and knocks again, louder this time. "Annie!" he calls softly. He can hear something inside – movement on the stairs – and soon the door swings open. Annie stands there, her face pale, her dark hair disarranged. She is still in her dressing gown. "He's gone," she says.

Ernest hurries upstairs. The figure in the bed has a shawl wrapped round his shoulders, as if he can yet feel the cold, and his body appears so small under the coverlet that he might be a child. "I brought you some whisky," he whispers, and chokes on the last word as tears blur his eyes. He goes to the bedside and kneels, reaching out to hold his father's bony hand, which is still warm.

After a long minute, he rises and bends to plant a kiss on the old man's weathered forehead. His eyeglasses have fallen on the pillow beside him and he sets them on the table by the bed, within reach, as if they might be needed when he wakes. Beside them lies a manuscript, scrawled with notations, and Ernest looks to see what his father was reading before he breathed his last. *Esther Waters* – it is George Moore's latest novel, due for publication in the spring. He will be touched.

On the desk, he finds Henry's memoir, *Glances Back Through Seventy Years*. It was published just before Christmas, and this is the first time Ernest has seen it in finished form. It looks suitably elegant in green buckram covers, lettered and decorated in gilt. There are five copies of the two-volume set, stacked together –

Henry's parting gifts to his children. Ernest opens the first and sees his own name inscribed in his father's generous hand, and the simple message: "With gratitude".

He turns to the last page of the second volume, expecting the narrative to end when Henry quit Paris in 1878, only to discover that his father added a final page, as he had long urged him to do, touching on "the *affaire* Zola". He must have done so immediately before sending it to the printers, while Ernest was preoccupied with Zola's recent visit. He writes of the irony that he is "penning these concluding lines" just as Zola is being welcomed in London "with rounds of ringing cheers". In reference to the last turbulent chapter of his life, he says, "The occurrences, however, in which I have been mixed up during the past twenty years, if more than glanced at, would form far too long a story to be told at the fag-end of two sufficiently bulky volumes." The few short lines in which he then summarises the last two decades say everything:

> I also introduced to English readers hundreds of volumes translated from foreign authors whose writings until then had been sealed books to the multitude, when my publication of the works of M. Zola, and the persecution of a band of fanatics, brought about my pecuniary ruin.

That is the sum of it, Ernest thinks. It is for this he will be remembered.

Henry Vizetelly, circa 1893.

Coda

It is absurd to have a hard and fast rule about what one should read and what one shouldn't. More than half of modern culture depends on what one shouldn't read.

OSCAR WILDE, "The Importance of Being Earnest"

HENRY VIZETELLY's obituary in *The Times* celebrated him as a founder of the illustrated press, an author of books on history and wine, and "a well-known engraver and publisher", adding, "and it is not long since his issue of some of Zola's works got him into trouble." It also announces that his autobiography, *Glances Back Through Seventy Years,* has just been published.

ERNEST VIZETELLY continued to translate Zola's novels for Andrew Chatto. He went on to write several books himself, including a book on French wine with his younger brother ARTHUR, and a biography titled *Émile Zola, Novelist and Reformer,* as well as *With Zola in England,* an account of Zola's year in exile in 1899, when he fled France during the Dreyfus Affair, after being tried and convicted for criminal libel. Ernest was instrumental in helping Zola during this period, finding him accommodation, bringing him letters and news of home, and enabling both his wife and his mistress and children to visit him.

Within seven years of Henry's death, Ernest and his brother Edward had a public falling-out in a series of letters to *The Times,* from which a libel case arose. It was only forestalled by Edward's early demise in April 1903 at the age of fifty-four, in what the *New York Times* reported as "straitened circumstances". Ernest continued to publish translations and non-fiction works until he died in 1922 at the age of sixty-nine. ANNIE VIZETELLY died in 1930 at the age of sixty-eight, and was outlived by her brother FRANK, who became a naturalised American citizen and worked as a lexicographer and editor in New York until he died in 1938.

W. T. STEAD left the *Pall Mall Gazette* in 1889 and founded the journal the *Review of Reviews* before going on to become a publisher of popular novels and an international advocate of causes that "defended woman's virtue". He was ever a social campaigner full of contradictions: for example, despite a long association with the "moral majority", when asked by a friend for his view of Oscar Wilde at the height of the sensational trial of 1895, he replied, "He is guilty of only a little more than what most English schoolboys indulge in." Stead died on the *Titanic*, on 15 April, 1912. Survivors reported that he helped move women and children into the lifeboats and then gave up his life jacket to a fellow passenger. There are monuments to his memory at the Peace Palace in The Hague, in Central Park and in London on the Victoria Embankment.

GEORGE MOORE published his anti-censorship novel *Esther Waters* in 1894, not long after Henry Vizetelly's death. In a tribute to his friend, he created a character in the novel called William Larch, a publisher twice prosecuted for moral crimes by crusading vigilantes; the book has remained consistently in print. He moved between Dublin and London in subsequent years, an influential figure in the literary scene of both cities, writing numerous novels, short stories, stage plays and essays. His final novel was published in 1930 and he died in London soon after. His ashes were returned to his family home in Ireland.

ÉMILE ZOLA continued to write novels and live his double life for another decade; he was never at ease with this, writing in a letter to Jeanne in 1894, "This is making me despair. I had dreams of making everyone around me happy but I see quite clearly that this is impossible." In 1898 he was drawn into the Dreyfus Affair when he took it upon himself to write an open letter titled "*J'Accuse*" in the newspaper *L'Aurore*, confronting the President of the Republic about a miscarriage of justice involving a Jewish officer in the French Army. The resulting trial and scandal caused him to leave for England, where the public were sympathetic to Dreyfus, and where he remained in exile for just under a year.

In stark contrast to his celebrated visit to London five years earlier, he crept into the city using the pseudonym "Monsieur Pascal", and relied on Ernest Vizetelly to help him find safe havens from prying journalists and his enemies. In order to avoid extradition, he kept a low profile, and moved between various locations in suburban South London, allowing few visitors. There he wrote a diary of his experience, describing his frustration with political circumstances in France, the wrenching separation from his loved ones, the monotony of his solitary life and the poor quality of English food ("Good God," he says, "English bread! Barely cooked!"). Returning to France as soon as the scandal subsided, Zola continued his work as a social reformer, while completing three more novels.

On 29 September, 1902, he and his wife returned to Paris after a spell at Médan. In the middle of the night, they both woke, unable to breathe. Zola rose and tried to open a window, fell to the floor and was asphyxiated by fumes from the blocked chimney. As in his worst nightmares, he suffocated to death. Fifty thousand people flocked to his funeral.

Though he would never know it, Zola was nominated twice for the Nobel Prize in Literature, in 1901 and 1902, but his candidacy was hindered by the influential French Academy, who had never given him their seal of approval. In 1908, his body was transferred from the cemetery at Montmartre to the Pantheon, a secular museum containing the remains of France's most distinguished citizens, where he was placed alongside Voltaire, Rousseau and Victor Hugo.

JEANNE ROZEROT, whose children were eleven and thirteen at the time of Zola's death, survived her lover by twelve years, and was convinced he was murdered by anti-Dreyfusards. To this day, the truth is uncertain.

ALEXANDRINE ZOLA was overcome by the fumes from the chimney that September night and was found unconscious in her bed in the morning, but survived her husband and became a fierce defender of his literary legacy. As was Zola's wish, she recognised his children by Jeanne after his death, and according to their own reports, they came to think of her as "a beloved aunt". She arranged for the house at Médan to become an orphanage for unwanted children; today it has been preserved as a museum which honours both Zola and Dreyfus. Alexandrine died in 1925.

REGINA V. VIZETELLY'S LEGAL LEGACY was to set a precedent for three generations of writers and artists to come: English courts would actively disallow an artistic merit defence should anyone be required to defend their work against allegations of obscene libel. This endured until 1960 and the trial at which

D. H. Lawrence's *Lady Chatterley's Lover* was tested under Parliament's new obscenity Act of 1959, which finally introduced the concept of publications "for the public good" and "in the interests of science, literature, art or learning, or other objects of general concern". The new legislation also scrapped the 1857 Act's ability to give destruction orders to literature without the right of recourse by the publishers, thereby withdrawing vital fuel for the book-burning descendants of the N.V.A.

One of the thirty-five expert witnesses called in the *Lady Chatterley's Lover* trial made a defence of Lawrence and his publisher that might have been mounted for Vizetelly, if only Henry had had a similar calibre of legal representation. The salient point of sociologist and cultural historian Richard Hoggart was that *Lady Chatterley's Lover* was "puritanical" in the true definition of the term. The book (and its author) had an intense sense of conscience and personal responsibility. Lawrence was depicted as a teacher, a voice decrying corruption in his society; the very same could have been said of Zola.

In the decades between these two trials, there were numerous important markers on the censorship trail and in the life of Zola's works in England, as well as in America, where events and court judgments often moved in parallel. For further reading on this subject, there are sundry texts cited in the bibliography. Some highlights on the seventy-year timeline are:

1894: The Lutetian Society, a literary group led by proponents of the "Decadent Movement", Ernest Dowson and Arthur Symons, published six unexpurgated Zola novels including the banned books, all re-translated and introduced by academics and authors. Ernest Vizetelly was furious when he heard of it, but he could do nothing in the face of Zola's approval of the project. How was this possible, just five years after Henry's incarceration? Once again, it was all about the readership. The "secret literary society", as it was styled, offered the books in exclusive, illustrated, beautifully bound limited editions to private member subscribers, with an explicit statement that the books were "not to be sold to the ordinary English public". The prices for these books were at least twenty times more than those of Vizetelly & Company's publications. By pursuing this strategy, The Lutetian Society were unhindered by the law.

Despite all the fanfare attending his visit in 1893, it would be wrong to assume that Zola was rehabilitated then; it was a conciliatory act by the Institute of Journalists but not by the British public as a whole. He was, as he said himself, being celebrated as a journalist, rather than being forgiven for his fiction. When Zola's first novel since the last of the Rougon-Macquart saga was published by Chatto in 1894 it was "carefully and extensively revised" by Ernest Vizetelly – to an even greater extent than his earlier work had been. *Lourdes* was the first of his "Three Cities trilogy", and offers a sceptic's view of the Catholic shrine and the pilgrims who flock there. The work caused enormous controversy, and so outraged the Catholic Church that his complete works were immediately placed on the Index of Prohibited Books by the Vatican – at that time a roster of some five thousand titles. The government censors of several Catholic countries, including

Ireland, soon followed suit. Their bans on Zola's books would not be lifted until the late 1960s.

1895: With his play "The Importance of Being Earnest" still selling out in the West End, Oscar Wilde prosecuted his lover's father, the Marquess of Queensberry, for libel after the man accused him in writing of being homosexual, or rather, "a Somdomite". A written statement, even misspelled, is not libellous if it is proved true, and this is precisely what the defence achieved, in a series of trials. Ironically, Wilde was represented by the same Q.C. who so effectively prosecuted Henry Vizetelly, the ferocious Sir Edward Clarke. Wilde had assured the high-principled advocate "on my word as a gentleman" that the libel was untrue, and on that promise Clarke not only took on the case but also waived his fee as the process continued. It is hard not to wish that Henry Vizetelly could have lived to see this farce play out, despite its tragic end: Wilde was ultimately convicted for indecent behaviour and sentenced to two years in prison with hard labour. He died in self-imposed exile in France, three years after his release.

1899: The Public Morality Council (P.M.C.) was founded in London as a municipal body which, like the N.V.A, concerned itself with the reporting of and prevention of irregular conduct and immorality. The group continued to thrive until the late 1960s, ultimately targeting theatre, cinema, radio and television. The P.M.C. was echoed and supported by Mary Whitehouse's National Viewers' and Listeners' Association, formed in 1965.

1905: James Joyce, a successor to Zola in many respects, though he professed to dislike Zola's novels, became the next most prominent literary figure to suffer from the effects of English obscenity laws, not initially by prosecution, but by suppression of his work. In a salutary tale of authorial perseverance, he submitted his short story collection *Dubliners* eighteen times over eight years to fifteen different publishers without success. One London publisher did agree to take it on in 1905, but had to back out when the printers would not set the type. The same thing happened in Dublin four years later. The compositors there took it upon themselves to burn the initial page proofs when they realised what they were setting. It was not published until 1914, by the London firm of Grant Richards.

DURING THE EDWARDIAN PERIOD, Paris, with its established liberty of freedom of expression, became a new centre for the publication of banned books. It would provide a haven for expatriate publishers fleeing literary censorship for years to come, among them Lord Carrington, who published authors including Oscar Wilde, as well as a good deal of erotica. The "serious texts" provided him with what some critics called "a veil of legitimacy" for the more graphic majority of his output – a business model which would be followed by others in subsequent decades.

AFTER THE FIRST WORLD WAR the American Sylvia Beach, together with her lover Adrienne Monnier, founded the famed Shakespeare & Company bookshop and lending library in Paris. They would go on to publish Joyce and others, as well as supporting many aspiring American and British expatriate writers until the shop was shut down during the German occupation in the Second World War.

1928: London publishers Jonathan Cape Ltd were summoned to Bow Street, just as Henry Vizetelly had been three decades earlier, to defend the publication of an obscene libel: *The Well of Loneliness* by Radclyffe Hall, which "described unnatural and criminal acts between women". Their defence attempted to argue that it was well-written, "with no filthy words", but the prosecutor's response, as in the Vizetelly trials, was dismissive: "The more palatable the poison, the more insidious it is." An order to destroy all copies of the novel was issued. Dismayed by this defeat, Hall was reported as saying to friends on leaving the courtroom, "Believe me, the end is only beginning." Her comment was prophetic: the next quarter-century was characterised by repeated assaults on literary material by British moralists and politicians.

IN THE 1930S, the Mancunian Jack Kahane founded the Parisian publishing house Obelisk Press, bringing out books which could not be published in England, where somehow, as his son put it in his memoirs, "a whole generation of men had been through the toughest of wars – and won – only to be reduced to the level of schoolchildren, and told what to read and not to read by a conglomerate of spinsters and bowler-hatted policemen". Kahane was the first to publish Henry Miller, Anaïs Nin, Cyril Connolly, and what he called "that cosmic monument to sexo-journalistico-literary bombast", *My Life and Loves,* the memoir of the Vizetelly's "angel" Frank Harris. In Britain, only smuggled editions of Kahane's publications could be read. Obelisk Press foundered during the Second World War.

POST-WORLD WAR TWO: In Paris, Maurice Girodias, Jack Kahane's son (who took his mother's surname during the war to avoid Nazi interest in his Jewish roots) revived his father's publishing business with new printings of Henry Miller's books. But national attitudes had swung to the right, and he was soon prosecuted, in the first literary censorship trial in France since Flaubert's almost a century earlier. In what became known as "*l'affaire* Miller", French intellectuals rallied to the cause of freedom of expression and the case was ultimately dropped by the Ministry of Justice, but Girodias, like Henry Vizetelly before him, was seriously financially damaged by the process.

IN THE 1950S he founded Olympia Press, and in 1955 he published Vladimir Nabokov's *Lolita*. This would again put the publisher at risk of prosecution in France; in Britain, the Home Office instructed all customs officers to seize copies of the book being brought into the country. Sounding much like Zola, Nabokov wrote to his embattled publisher: "On the ethical plane, it is of supreme indifference to me what opinion French, British or any other courts, magistrates or philistine readers in general, may have of my book."

In the same period, Samuel Beckett, also first published in Paris, was widely banned elsewhere, and has been on and off ever since (most recently in Guantánamo Bay prison, where inmates wished to stage a production of "Waiting for Godot"!). In Beckett's case it was the British censor, rather than judges and juries, that prevented his work from being performed. Under the Licensing Act of 1737, the Lord Chamberlain still acted as the moral controller of all plays performed in Britain. He insisted, on the grounds of "preserving the public peace", on script changes to Beckett's work before finally giving it a performance licence. His powers went unchanged until 1968. With reference to Henry Vizetelly's story, it is notable that the first performance of Beckett's "Endgame" was staged at London's Royal Court Theatre in 1957 and was not subjected to the censor's interference. This was presumably because they performed it in the original French, and the refined, French-speaking audience were considered above corruption.

IN AMERICA, Girodias' sometime business partner, Barney Rosset, founded the maverick imprint Grove Press, with the aim of introducing avant-garde European literature and drama to the American public, alongside the Beat Poets of the '50s and '60s, and likewise challenging prevailing attitudes about sex, culture and politics. They published Lawrence, Henry Miller and Burroughs, and took their defence of these works as far as the Supreme Court, ultimately winning the right to publish them.

1954: In London, publisher Paul Elek, immigrant son of a Budapest printer, became a latter-day version of Vizetelly. He moved from printing to founding a small and under-resourced family publishing house, bringing out modern fiction as well as illustrated English classics, sold in series, before turning to Zola. Between 1950 and 1960, he brought out unexpurgated new translations of sixteen out of the twenty Rougon-Macquart novels. When he tried to publish *The Soil* (under the title *The Earth*), the suppression of 1888 was almost repeated because so many printers refused to take the book on. On 18 June, 1954, in the spirit of Henry Vizetelly, he wrote an open letter to *The Times* to complain of this, and he soon overcame objections. Unlike his predecessor, he was not threatened with prosecution. It was no doubt helpful that the N.V.A., Henry's old foe had finally folded in the early 1950s, after a series of internal financial scandals. The scholars' consensus is that his versions are far superior to the Vizetelly translations, with the principal difference being a more faithful, lyrical quality of prose, and of course, a lack of the severe Victorian expurgations of sexual and other content. By way of example, *Joie de Vivre*, the twelfth book in the saga (titled *How Jolly Life Is!* by Vizetelly and *Zest for Life* by Elek) has, in the Elek version, almost the same number of words in English as in the French – whereas the word count in Vizetelly's version is halved.

1957: British customs officers seized the complete works of Jean Genet in French when the Birmingham Public Library ordered them. Was foreign language no longer a defence against the law, or was this one of the last gasps of officialdom's long vendetta against pernicious French literature? Already action was being taken to repeal Lord Campbell's long-outdated Obscene Publications Act of 1857, and halt the censorship which had resulted from it. Ministers were preparing a new Act which would allow for a literary merit defence, as well as the right to take the reputation of the publisher and the author into account. They would also include a right to appeal against destruction orders, although still encouraging the prosecution of pornography. By

1959 this new law would be enacted, only to be tested in 1960 by the watershed *Lady Chatterley's Lover* trial.

1964: This did not mean the end of prudery or censorship in the Anglo-Saxon world – far from it. One of the best proofs of this in the context of our story regards John Cleland's *Fanny Hill* (subtitled *Memoirs of a Woman of Pleasure*). First published in England in 1749 (upon which both author and publisher were arrested and jailed), and first censored in America in 1821, it came back into the spotlight four years after the *Lady Chatterley's Lover* trial. The American publisher G. P. Putnam brought out the first commercial edition since the eighteenth century, in the wake of Grove Press' success with *Tropic of Cancer* and *Lady Chatterley's Lover*. They were prosecuted, publicly lambasted by moral campaigners who doubtless though it "fit for swine", with its scenes of orgies, sodomy, cross-dressing and sex between women. The book was published in paperback for ninety-five cents per copy. As with Zola in Britain, American vigilantes moved to protect the young and the working class from such filth. The case went all the way to the Supreme Court, where the book was eventually found to be protected by the First Amendment: the right to free speech. In the decades that followed, this ruling would be tested many times. No doubt the definition of freedom of speech will forever be contested by those who consider themselves guardians of morality.

Appendix
Les Rougon-Macquart

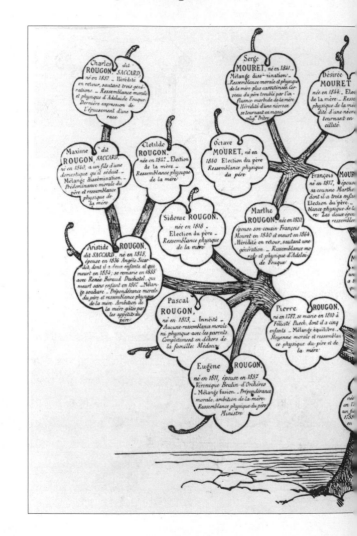

Charles dit
ROUGON - SACCARD,
né en 1857 – Hérédité
en retour, sautant trois générations. – Ressemblance morale
et physique d'Adélaïde Fouque.
Dernière expression de
l'épuisement d'une
race.

Serge
MOURET, né en 1841.
Mélange dissémination. –
Ressemblance morale et physique
de la mère plus caractérisée. Cer-
veau du père troublé par l'influence morbide de la mère.
Hérédité d'une névrose
se tournant en manie
relig.e Prêtre.

Désirée
MOURET
née en 1844. – Élec
de la mère. – Resse
physique de la mè
dité d'une névro
tournant en
cillité.

Maxime dit
ROUGON, SACCARD,
né en 1840, a un fils d'une
domestique qu'il séduit. –
Mélange dissémination. –
Prédominance morale du
père et ressemblance
physique de
la mère.

Clotilde
ROUGON,
née en 1847. – Élection
de la mère. –
Ressemblance physique
de la mère.

Octave
MOURET, né en
1840. Élection du père.
Ressemblance physique
du père.

François MOU
né en 1817, épouse
sa cousine Marthe
dont il a trois enfan
Élection du père. –
blance physique de la
re. Les deux épou
ressemblent.

Sidonie ROUGON,
née en 1818. –
Élection du père. –
Ressemblance physique
de la mère.

Marthe
ROUGON née en 1820,
épouse son cousin François
Mouret en 1840 et meurt en 1864.
Hérédité en retour, sautant une
génération. – Ressemblance morale et physique d'Adélaïde Fouque.

Aristide ROUGON,
dit SACCARD né en 1815,
épouse en 1836 Angèle Sicar
dol, dont il a deux enfants et qui
meurt en 1854; se remarie en 1855
avec Renée Beraud Duchatel, qui
meurt sans enfant en 1867. – Mélange soudure. – Prépondérance morale
du père et ressemblance physique
de la mère. Ambition de
la mère gâtée par
les appétits du
père.

Pascal
ROUGON,
né en 1813. – Innéité.
– Aucune ressemblance morale
ni physique avec les parents.
Complètement en dehors de
la famille. Médecin.

Pierre ROUGON,
né en 1787, se marie en 1810 à
Félicité Puech, dont il a cinq
enfants. – Mélange équilibre.
Moyenne morale et ressemblance physique du père et de
la mère.

Eugène ROUGON,
né en 1811, épouse en 1857
Veronique Beulin-d'Orchères
– Mélange fusion. – Prépondérance
morale, ambition de la mère.
Ressemblance physique du père.
Ministre.

née
en 18
un fi
1756
en

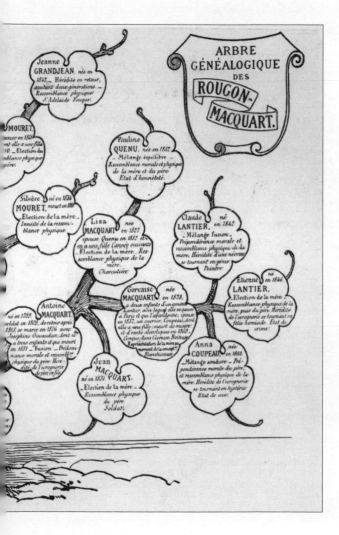

ARBRE
GÉNÉALOGIQUE
DES
ROUGON-
MACQUART.

Jeanne
GRANDJEAN, *née en
1842. — Hérédité en retour,
sautant deux générations. —
Ressemblance physique
d'Adélaïde Fouque.*

...MOURET,
*...pouse en 1841
...ent elle a une fille
...50. — Élection du
...mblance physique
...père.*

Pauline
QUENU, *née en 1852.
— Mélange équilibre.
Ressemblance morale et physique
de la mère et du père.
État d'honnêteté.*

Silvère | *né en 1834,
MOURET, meurt en 1851.
— Élection de la mère. —
Innéité de la ressem-
blance physique.*

Lisa | *née
MACQUART, en 1827,
épouse Quenu en 1852 et
en a une fille l'année suivante.
Élection de la mère. — Ressemblance physique de la
mère.
Charcutière.*

Claude | *né
LANTIER, en 1842.
— Mélange fusion.
Prépondérance morale et
ressemblance physique de la
mère. Hérédité d'une névrose
se tournant en génie.
Peintre.*

Étienne | *né en 1846.
LANTIER. — Élection de la mère.
Ressemblance physique de la
mère, puis du père. Hérédité
de l'ivrognerie se tournant en
folie homicide. État de
crime.*

Antoine
MACQUART, *né en 1789.
...oldat en 1809, de retour après
1815, se marie en 1826 avec
Joséphine Gavaudan, dont il
a trois enfants et qui meurt
en 1851. — Fusion. — Prédominance morale et ressemblance
physique du père. Héré-
dité de l'ivrognerie
de père en fils.*

Gervaise | *née
MACQUART, en 1828.
a deux enfants d'un amant,
Lantier, avec lequel elle se sauve
à Paris et qui l'abandonne; épouse
en 1852, un ouvrier, Coupeau, dont
elle a une fille; meurt de misère
et d'excès alcooliques en 1869.
Conçue dans l'ivresse. Boiteuse.
Représentation de la consom-
mation et de l'amour.
Blanchisseuse.*

Anna | *née
COUPEAU, en 1852.
— Mélange soudure — Pré-
pondérance morale du père
et ressemblance physique de la
mère. Hérédité de l'ivrognerie
se tournant en hystérie.
État de vice.*

Jean
MACQUART, *né en 1831.
— Élection de la mère.
Ressemblance physique
du père.
Soldat.*

293

These twenty novels are much more and much less than an "epic family saga" – more, because it is also Zola's history of the Second Empire, and it moves through so many different social spheres, unrestricted to single lives or settings; less, because despite its scale, Zola was charting the stories of just one family, the illegitimate and legitimate descendants of one woman, Adelaide Fouque, and their genetic inheritance: insanity, obsession, alcoholism and, above all, "appetite". The legitimate family, led by her first son Pierre, are the Rougons, and her illegitimate children Ursule and Antoine come from an affair with the drunken smuggler Macquart. The "third branch" is the Mourets, from Ursule's marriage into the middle classes.

When he first made his plan for the works, much inspired by Balzac's *Human Comedy*, Zola envisioned ten "episodes". His stated intention was to make a study of a family from the coup d'état of Napoleon III in December 1851 to "nowadays", meaning France as it was in 1868. He would differentiate his work by writing the first scientific analysis in fiction of the effect of heredity and environment on human behaviour. By the time the seventh book, *L'Assommoir*, had firmly established the project as a commercial success the list grew to twenty.

It is not a tidy series; some of the novels follow on from each other, others do not; major characters in one book may be glimpsed in another, or might not be seen for years; and although the birthplace of the clan, the fictional "Plassans" (a version of Zola's own birthplace, Aix-en-Provence), features in a number of the books, there are as many stories set in Paris, and others taking place along the northern coast or in the rural west of France. It is impossible to arrange the books chronologically due to the degree of overlap. As if to reflect on this, the author issued a recommended reading order, differing from the publication order, within the introduction of the final book, *Doctor Pascal*. He also offered a family tree within the texts of the first and last books, then released several altered versions en route, as suited his and the stories' changing needs. From the outset, every book had a pre-ordained concept which would allow the author to roam across the entire social and political landscape of mid-nineteenth century France, from "the political novel" to the "the art novel" to "the worker's novel", the "scientific novel" and "the novel of the defeat".

The tree gives the name and date of birth of each family member, and was originally colour coded by family lines and traits, as well as detailing whom each character most resembled (favouring father or mother for example), their job, and important facts of their life. As Patterson writes in his *Zola Dictionary*, "they do not form an edifying group, these Rougon-Macquarts, but Zola was not on the outlook for healthy subjects." To some readers it might seem that the writer limited himself by drawing the tree before writing the novels, especially as he had little idea of the plots he would go on to create. But Zola was a wilful gardener, performing tree surgery as necessary, lopping off a limb here or there along the way (for example a long envisioned "novel of the war in Italy" never saw the light of day), and had no qualms about grafting on new branches or leaves as he progressed, such as Jacques Lantier of *The Human Beast*. Lantier was "spliced in" to his family line long after his mother's (Gervaise Macquart) death, because Zola required the tortured maniac to descend from her contaminated bloodline. Gervaise herself is unmentioned in the first edition of the first novel when we meet her parents and siblings, and was worked in later, when Zola conceived *L'Assommoir*.

Other than the first and last novels, which give overviews of the whole saga in their different ways (the former functions like a musical overture, the latter as a summary), the Rougon-Macquart novels can be read in virtually any sequence, but they are briefly described here in Zola's own recommended order, with French titles and publication dates.

1   *The Fortune of the Rougon* (*La Fortunes des Rougon*, 1871): Published just after the fall of Napoleon III's Second Empire, it follows both the events of the *coup* and imagines its effect on the fictional village of Plassans, but also flashes back to tell the story of young Adelaide Fouque's involvement with both Rougon and Macquart. Now aged and infirm in mind and body, she is known as "Tante Dide". At this story's centre is the rivalry of her adult children; Pierre Rougon and his wife Felicité become avid supporters of Napoleon III in order to gain social advantage, while the Macquarts descend into squabble and squalor, unable to overcome their hereditary predilection for drink. The Mourets are represented by Adelaide's grandson, Silvère, young hero of the local Plassans militia, who, together with his beloved Miette, meets a tragic end. For the first-time Zola reader, it is a

challenging but absorbing read – the plaiting of epic, romantic, and farcical elements in this historical novel recalls Victor Hugo's *Les Misérables*. In the first ten pages of *The Fortune of the Rougon*, Zola plants the roots of his great family tree by describing a defunct graveyard, heavy with history. The senses are engaged at once:

> The rich soil, in which the gravediggers could no longer delve without turning up some human remains, was possessed of wondrous fertility . . . Beneath one's feet amidst the close-set stalks one could feel that the damp soil reeked and bubbled with sap . . .

2 *His Excellence Eugène Rougon* (*Son Excellence Eugène Rougon*, 1876): The avaricious son of Pierre and Felicité Rougon has been instrumental in Napoleon III's successful *coup*. This book finds him living in Paris where he has been appointed Minister of the Interior, but struggles to maintain his position while satisfying both his greedy family and an Italian adventuress, Clorinde Balbi, whom he rejects as a wife for her lowly status only for her to become the Emperor's mistress. A story of powerlessness in the corridors of power, it reveals Zola's low opinion of politicians and their methods, and ends cynically with Eugène, after many setbacks, gaining new influence and becoming the special "Minister without Portfolio".

3 *The Kill* (*La Curée*, 1872): Set in Baron Haussmann's new Paris, a city rebuilt on the Emperor's command during the 1850s,

this is a story about property speculators and the corrupting influence of money, as well as a retelling of Euripides' "Phaedra". The title refers to the meat that is thrown to dogs after the hunt; this book has also been titled in English as *The Rush for the Spoil* (Vizetelly edition), *The Contest for the Spoils* and even *The Hounds' Fee*. It is a "tragi-farce" of life among the *nouveaux riches*, in which we see the commercial exploits of money-mad Aristide Rougon, youngest son of Pierre and Felicité, who has taken on the surname "Saccard" at the urging of his politician brother Eugène (who wants to distance himself from him). While he makes his ruthless way to the top of the property market in Paris, his unhappy young wife has a torrid affair with his son by his first marriage.

4 *Money* (*L'Argent*, 1891): Written nearly twenty years after *The Kill*, this is nonetheless the direct sequel. It opens soon after the death of Aristide Saccard's wife, when his fortunes are on the wane; he decides to set up a bank to offer finance to the Emperor's ever-expanding capital projects and with Enronesque duplicity, manipulates the price of the bank's stock in order to establish himself. As ever, he is locked in a bitter rivalry with his politician brother, and when his bank's stock soars, he buys up newspapers as well, both to bolster the bank and his financial agenda, and to attack Eugène. Ultimately his enemies conspire against him and the bank, which has become "too big to fail". It collapses with disastrous results for the entire nation.

5   *The Dream* (*Le Rêve*, 1888): Another book composed much later in the series, which Zola moves to the front of his reading order to follow *Money*. The heroine Angelique's mother Sidonie is the sister of Eugènc and Aristide Rougon (Saccard). The story, a departure from the more materialistic and gritty books that precede it, moves to a new location beyond the established locales of Plassans and Paris, unfolding some ten years into the Second Empire, and features an "experiment of adoption" which allows Zola to examine nature v. nurture. The angelic main character is a dreamy, romantic girl raised in idyllic circumstances who nonetheless suffers from similar obsessive-compulsive tendencies to her forebears – in this case the desire to marry a handsome prince. A careful miniature of a story rather than one of Zola's sprawling epics.

6   *The Conquest of Plassans* (*La Conquête de Plassans*, 1874): The main character of this novel, also titled (by Elek, in the 1950s) *A Priest in the House*, is the "mentally feeble" Marthe Rougon, another child of Pierre and Felicité, whom we met in the first novel, *The Fortune of the Rougon*. She has a settled life with her husband, her cousin François Mouret, and their three children, until things unravel when they take a visiting priest as a lodger. The sinister Rasputin-like Abbé Faujas, a man with dubious political intentions, is the embodiment of Zola's loathing for the corruption of the Catholic Church in France.

7   *Piping Hot!* (*Pot-Bouille*, 1882): Variously translated as *Pot Luck*, *Restless House*, *Lesson in Love* and *The Stew Pot*, the family character in this novel is young Octave, the rakish twenty-two-year old son of Marthe and François Mouret, who moves into a fine Parisian apartment building (a new concept at the time) only to discover that beneath its respectable façade the place is seething with bourgeois passion. Octave resembles his power-mad uncle Eugène Rougon, but in his case the power he desires is over women. This is arguably the lightest of the twenty books, a bedroom farce with dark undertones.

8   *The Ladies' Paradise* (*Au Bonheur des Dames*, 1883): A *Piping Hot!* sequel, also known as *The Ladies' Delight*, this novel is set in a department store which Zola based on Paris' newly launched Le Bon Marché, which revolutionised the world of French retail. Set between 1864 and 1869, it follows the rise and rise of Octave Mouret's career; he is a charismatic, handsome salesman and manager who tries to control and manipulate everything, particularly the women, until he is "tamed" by falling in love with Denise, a young shop girl.

9   *The Sin of Father Mouret* (*Le Faute de l'Abbé Mouret*, 1875): Translated by Vizetelly as *Abbe Mouret's Transgression* and by Elek, six decades on, as *The Sinful Priest*. The offending protagonist is Serge Mouret, son of Marthe Rougon Mouret, and brother of Octave, last seen in that other great anti-clerical novel, *The Conquest of Plassans*. His obsession with religion leads him

to a nervous collapse and total amnesia, moving the novel into a surreal if not supernatural realm. His uncle, Doctor Pascal Rougon, arranges for his care, but he falls in love with the girl who attends him, with – as is often the case for priests in Zola's oeuvre – disastrous results.

10 *A Love Episode* (*Un Page d'amour*, 1877): Another tale, like *Piping Hot!*, of love and betrayal in suburban Paris, this time featuring a relatively "normal" Rougon-Macquart protagonist, Hélène Mouret (sister of François, from *The Conquest of Plassans*, and Silvère, hero of *The Fortune of the Rougon*), whose young daughter Jeanne has unfortunately inherited the now-familiar familial obsessive tendencies and a neurological disorder akin to epilepsy. Young widow Hélène asks her neighbour Doctor Henri Deberle to attend when her child has a seizure, and finds herself falling in love with him. But their happiness is thwarted by her daughter's possessive jealousy.

11 *The Belly of Paris* (*Le Ventre de Paris*, 1873): First translated into English as *The Fat and the Thin*, this is a populous, sensory novel set in Les Halles, the recently rebuilt food market in Paris. Originally published as the fourth in the series, it is Zola's first novel to focus entirely on the working class. The family connection here is through Lisa Quenu, daughter of Antoine Macquart, now a butcher's wife, who arranges for her brother-in-law Florent to get a job in the market. He is a Republican who is in and out of trouble with the law. He attempts to foment revolution, but his

plot is thin compared to the "odes to food" that make this novel both fat and famous – look out for the "Cheese Symphony".

12 *The Joy of Living* (*La Joie de Vivre*, 1884): Vizetelly published this, with characteristic punctuation, as *How Jolly Life Is!* Later versions were called *The Joy of Life* and *Zest for Life*. Set between 1863 and 1873, the action moves from Paris by way of Provence to Bonneville, a seaside town in Normandy, and features the adult daughter of "the Quenu of Les Halles", Pauline. Orphaned at ten, this jolly optimist comes to live with her father's miserable relatives, bearing an inheritance which her greedy aunt soon "borrows" to try and improve her family's fortunes – to no avail. Pauline is the least typical of her family line, facing her many travails with altruism and decency, and a sense of *joie de vivre*. The novel is less a study of heredity than the others and, interestingly, focuses on one of Zola's own maladies, hypochondria, a problem writ large in Lazare, the cousin whom Pauline is expected to marry.

13 *The Dram Shop / The Drinking Den / The Gin Palace* (*L'Assommoir*, 1877): Commonly known in English by its colloquial French title, this was Zola's "breakthrough" book when it was published (the seventh in the saga), reaching a mass audience and establishing him as a household name in France. An urban tale of the working class, it shares some themes of *The Belly of Paris*, but focuses specifically on the effects of alcoholism and poverty through the life story of Gervaise Macquart, sister of Lisa Quenu,

and daughter of Antoine Macquart (the feckless drunken son of matriarch Tante Dide). Gervaise is now a washerwoman in Paris, abandoned by Lantier, father of her children; in the first half of the novel she marries the industrious teetotaller Coupeau in a colourful wedding set piece, and manages to buy her own washhouse. Sadly, from this high point, Gervaise begins to fall, as Coupeau is injured in a fall at work, takes to drink and becomes a version of her vicious father; broken by it all, Gervaise joins him in his rapid descent.

14 *The/His Masterpiece* (*L'Oeuvre*, 1885): The fourteenth novel published, as well as the fourteenth in Zola's reading order, this is his "art novel" describing life in bohemian Paris as lived by Zola himself, who lends his experiences to one of Gervaise's children, Claude Lantier. He is a gifted Impressionist painter whose version of familial obsession centres on his desire to paint a great work. Featuring a writer much like the author, and evidently one of Zola's personal favourites in the series, the novel is said by some to have ended his lifelong friendship with Paul Cézanne, who recognised himself in the tortured Claude.

15 *The Human Beast* (*La Bête Humaine*, 1890): Zola came up with one hundred and fifty titles before settling on this for his "railway novel"; it has been rendered in English as *The Beast Within*, *The Beast in Man*, and even (by Edward Vizetelly, circa 1901) as *The Monomaniac*. The beast of the title is Jacques Lantier, brother to the tragic painter Claude. He is the belatedly

invented son of Gervaise Macquart (she does not actually have a son called Jacques in *L'Assommoir*, which ends with her death). He is a railway engine driver tortured by murderous desires who falls for Séverine, an avaricious woman who has also conspired to kill. This is an astonishing portrait of obsession, even compared to the others that surround it, and a psychological thriller to rival any that followed, with fantastic sensory detail bringing to life the railway and the "industrial beast" of man-made machines. The story also allows the author to criticise the French legal system, as politicised and as corrupt as ever.

16 *Germinal* (*Germinal*, 1885): The title is the name that was given after the Revolution of 1789 to the first month of spring in the French Republican Calendar, until it was abandoned in 1805. The bestselling of all of Zola's novels since publication, it is a masterwork by anyone's reckoning: an epic story of labour v. capitalism. The hero is Étienne Lantier, brother of Jacques and Claude. Coming to work in a grim mining community in the far north of France in the mid 1860s, a time of escalating economic crisis in France and throughout Europe, Étienne is stirred to action by the foul conditions and desperate poverty he finds, which leads him to organise a miners' strike. Though the workers do not triumph (after all, Zola was a ralist) a seed has been planted. At his uneral, crowds of workers chanted "Germinal! Germinal!" as they followed his coffin.

17 *Nana* (*Nana*, 1880): A much earlier novel, written just after *A Love Episode*, and another huge success – the first French edition of more than fifty thousand copies sold out in a day. When he revised the reading order, Zola put this tale charting the fate of Gervaise Macquart's lovely daughter after the novels that describe the fates of her three brothers, because it is set nearer to the end of his Second Empire timeline. We find Nana working at the colourful Varieties Theatre, where at just fifteen years of age, she is a popular actress and courtesan, kept by some of the great men of Paris. (In turn she keeps as pets some yappy little dogs, one of whom Zola christened "Lou-lou", which was his nickname for his wife!) Nana is a voracious, self-destructive force, a bewitching beauty who ruins the legion of suitors who fall for her, before losing her son and dying a gruesome death from smallpox. The book can be read as a salutary moral tale from this "most moral of authors", and it is a poke in the eye of the hypocritical upper classes who tout integrity but secretly keep underage cocottes for their pleasure. It is also a metaphor for the advanced moral contagion of the Second Empire, which collapses as Nana dies.

18 *The Soil / The Earth* (*La Terre*, 1887): The fact that Zola penned the gritty, brutal novel that effectively broke Henry Vizetelly in between composing his "art novel" *His Masterpiece* and the delicate romance of *The Dream* is a testament to his intellectual and creative dexterity – it could not be further removed from either, and stands closer to *Germinal* in its themes and tone.

Set in central France in the "bread-basket" of the Beauce, its Macquart protagonist is Jean, another son of the drunken Antoine Macquart, whose inheritance from his benighted clan is manifest in a desire for family and home. Unfortunately he has come to the wrong place. Arriving in a small farming community, he falls in love and becomes entangled with a complex family feud involving Fouan, an old man who, Lear-like, splits his fortune between his greedy, unkind children. Although it describes the physical and moral poverty of characters worn down by the inhumanity of the Second Empire, this novel still has the power both to shock and resonate today, as a tale of the inevitable cruelty and violence that is born from sustained deprivation.

19 *The Downfall* (*La Débâcle*, 1892): Written in three parts, this epic novel describing "the confusions and futility of war" is a sequel to *The Soil* in as much as it follows directly in time, and its protagonist is once again Jean Macquart, who joins the army when war is declared against Prussia in 1870. Part One sees Corporal Macquart deployed around the country as the generals struggle to combat the enemy; Part Two tells the story of the disastrous Battle of Sedan, in which the French were roundly defeated; and in Part Three, Jean and his best friend escape and take refuge in Sedan and Paris respectively, before they are brought together on opposite sides of the battle, as the Second Empire finally comes to an end.

20 *Doctor Pascal* (*Le Docteur Pascal*, 1893): Zola called this final novel "my defence of all that I have done, before the court of public opinion". It can be unfairly dismissed as a mere summary or a "metanovel", when in fact it also serves up a good self-contained story addressing what it is like to be reborn by love in middle age, and how families are torn apart by shame and envy. In a finale that features cameos from virtually all the Rougon-Macquart descendants, Zola gets in some final digs at the Church and the political establishment and conjures up a few breathtaking set pieces along the way, including the death of a young haemophiliac at the bedside of his now centenarian and mute great-great grandmother Tante Dide, and the spontaneous combustion of Antoine Macquart due to alcoholism, in the vein of Krook in *Bleak House*. Not to be missed. The final pages leave us with the last of the Rougons, the son of Dr Pascal, as a babe in arms:

> And in the warm silence, in the solitary peace of the workroom, Clotilde smiled at the child, who was still nursing, his little arm held straight up in the air, like a signal flag of life.

Bibliography

ÉMILE ZOLA

The wealth of material I have read began with the complete works of Émile Zola – and with apologies to Ernest and Henry, I suggest to any reader the more recent the translation the better, by all means using Paul Elek's 1950s versions if nothing more current can be found. The full saga is also available in various versions through Project Gutenberg.

The original manuscripts of Zola's novels as well as his preparatory notes were given by his widow to the National Library of France in 1904; some of these have been made available via their digital library Gallica at http://gallica.bnf.fr

Further resources that may be of interest can be divided between the two heroes of our story as follows:

VIZETELLY, THE VICTORIANS AND PUBLISHING

Few records remain of Henry Vizetelly's company and we must rely heavily on the memoirs written by himself and his son, and any contemporary accounts in the press or by colleagues and friends, all of which have their own natural biases. Among the current references I was able to find, I cannot recommend too highly Anthony Cummins' witty and learned academic studies on the subject, as well as the superb catalogue from an exhibition on Vizetelly's company mounted in 2003, at the University of Toronto (listed under M. Korey below). The university also houses the Zola Research Program, with the largest repository of Zola's correspondence to be found in North America, and is open to the public.

ASQUITH, H. H. *Memories and Reflections.* London: Cassell & Company (1928)

BECKER, G. J. (ed) *Documents of Modern Literary Realism.* Princeton: Princeton University Press (1967)

BLAND, L. *Banishing the Beast: Sexuality and the Early Feminists*. London: Penguin (1995)

BRADSHAW, D., and POTTER, R. (eds) *Prudes on the Prowl*. Oxford: Oxford University Press (2013)

CALDER, J. *Garden of Eros*. Edinburgh: John Calder Books (2014)

CORREA, D. *The Nineteenth-Century Novel: Realisms*. London: Routledge (2001)

CUMMINS, A. *Émile Zola's Cheap English Dress*. Oxford: Oxford University Press (2008)

CUMMINS, A. "From *L'Assommoir* to 'Let's ha' some more': Émile Zola's Early circulation on the Late-Victorian Stage". *Victorian Review* (2008)

CURTIS, S. "Henry Vizetelly and Vizetelly & Co.". *Poetry Nation Review* (1983)

DE GRAZIA, E. *Girls Lean Back Everywhere: The Law of Obscenity and the Assault on Genius*. New York: Random House. (1993)

ECKLEY, G. The *Maiden Tribute: A Life of W. T. Stead*. Philadelphia: XLibris (2007)

FLEMING, B. "An Assessment of the Letters from Vizetelly & Co. to Émile Zola". *Publishing History* (2001)

GIRODIAS, M. (ed) *The Olympia Reader*. New York: Grove Press (1965)

HARRIS, F. *My Life and Loves* (Vols 1–4). Paris: Obelisk (1931)

HEATH. D. *Purifying Empire: Obscenity and the Politics of Moral Regulation in Britain, India and Australia*. Cambridge: Cambridge University Press (2014)

HYLAND, P., and SAMUELS, N. (eds) *Writing and Censorship in Britain*. London: Routledge (1992)

HYNES, S. The *Edwardian Turn of Mind*. London: Random House (1992)

JONES, M. *Translations of Zola in The United States Prior to 1900*. Baltimore: Johns Hopkins University Press (1940)

KEATING, P. *The Haunted Study: A Social History of the English Novel.* London: Secker &Warburg (1989)

KENDRICK, W. *The Secret Museum: Pornography in Modern Culture.* Berkeley: University of California Press (1997)

KOREY, M., and LANDON, R. (eds) *Vizetelly &Compan(ies): A Complex Tale of Victorian Printing and Publishing.* Toronto: University of Toronto (exhibition catalogue) (2003)

LIECK, A. *Bow Street World.* London: Robert Hale (1938)

MacLEOD, K. *Fictions of British Decadence.* London: Palgrave Macmillan (2006)

MERKLE, D. (ed) *The Power of the Pen: Translation and Censorship in Nineteenth-Century Europe.* Munster: Lit Verlag (2010)

MILTON, J., and BANDIA, P. F. *Agents of Translation.* John Benjamins: Philadelphia (2009)

MOORE, G. *Circulating Morals or Literature at Nurse.* London: Vizetelly and Company (1885)

ROBINSON, W. S. *Muckraker: The Scandalous Life and Times of W. T. Stead.* London: Robson Press. (2013)

RODENSKY, L. *The Oxford Handbook of the Victorian Novel.* Oxford: Oxford University Press (2013)

SHULTS, R. L. *Crusader in Babylon: W. T. Stead and the Pall Mall Gazette.* Lincoln: University of Nebraska Press (1972)

SOVA, D. *Literature Suppressed on Sexual Grounds.* New York: Infobase (2006)

SUTHERLAND, J. *Victorian Fiction: Writers, Publishers, Readers.* London: Palgrave Macmillan (2006)

THOMAS, D. *Long Time Burning.* New York: Praeger (1969)

VIZETELLY, H. *Extracts Principally From English Classics.* London: Vizetelly & Company (1888)

VIZETELLY, H. *Glances Back Through Seventy Years* (Vols 1–2). London: Kegan Paul, Trench, Trubner & Company (1893)

WEEKS, J. *Sex, Politics and Society: The Regulation of Sexuality since 1800*. London: Longman (1989)

ZOLA

Most of my sources were works available in English, with the exception of M. Bloch-Dano's excellent biography of Alexandrine, and Zola and others' letters, as well as some contemporary press articles, notably from *Le Figaro*. His collected works are available in French in the updated Classiques Garnier edition of 2013, and his complete preparatory notes are gathered in Champion's 2003 edition; for further reading in French, look for acknowledged experts Alain Pages, Henri Mitterand and Colette Becker.

For the Anglo-Saxon aficionado, The Émile Zola Society in London http://www.Émilezolasocietylondon.org.uk and the AIZEN in Canada https://www.ualberta.ca/~aizen/about are learned groups that publish and meet regularly, creating useful articles, bulletins, lectures and colloquia covering aspects of Zola's work and life. The work of Cahiers Naturalistes is also invaluable for any student of his writing. http://www.cahiers-naturalistes. com/

There are many other "unofficial" resources including blogs for enthusiasts such as readingzola.wordpress.com and swiftlytilting-planet.wordpress.com. If you were to read only one book in English on Zola's life and reception in Britain, it would have to be Graham King's (see below); for those who wish to undertake to read the complete Rougon-Macquart Saga, it is useful to have Patterson's dictionary of Zola on hand (see below), which contains a breakdown of story and a full index of characters.

ALEXIS, P. *Notes d'un Ami*. Paris: Charpentier (1882)

BAKKER, B., and BECKER, C. *Correspondance d'Émile Zola* (Vols 1–3). Montreal: Montreal University Press. (1982)

BLOCH-DANO, E. *Madame Zola*. Paris: Editions Grasset (1997)

COLBURN, W. *Zola in England, 1883-1902*. Urbana, IL: University of Illinois (1952)

DECKER, C. "Zola's Literary Reputation in England". *Publications of the Modern Language Association of America* (1934)

ÉMILE-ZOLA, B., and PAGÈS, A. (eds). *Émile Zola: Lettres à Alexandrine*. Paris: Gallimard (2014)

ÉMILE-ZOLA, B., and PAGÈS, A. (eds). *Émile Zola: Lettres à Jeanne Rozerot*. Paris: Gallimard (2004)

HEMMINGS, F. W. J. *The Life and Times of Émile Zola*. Oxford: Clarendon (1997). This is a follow-up to his literary analysis titled simply *Émile Zola*. London: Paul Elek (1953)

HOWELLS, W. D. *The Works of William Dean Howells: Émile Zola*. Project Gutenberg (1996)

JOSEPHSON, M. *Zola and His Time*. London: Victor Gollancz (1929)

KING, G. *Émile Zola and His Novels for English Readers*. London: Barrie & Jenkins; New York: Harper & Row (1978)

KLEEBLAT, N. L. "Merde! The Caricatural Attack against Émile Zola". *Art Journal* (1993)

LANOUX, A. *Bonjour, Monsieur Zola*. London: Staples Press (1995)

NELSON, B. (ed). *The Cambridge Companion to Zola*. Cambridge: Cambridge University Press (2007)

PATTERSON, J. G. *A Zola Dictionary*. Project Gutenberg (1912)

REWALD, J. (ed) *Paul Cézanne Letters*. London: Bruno Cassirer (1941)

SCHOM, A. *Émile Zola: A Biography*. London: Macdonald: Queen Anne Press (1987)

SHERARD, R. *Émile Zola: A Biographical and Critical Study*. London: Chatto & Windus (1893)

SPEIRS, D., and PORTEBOIS, Y. (trans/eds). *Notes from Exile by Émile Zola*. Toronto: University of Toronto Press (2003)

VIZETELLY, E. *Émile Zola, Novelist and Reformer*. London: John Lane (1904)

VIZETELLY, E. *With Zola in England: A Story of Exile*. London: Chatto & Windus (1899)

WILSON, A. *Émile Zola: An Introductory Study of His Novels*. London: Secker & Warburg (1952)

Illustration Credits

PART ONE

Zola's house in Médan, engraving of 1902 (Mary Evans Picture Library / Iberfoto / Coleccion Gasca)

"King of Pigs" lithograph by Jules Eugène Lenepveu from *Museum of Horrors*, 1900 (Bridgeman Images / Private Collection)

"Pity the Poor Speaker" cartoon engraved by Harry Furniss from *Punch* of December 1888

Henry Vizetelly in an 1863 heliogravure after a photograph (National Portrait Gallery, London)

Ernest Vizetelly photographed circa 1900

"Sancta Simplicitas" cartoon by George du Maurier in *Punch*, November 1885

W. T. Stead, photograph of 1890 (National Portrait Gallery, London)

Newspaper vendors outside the offices of the Pall Mall Gazette in 1885 by Arthur Twidle

PART TWO

Title page of Vizetelly's 1885 edition of *Nana*.

Herbert Henry Asquith in a photograph circa 1900 (Getty Images / Popperfoto)

Caricature of George Moore by Walter Sickert from *Vanity Fair* January 1897 (Bridgeman Images / Peter Jackson Collection)

Zola in his study in an engraving from an Italian magazine of 1892 (A.K.G. Images / De Agostini)

Jeanne Rozerot, Zola's mistress from 1888 (Bridgeman Images / Tallandier)

Old Bailey courtroom in 1879, drawing by William Powell Frith (© Trustees of the British Museum)

Edward Clarke in a photograph circa 1890 (Getty Images / Hulton Archive)

PART THREE
The Vizetelly colophon
Nana in mirror engraved by Bellenger after Gill, from the French edition
    of *Nana*
Drawing of Frank Harris by Max Beerbohm, 1896
Holloway Prison, general view, 19th century engraving (Bridgeman Images /
    Peter Jackson Collection)
Alexandrine Zola in an undated photo (Getty Images / Ullstein)
Holy Family circa 1895 (© Association du Musée Emile Zola)
Henry Vizetelly circa 1893 (University of Sussex Library Special Collections /
    Vizetelly Archive)
Institute of Journalists' Annual Conference Dinner invitation
Zola with the Lord Mayor in London, 1893

CODA, APPENDIX and BIBLIOGRAPHY
"Oscar Wilde at Work" by Aubrey Beardsley, circa 1895 (Getty Images /
    Private Collection)
Emile Zola as a naturalist by Andre Gill from *L'Eclipse*, 1876 (Bridgeman
    Images / Musee de la Ville de Paris, Musee Carnavalet)
Genealogical tree of the Rougon-Macquart family (Bridgeman Images /
    Archives Charmet)

The publishers have made every effort to contact all copyright holders, but if
in any case they have been unsuccessful please get in touch directly.

Acknowledgements

I am indebted to Chantal Morel of the Émile Zola Society in London and her colleague Professor Geoff Woollen, as well as Professor Brendan Fleming, who gave so generously of their time and knowledge to me. Much gratitude also goes to experts in translation and printing including David Bellos, Richard Lawrence, Rob Richardson and Mick Clayton, and to Teri Chace, Tanya Chianale, Frank and Caitlin Blau for their specialist input. In addition I thank Peter Ransley for the life-changing introduction to Zola half a lifetime ago, and Lee Sandlin for honesty and inspiration, even from the beyond. Many thanks also to my editors, readers and champions: Sophie Lambert, Katharina Bielenberg, Christopher MacLehose, Katri Skala, Sarah Dunant, Lu Spinney, Frances Soulé, Jude and MaryJane Blau, Jill Goldstein Baldasseroni, Pip Broughton, Clive Brill, Georgia de Chamberet, Sheila Corr, Richard Rockwood, Judy Counihan, Nina Sandlin, Giles Goddard, Nancy Crane, Oliver Morgan.

And above all, heartfelt thanks to Gregory Horne and Lily Teresa Slater, always.

EILEEN HORNE was born in California, and has lived in Italy and London for thirty-five years. She spent two decades as a television producer in the UK, founding her own production company in 1997 and making over a hundred hours of drama, among them two projects inspired by Zola's novels. She now combines writing, including adaptations for radio and television, with teaching and editing. Her first book, *The Pitch*, was published by Faber in 2006 and she translated an Italian novella for the MacLehose Press collection *Judges* (2014). She lives in London and Umbria with her husband and daughter.